THE STORM

THE STORM

ONE VOICE FROM THE AIDS GENERATION

CHRISTOPHER ZYDA

RARE BIRD BOOKS
LOS ANGELES, CALIF.

THIS IS A GENUINE RARE BIRD BOOK

Rare Bird Books
453 South Spring Street, Suite 302
Los Angeles, CA 90013
rarebirdlit.com

FIRST HARDCOVER EDITION

Rare Bird Books Subsidiary Rights Department
453 South Spring Street, Suite 302
Los Angeles, CA 90013

Set in Minion
Printed in the United States

10 9 8 7 6 5 4 3 2 1

Publisher's Cataloging-in-Publication Data

Names: Zyda, Christopher, author.
Title: The Storm: One Voice from the AIDS Generation / Christopher Zyda.
Description: Includes index. | First Hardcover Edition | A Genuine Rare Bird Book | New York, NY; Los Angeles, CA: Rare Bird Books, 2020.
Identifiers: ISBN 9781644281680 (Hardcover) | 9781644281888 (ebook)
Subjects: LCSH Zyda, Christopher. | Gay men—United States—Biography. | Gays—United States—Biography. | AIDS (Disease) | Los Angeles (Calif.)—Biography. | BISAC BIOGRAPHY & AUTOBIOGRAPHY / Personal Memoirs
Classification: LCC HQ75 .8.Z92 2020| DDC 306.76/62092—dc23

This book is dedicated to Stephen, the first love of my life; to my sister, Joan; to my friend Bryn; and to everyone else who was lost during the storm.

CONTENTS

PREFACE

THIS BOOK IS MY true story. I know, because—against all odds—I lived through all of it. This book is a memoir, not an autobiography, because it focuses primarily on fifteen years of my life—the years of 1983 through 1998—and not on my entire life. And memoirs have rules. In today's Age of Truthlessness, I want to disclose the rules that I have followed in writing it.

Most of the people in this memoir are referred to by their first names. For persons who I am certain are dead, who constitute most of the people in my story, I have used their real first name as a means of honoring their memory and legacy in my life. For persons who are still alive, or who possibly still may be alive, I have also used their real first name unless they are villains. Villains are not referred to by their names at all, only by their roles in my story. I have used the full names of all public figures. There is one non-villain whose identity I disguise in order to protect him and his family.

I have painstakingly, and quite painfully, recreated this period of my life based upon notes, writings, interviews, photographs, home movies, obituaries, ticket stubs, invitations, scrapbook contents, Post-it notes, therapy notes, legal filings, income tax returns, address books, memory boxes in my bedroom closet and my warehouse, family genealogy research, Social Security Death Index searches, Google searches, discussions with family members and friends and former work colleagues, *Billboard Magazine*'s annual top 100 songs lists, and historical events (AIDS medical and social history, US history, California history, and Los Angeles history)—but most of all, my *memory*. I have tried to be accurate and honest and also fair, even with respect to the villains and with respect to events that portray me in a negative light, because truth-telling is powerful. My memory is much better than I thought it would be when I embarked on this writing journey, but please understand that it is not perfect and these events happened a very long time ago.

In the passages with actual dialogue, the content and tone is accurate, but these may not be the exact words that were said.

There is one section in which the narrative delves into fantasy, which I clearly state.

In the sections in which I write about my inner thoughts, please know that these sections convey my thoughts at the time but also layer in a more seasoned perspective as I look back from the vantage point of an older man. After all, one of my goals in writing this memoir was to contemplate this story of my youth, examine my flaws, and to understand how my life experience shaped me into the man I am today. This process was incredible therapy for me.

Finally, my story is just one of many stories from the AIDS generation. In it, I speak only for myself, and not in any way for the gay and lesbian community, not for AIDS activists, not for any other groups, not for anyone else. I speak only for myself and my own life experience. As you will see, I don't look very good or even likeable in several parts of this memoir, but I admit that I am a flawed human being. This story is the way it all happened and it is my history.

ACKNOWLEDGMENTS

MICHAEL WIELAND, MY HUSBAND, for believing in me and for supporting me whole-heartedly while I wrote this memoir.

James Devoti and Karen Kraft, for convincing me that this was a story worth telling.

My friends and family members who provided feedback and encouragement on various chapters along the way: Marc Albert; Robert Amend; Max Angst; Guy Baldwin, LMFT; Dana Baron; Marty Bartolac, MD; Hal Bastian; Jackie Black, PhD; Sonja Beals-Iribarren; Elizabeth Boykewich; Gail Boykewich; Stephen Boykewich Jr.; Stephen Boykewich Sr.; Vera Boykewich; Lynn Bukowski; Dillon Ceglio; Terri Chapman; Wayne Chavez; Megan Chernin; Peter Chernin; Barbara Cimaglia; Karen Coler-Castaneda; Trevor Coran; Briana Corcia; Valerie Cohen; JoAnn Cort; Michael Cort; Carol Costanzo; Drew Dees; Stephanie Dees; James Devoti; Marcia Diamond; Mindy Dodge; Douglas Dye; Jane Eisner; Michael Eisner; Caleb Ellis; Jane Engle; Mary Estrin; Robert Estrin; Kristina Forest; Connie Frank; Lowell Gallagher; Roslyn Gaudin; Erica Giovinazzo; Ruth Gitlin; Gregg Gonsalves; Chuck Gordon; Larry Gordon; Lynda Gordon; Maggie Gordon; Bryan Gregory; Scarlett Hammett; Tom Hansen; Hope Heaney; Ursula Heise; Andy Henry; Judy Hofflund; Jeff Hoffman; Virginia Hough; Nike Irvin; Sandy Itkoff; William Jarvis, MD; Janine Jason, MD; Gigi Johnson; Lynsy Karrick-Wikel; Barbara Kellams; Dorcas Kelley; Karen Kraft; Richard Kron; Joel Lambert; Adriel Lares; Robert Laurita; Andrew Marsh; Michael Marsh, MD; Christine Masterson; David McCarthy; Martha Miller; Francois Mobasser; Alexandrea Morelock; Ryan Morelock; Sarah Murphy; Marcie Musser; Robert Musser; Richard Nanula; Larry O' Shell; Linda Palmor; Erika Pardo; Frank Paschal;

11

Christopher Plourde; Noel Plourde; Tamer Qafiti; Natacha Rafalski; Jason Reed; Marsha Reed; Daria Roithmayr; Karen Rowe; Suzanne Russell; Kelley Ryan; David Schaberg; Greg Scott; Margaret Snow; Parsa Sobhani; Melrose Sprague; David Thompson; Jeanne Thurber Tierno; Rus Tokman; Evan Tompkinson; Valerie Townsend; Liz Tractenberg; Stephen Tschida; Mark Tucci; Elizabeth Wall-Macht; Louise Wasso-Jonikas; Kim Wieland; Michael Wieland; Shirley Wieland; Steve Wieland; Meryl Witmer; Gloria Wolper; Israel Wright; Elaine Wynn; Gillian Wynn; Kevyn Wynn; Cid Zaima; Alysa Zyda; Fred Zyda; Greta Zyda; Michael Zyda; and Tyerin Dennis Zyda.

My friends and family members who helped me remember pieces of my history: Robert Amend, Hal Bastian, Jane Engle, Andrew Greenebaum, Joan Hemmann, Nike Irvin, Sandy Itkoff, Erika Pardo, Noel Plourde, Margaret Snow, Dan Wolf, and Tyerin Dennis Zyda.

For helping with medical terminologies, references, and footnotes: Leslie Weinstein, MD.

For editing my manuscript: Dan Wolf.

My agent, John Mason, and Mary Bonventre at Copyright Counselors, LLC.

My publishing team at Rare Bird Books: Tyson Cornell, Guy Intoci, Hailie Johnson, and Julia Callahan.

And Bob Merrill, who wrote *Funny Girl* and who taught me playwriting at UCLA in 1983, who said, "Just pay attention to the world around you and your stories will write themselves." Wherever you are in the universe today, Bob, you were right.

CHAPTER 1
SUN

O N A COLD AND clear Monday evening in early January 1984, I stood, scared, dressed in my suit and tie, at the bottom of the steps to the UCLA Delta Sigma Phi Fraternity house located at 620 Landfair Avenue in Westwood, California. Tonight, I would tell the truth to my eighty-plus fraternity brothers at our Monday night chapter meeting.

The truth about my sexual orientation. A subject about which I had artfully avoided any public discussion throughout my childhood, adolescence, and even college, until this moment in time when I was a twenty-one-year-old senior two quarters from graduation. And for my first public discussion of this subject, I had decided that these eighty-plus fraternity brothers—close friends of mine for the past nearly four years—were the right audience. I would tell them that I was gay. A truly fateful moment in my life. Yes, I was terrified of what might happen. After all, it was January 1984, a lifetime before the greater acceptance of gays and lesbians that exists today. 1984 was just a few years after the groundbreaking gay character Jodie Dallas appeared on the television show *Soap*, but still long before the *Golden Girls* episode about Dorothy's lesbian college roommate, long before the *Friends* episode named "The One With the Lesbian Wedding," long before the groundbreaking coming out "Puppy Episode" on *Ellen*, and long before the gay-centered comedy series *Will and Grace*.

I stood at the bottom of those fraternity house steps because of a fuse that I had lit eight months earlier, when I had come out of the closet to Kevin, a friend from UCLA student government's Spring Sing Committee and a member of the fraternity two doors up the street from mine. Kevin was handsome, with brown hair, dark eyes, and a great smile. Kevin and I had forged a close friendship, and regularly we would get together for dinner, movies, and to hang out. One night in May 1983, Kevin and I went to see *Sophie's Choice* along with Kevin's male roommate, who brought along a male friend. During the film, I noticed that Kevin's roommate and his friend held each other's hands, so after we returned to Kevin's apartment on Oakwood Avenue in Hollywood, I asked Kevin about it. His demeanor suddenly changed and he looked at me with a serious expression from across the coffee table.

"Chris, my roommate is gay," said Kevin. Then a pause. "I have been trying for a while to tell you that I'm gay, too."

I swallowed hard. "I, I um," but he interrupted me.

"Chris, I'm wondering when you are going to tell me that you also are gay."

Boom! My anxiety skyrocketed through the roof. Suddenly, the big elephant in the room occupied the coffee table between the two of us, completely unavoidable. Kevin had scored a bullseye. No amount of pivoting or tap-dancing could get me out of this situation, unless I lied. I knew that I couldn't lie. I took a deep breath to answer him, when he added:

"Chris, I like spending time with you. I want us to be together."

Kevin then moved closer to me and held my hand. We had been on an actual date at *Sophie's Choice* and I didn't even know it! (In retrospect, my experience with Kevin serves as Exhibit A of my lifelong challenge of having the world's worst gaydar.)

The situation with Kevin terrified me. You see, I had almost always known that I was gay. Before I understood sexual orientation, I simply knew that I was "different." Different from everyone else. Different thinking, different perspectives, different interests, just plain different. Not like any others around me. A few of my differences:

1. Breech baby, born left foot first, and delivered without cesarean section.
2. Left-handed in a right-handed world.
3. INTJ,[1] a rare Myers-Briggs personality type.
4. Easily bored.
5. Occasionally stubborn.

---

1   The Introverted Intuitive Thinking Judgmental (INTJ) personality type, also referred to as "the architect" or "the mastermind," appears in approximately 2 percent of the population according to the Myers and Briggs Foundation.

6. I play the piano by ear, and at age seven I drove my piano teacher nuts by adding notes and chords to my assigned piano recital pieces to make them sound better.

7. Also at age seven, the State of California classified me as a "gifted" student after Dr. Sobel, my public elementary school psychologist, tested my IQ and I scored over 138, the highest score possible on the test he administered.

8. The Pope demoted my Roman Catholic namesake, Saint Christopher, from official sainthood to "folk hero" status around 1969, far too late for my religious parents to rename me with a proper saint name. My catechism teachers at Our Lady of Lourdes Roman Catholic Church in Northridge, California, regularly pointed out my patron saint's demotion, highlighting my difference. I was then, and I still am, different on so many levels.

When puberty hit, I knew for certain that I was attracted to boys, but society programmed me to believe that same-sex attraction was wrong, so I stuffed everything deep down inside. Junior high school for me was a painful desert. By high school, I decided that I would come out of the closet someday, but not until after I finished college. I know that it sounds silly today, but I feared that if I came out, the resulting distractions would hurt my GPA and reduce my chances of acceptance into graduate school if I ever wanted to attend one. So, I bolted my closet door shut. As part of my cover, during college I even very casually dated women, including a nice young woman, Joanne, from a UCLA sorority. I exhibited all the behaviors of a hugely mixed-up gay Roman Catholic young man trying to fit into a heterosexual world in the midst of a never-ending barrage of anti-gay messages from society. A pained existence, about to crumble.

In an instant, Kevin had come out to me, turned the tables on me, and yanked my closet door open. This terrified me. I knew that I had to tell him the truth. After all, I'm the one who brought up his roommate's hand-holding. So, I chose to take my first step forward.

"Yes, Kevin, I am gay. I've also never said this to anyone before. You are the first."

Then Kevin kissed me, and I spent the night at his apartment. My first sexual experience with another man, although I fumbled my way through it, was off the charts, butterflies included.

In the morning, I stared at the ceiling of the bedroom, Kevin quietly sleeping next to me, my mind racing about the Pandora's box that I had just opened. My panicked internal stream of consciousness raced like this: Who will Kevin tell about my being gay? Should I tell Joanne? No, I can't tell Joanne because her sorority sister Pellie is dating Dave, one of my fraternity brothers, and I don't want this news getting back to my fraternity. Should I just stop seeing Joanne? Do I owe her any sort of explanation? Should I tell my parents? Goodness, no. Is it possible for me to stay mostly in the closet and have no one know about this? How does this gay world work? Do I want to be Kevin's boyfriend? Am I even ready to be someone's—any man's—boyfriend? Kevin is gorgeous, and smart, and funny, and kind, why wouldn't I want to be his boyfriend? What if he wants to hold hands in front of Royce Hall? Will coming out hurt my GPA? How can I continue living in my fraternity house if I'm now out of the closet? Ugh, now I will need to move out and rent an expensive apartment. Good God, for the rest of my life *Sophie's Choice* will always be my "coming out" movie. That's so messed up! I love Meryl Streep, but why couldn't it be a more uplifting film? I'm getting anxious. I need to get out of Kevin's apartment as quickly as possible so that I can regroup.

I'm afraid I need to state what should be obvious to everyone (but apparently isn't): people are born gay or straight. No one chooses to become gay any more than anyone chooses to have blue or brown eyes. But when you are gay, at some point you do have to choose whether you want to live a truthful life or remain bolted tightly inside the closet. Many men and women from my generation chose to live with the bolts firmly in place out of fear and self-preservation. By admitting to Kevin that I was gay, those bolts disintegrated and my closet door creaked open. Once that door opens even a crack, it nudges life into a cascading series of events that can't be reversed, like the ripples that expand from a stone thrown into a lake. By making my choice, I could see my life already rippling beyond Kevin, and this amplified my fears.

I stirred around in the bed enough to wake him up.

"Good morning, I need to get going," I said. "Last night was a big night for me, and I need some time to think about everything."

Kevin looked sad. His new hoped-for boyfriend was leaving him, even before breakfast.

"Kevin, I don't know that we can be together, at least not right away, because I need to sort things out," I continued. "I need to figure out how this new world works for me and what it means for my life. I hope that you can understand this."

Kevin now looked crushed. My mind still raced. I dressed, hugged him goodbye, and left. Over the next few weeks, we spoke on the phone a number of times, but we never got together. I kept him at a distance. Our moment of possibility had passed. His calls slowed, then stopped. He graduated and went to work on a cruise ship. Eventually, we drifted apart into a distant, fading friendship. I didn't see Kevin again until eleven years later.

Meanwhile, the summer of 1983 rocked my world. With no summer school, I worked full-time as a library researcher for the *Los Angeles Herald-Examiner* newspaper, and on evenings and weekends I learned about this new gay world that I had finally allowed myself to join. I immediately stopped seeing Joanne, of course. I discovered the gay neighborhood of West Hollywood— also known as "Boystown" or the "Swish Alps," but not yet as WeHo—and its many gay bars, dance clubs, and restaurants. At that time, old Red Car trolley tracks still occupied the center of West Hollywood's main thoroughfare, Santa Monica Boulevard. That summer, I gained self-confidence when I learned that scores of handsome men found me attractive, something I had never believed was true about me. I collected dozens of phone numbers from men who wanted to date me, and I saved these phone numbers in a jar on the top of my dresser. I made many new gay friends, including fellow students from UCLA and USC, and we all met up in West Hollywood's gay dance clubs and bars on weekends. Or we would meet at the gay sections of beaches: Venice Beach, Will Rogers Beach (nicknamed "Ginger Rogers Beach"), and Laguna Beach. My new friends invited me to lavish pool parties in West Hollywood, the Hollywood Hills, Bel Air, Holmby Hills, and Malibu. These gays had incredible homes with gorgeous views! I fell in love with the Hollywood Hills and its canyons, and I dreamed of someday owning a home in the Hills with a great view, too. I danced many nights at the Studio One disco, followed by late-night breakfasts at Canter's Deli. I saw up-and-coming vocal stars perform at the Backlot and the Rose Tattoo restaurants during Monday talent nights. I watched the hit television show *Dynasty* on Wednesday nights at the Revolver video bar, as its stars Linda Evans and Joan Collins would wrestle around in mud or endure some other humiliation and the entire bar packed with men would erupt into cheers. I joined and worked out at the exclusively gay Athletic Club gym, owned by the openly gay bodybuilding legend Jim Morris, alongside the fittest men in Los Angeles. A major television star from *Dynasty*, closeted at the time, worked out at the Athletic Club and everyone kept his secret. In the summer of 1983, West Hollywood was gay Camelot. Life was simple and sunny, and I felt so alive.

Some of the best songs from the playlist of my life come from that summer. "Billie Jean," "Flashdance," "Beat It," "Maniac," "She Works Hard for the Money," "The Safety Dance," "1999," "Always Something There to Remind Me," "Cool Places," "Our House," "Wanna Be Startin' Somethin'," "I'm Still Standing," and "It's Raining Men."[2] Songs that instantly transport me back to my time-capsule summer of wild fun, exploration, hope, and the moment when everything in life for me, and so many others, seemed possible.

Eventually I met Marty, a stunningly handsome blond-haired, blue-eyed man from Michigan who worked as a waiter at Restaurant Muse on Beverly Boulevard. Marty had apparently followed me a bit around West Hollywood, and finally summoned the courage to say hello to me at the corner of Santa Monica Boulevard and San Vicente Boulevard. Not creepy at all, right? I dated Marty for the second half of the summer of 1983.

My favorite memory involving Marty: we were invited to a party on a yacht in Marina del Rey, but I couldn't leave my work in time to get to the boat before it departed for Malibu. Marty wanted me to come to the party so badly that he asked me to meet the yacht later that day at the Malibu Pier. When I finished at work, I drove to Malibu but, unfortunately, the yacht could not dock at the pier to pick me up. So, I stripped down to my bathing suit, jumped into the ocean, and swam out to join everyone. I made quite an entrance climbing up the ladder on the side of the yacht, a wet and shirtless twenty-one-year-old, with a group of fully dressed gay men applauding me. To this day, that remains my best party entrance ever. I fell in love with yachts that afternoon, and I dreamed of owning one someday. When the party ended, I dove off the boat, swam back to shore, and drove home.

Although I am a California and Los Angeles native, Marty was the first person I met who embodied California's New Age spiritual philosophy. He

---

2   Throughout this memoir, I reference songs, particularly ones from the 1980s and 1990s, to provide a contemporaneous musical context to my story for the reader. My mind fuses songs with my memories, so the inclusion of them in this memoir also helped me remember details of my story.

opened my eyes to new forms of spiritual and philosophical thinking, and he introduced me to Louise Hay's[3] writings about the power of positive affirmations and to the New Age Bodhi Tree Bookstore on Melrose Avenue.

One morning, as we lay in bed in Marty's studio apartment on Ozeta Terrace in the hills above the Sunset Strip and the iconic Tower Records store, Marty turned to me and said, "You know, Chris, the world is about to go through huge changes. A lot of people will be leaving it. And they will serve as angels for the rest of the people that stay here."

It was a typical New Age Marty–style comment, but this one stuck with me. In hindsight, Marty's comment foreshadowed the future.

I had a wonderful summer whirlwind romance with Marty. He was sweet and kind and incredibly sexy, but not a match for me. As I began my senior year at UCLA, I stopped dating him. I also moved out of my fraternity house and into an apartment at the corner of Kings Road and Fountain Avenue in the heart of West Hollywood with Chris, a friend from UCLA, and John, a friend from USC, both of whom were gay.

Well, that started the rumor about me. My fraternity brothers knew that Chris was gay, and they connected the dots. In early January 1984, one of them told me that a rumor was spreading that I was gay. I froze in shock and terror. I should have known that closet doors can't be kept partly open.

I could have ignored the rumor, avoided my friends in the fraternity for the next six months until graduation, and disappeared into the UCLA woodwork. After all, UCLA was a huge school with over 40,000 students. I couldn't live, however, with running away from my friends with whom I had shared so much. That's not my style. I decided that the best course of action, even though it absolutely terrified me, was to tell everyone in my fraternity the truth, in one fell swoop, at a Monday night chapter meeting, knowing full well that it could go incredibly badly. The fuse that I had lit eight months earlier had finally burned to its end.

So now, on this cold, clear night in January 1984, I stood, scared, at the bottom of the steps of my UCLA fraternity house, facing the moment of truth. I looked up to the stars above me for courage and then nervously

---

3   Louise Hay is known as one of the founders of the "self-help" movement, and published *Heal Your Body* in 1976, and *You Can Heal Your Life* in 1984. Both bestselling books discuss the connection between the mind and the body and how positive thought patterns can help reverse illness and improve health.

climbed those steps one last time. I knew that, one way or the other, when I descended these steps I most likely would no longer be a member of my fraternity. Even in Los Angeles in 1984, it was extremely unlikely that any fraternity would allow an "out" gay man to remain a member. My fraternity brothers and I would go our separate ways with our separate identities, just like Los Angeles had done earlier that month when the entire city split into two separate area codes with distinct identities. After tonight, I would be "213," and my fraternity brothers would be "818."

In the chapter room packed full of over eighty young men, I approached Dave, our president, and asked, "Would you mind if I make a quick announcement at the beginning of the chapter meeting? I need to leave early and head to the library."

Dave gave me the floor to speak. I took a deep breath and started.

"Hi, everyone, I have an announcement. It has come to my attention that a rumor is going around about my being gay, and I just want you all to know that it's true. Yes, I am gay."

Our fraternity meetings always operated with an undercurrent of side conversations, mumbling, joking, and other distractions. Not so tonight. Complete quiet now engulfed the room. You could hear a pin drop, all eyes fixed on me, and many mouths agape. I continued.

"Being gay is relatively new to me, and I'm figuring things out, but I hope that all of you understand that I'm still the same person whom you have known for the past four years. I'm still an English literature major. I'm still involved in student government. I'm still on the Dean's List. I'm still your friend. I'm just gay. I have known this almost my entire life, I just didn't act on it until a few months ago. I have tried for a long time to date women, but there just were no sparks for me. But with men, I have sparks. This is the honest truth. I hope that you won't judge me for anything but our friendship over the past four years."

The room still completely quiet, all eyes fixed on me, and mouths agape. Dave, our president, looked stunned but he didn't stop me. I kept going.

"Now, I know that because I'm gay, I probably shouldn't be a member of this fraternity anymore. It would be awkward for all of us. I fully expect for you to kick me out or to ask for my resignation, and so I hereby offer you my resignation."

The room still completely quiet, all eyes fixed on me, and mouths agape. It was turning entirely too serious. Think quickly, Chris. Then an idea popped into my head. I continued.

"Okay, then, that's my announcement. Oh, there's one more thing that I forgot to mention. Just in case you're all wondering—none of you are my type."

Suddenly the packed room roared with laughter, and then applause, and cheers, and the snapping of fingers. A huge icebreaking relief for everyone in the room. Especially me.

Then one of my fraternity brothers stood up and said, "Wow, Zydaman (my fraternity nickname), that took some real balls for you to say," which sent the room into groans and more rounds of laughter from his poorly timed sexual innuendo. Several more brothers stood up and took their turns to say encouraging words of support for me.

Then one of them proposed that instead of expelling me from the fraternity or accepting my resignation, they should vote me into "alumni status" instead, a creative solution. That way, I could come by the fraternity house whenever I wanted and still be part of the group, but without the normal obligations of membership. In an instant, the group voted me into alumni status, and then they all cheered and clapped for me as I left the meeting.

I couldn't believe the group's reaction—in 1984! Facing my fear and telling the truth that night turned an absolutely terrifying situation for me into an intensely exhilarating and uplifting moment of my life that I will never forget. I was on cloud nine. I learned an important life lesson: truth-telling is powerful.

I descended the steps of my fraternity, and continued my walk into my new life. I didn't set foot in that house again until nearly thirty years later.

Yes, these were sunny days for me.

As an English literature major, I had set my career sights on writing in Hollywood: movies, television shows, plays, novels, everything. I grew up in Porter Ranch in the San Fernando Valley, a conservative upper-middle-class suburb of Los Angeles with the entertainment industry all around me. Movies and television shows filmed regularly in my family's neighborhood, including *E.T. the Extra-Terrestrial*. In the famous scene where Elliot and E.T. and their friends escape on flying bicycles, they, in fact, at one point fly right over the office of Dr. Sloan, my orthodontist. Classmates of mine from elementary school through high school worked as extras and actors. In school, we made films as class projects, and we learned how to shoot scenes, edit, and even create soundtracks. Once we had our drivers licenses, on weekend nights my friends and I would drive our parents' cars to the Mullholland Drive overlooks to watch the twinkling lights of Hollywood and downtown Los Angeles far below us, and we would cruise Sunset Boulevard to see its distinctive movie billboards and the interesting nighttime pedestrians who walked the infamous Sunset Strip.

My dream of working in the entertainment industry began in 1977 when I was fifteen years old and my friend Karen, whose father worked as an executive at 20th Century Fox Studios, invited me to join her for a special screening of the original *Star Wars* movie at the studio lot in Century City. My first Hollywood screening, and it electrified me. From the moment that the opening credits rolled through the end of *Star Wars*, I sat there mesmerized and enchanted, and I vowed right then that someday I would work in Hollywood, even though my parents desperately wanted me to become a medical doctor. *Star Wars* changed my life. Coincidentally, my birthday, May 4, later became known as "Star Wars Day."

By my senior year at UCLA, I realized that I had some talent for creative writing. I had some early writing successes that encouraged me. I wrote the script for a student film that won first place in a film competition. I wrote the book, music, and lyrics for a musical that was selected for production by the theater arts department and the show received good reviews. In one of my screenwriting courses, I earned an A on my final screenplay, called *The Restitution*, in which mother Earth fights back against humankind's endless destructive environmental abuse by unleashing a gigantic and powerful storm to destroy humanity and reclaim the planet—long before climate change became a topic of global concern. I interned for Joan and Rima and Nadine at the Writers and Artists Talent Agency in Brentwood, where I learned the ropes about how to market film and television scripts. The UCLA English department selected me to work as an English composition tutor for other students. In that job, I advised on term papers, tutored members of the UCLA football and basketball teams in English composition, and critiqued and edited essays for graduate school applications. For students who asked, I even ran a side business in which I took a more active role advising them on their graduate school applications. I also worked as an entertainer, playing the piano professionally at parties, weddings, restaurants, and bars throughout

Los Angeles. I still worked part-time in the library at the *Los Angeles Herald-Examiner* newspaper, filing and researching information for articles. I had a file box filled with index cards of story ideas for films, television shows, plays, and novels. By 1984, nearly everything in my life focused on creative writing and on a writing career after college. I had even decided that I would hire Joan at the Writers and Artists Talent Agency to represent me when I landed my first big writing project. My future brimmed with exciting dreams and possibilities.

Interestingly, I earned the best grades of my college career during my senior year. Coming out hadn't hurt my GPA after all. Instead, it had cleared the distracting white background noise from my subconscious and I was able to perform at my peak, thereby securing options to attend a good graduate school if I ever wanted. But I certainly didn't plan on going.

Sunny days, indeed.

Then again, in the words of John Lennon's song "Beautiful Boy (Darling Boy)," "life is what happens to you while you're busy making other plans."

CHAPTER 2
CLOUDS

THE FIRST TIME THAT I learned about the acquired immune deficiency syndrome (AIDS) was during that carefree summer of 1983 when I worked at the *Los Angeles Herald-Examiner*. As a researcher in the newspaper's library, part of my job was to file the newspaper's articles and photographs in hundreds of cabinets that occupied two cavernous, windowless rooms bathed in fluorescent lighting at the *Herald-Examiner*'s Mission Revival headquarters in downtown Los Angeles, built for newspaper baron William Randolph Hearst by his architect, Julia Morgan, who also designed his famous "castle" in San Simeon. When a reporter needed background on a particular subject or person, I gathered the relevant information and delivered it to the newsroom. When the editors needed photographs, I provided a selection of relevant file photographs to consider. To do my job well, I had to read every article that ran in the newspaper each day so that I could quickly provide research on the latest breaking news stories. One of those stories was AIDS, a disease that was exploding in gay communities across the country. One *Herald-Examiner* reporter voraciously covered the AIDS beat, and I filed dozens of his articles and related photographs. Since I had recently come out of the closet, I read each AIDS article with a particular sense of dread, learning about a disease that was not some abstract news story but something that threatened my new world. Clouds on the horizon.

The early history of the AIDS virus that I learned from those 1983 news clips was both sketchy and terrifying.[4] The disease seemed to begin around

---

4   Throughout this memoir, I include historical and medical references for the benefit of readers who did not live through the early days of the AIDS pandemic, as I did, for whom such context may be helpful.

June 1981, when two doctors reported that five gay men in Los Angeles (ages twenty-nine, thirty, thirty, thirty-three, and thirty-six) developed a rare opportunistic infection called pneumocystis carinii pneumonia around the same time as another group of gay men in New York City and Los Angeles developed an unusual and also rare cancer called Kaposi's sarcoma.[5, 6] At first, the disease was called the "gay plague," "gay cancer," or "gay-related immuno-deficiency" (GRID), even though the disease also affected intravenous drug users.[7, 8, 9] By the end of 1982, those disease names were dropped in favor of AIDS, and according to the American Foundation for AIDS Research (amfAR), out of 771 reported cases in the US, 618 of them—a staggering 80 percent—had already died.[10,11] By 1983, AIDS had infected women, babies, hemophiliacs, and a seemingly large number of Haitians and Africans, too. Although AIDS didn't only infect gay men, gay men overwhelmingly bore the brunt of the disease's stigma. Total known AIDS infections at that time were still relatively small in number, but growing exponentially. In 1983, researchers discovered a retrovirus that likely caused AIDS—initially thought to be part of a virus family known as the Human T-cell Lymphotropic Virus, and was called HTLV-III—and they studied this virus in a laboratory.[12] In 1983, no one knew exactly how the AIDS virus was transmitted, but intimate sexual contact seemed highly suspect. Misinformation and fear ran wild. Discrimination quickly followed against people with AIDS, and also against the health professionals who treated them. In fact, the first

5   Centers for Disease Control and Prevention, June 5, 1981, "Pneumocystis Pneumonia—Los Angeles," *Morbidity and Mortality Weekly Report*, Volume 30, Number 21, 1–3.

6   Lawrence K. Altman, July 3, 1981, "Rare Cancer Seen in 41 Homosexuals," *The New York Times*.

7   Centers for Disease Control and Prevention, June 18, 1982, "A Cluster of Kaposi's Sarcoma and Pneumocystis Carinii Pneumonia among Homosexual Male Residents of Los Angeles and Orange Counties, California," *Morbidity and Mortality Weekly Report*, Volume 31, Number 23, 305–307.

8   Lawrence K. Altman, June 18, 1982, "Clue Found on Homosexuals Precancer Syndrome," *The New York Times*.

9   Michael VerMeulen, May 31, 1982, "The Gay Plague," *New York Magazine*.

10   Robin Herman, August 8, 1982, "A Disease's Spread Provokes Anxiety," *The New York Times*.

11   *American Foundation for AIDS Research* (amfAR), "Thirty Years of HIV/AIDS: Snapshots of an Epidemic," http://www.amfar.org/thirty-years-of-hiv/aids-snapshots-of-an-epidemic/. AIDS statistics from this same source are cited throughout this memoir.

12   Francois Barré-Sinoussi, F. et al, May 20, 1983, "Isolation of a T-Lymphotropic Retrovirus from a Patient at Risk for Acquired Immune Deficiency Syndrome (AIDS)," *Science*, Volume 220, Number 4599, 868–871.

US AIDS discrimination lawsuit was filed in 1983 by Joseph Sonnabend, a physician and AIDS researcher threatened with eviction from his cooperative apartment building because he treated AIDS patients—in, of all places, Greenwich Village, New York City, steps away from the Stonewall Inn, the birthplace of the US gay liberation movement in 1969.[13] The first safe-sex brochure, *Play Fair*, published by the San Francisco Order of the Sisters of Perpetual Indulgence, appeared in 1982,[14] followed by a more comprehensive safe-sex pamphlet in 1983, *How to Have Sex in an Epidemic: One Approach.*[15] AIDS charities, medical research foundations, and support groups quickly formed in major cities, including New York City's Gay Men's Health Crisis, founded in January 1982, and AIDS Project Los Angeles, which held its first board meeting in January 1983. In stark contrast, President Ronald Reagan and the US government did virtually nothing to respond. In 1983, no AIDS test existed yet, so people did not find out that they had the virus until the disease presented actual symptoms. In 1983, AIDS had no effective drugs or treatment protocols. As a result, AIDS killed people quickly, sometimes within a few months. People simply just disappeared.

Imagine, for a moment, the terror of being a twenty-one-year old gay man like me in 1983, or a gay man of any age at that time, and absorbing this barrage of devastating news about the AIDS virus. As I filed those articles in the *Herald-Examiner* library, my sense of dread skyrocketed because the gay community—my community—was ground zero for AIDS. I feared that AIDS would touch me someday. It would. AIDS would become the storm to land a direct hit on my life and the life of everyone around me. A superstorm caused by a virus that would alter my dreams and life forever. Because of all those terrifying AIDS articles, I made one important decision in the summer of 1983: I stopped having unprotected sex.

For me, the prospect of having sex in 1983 quickly became analogous to the predicament of the male black widow spider, who, more often than not, dies after he has sex. Before the first AIDS cases appeared in 1981, just like

13   Philip Shenon, October 1, 1983, "A Move to Evict AIDS Physician Fought by State," *The New York Times.*

14   Sister Florence Nightmare and Sister Roz Erection of the San Francisco Order of the Sisters of Perpetual Indulgence, 1982, *Play Fair!* The Sisters of Perpetual Indulgence is a community service organization run predominantly by gay men who dress up in drag as nuns.

15   Richard Berkowitz and Michael Callen, News from the Front Publications, copyright May 1983, *How to Have Sex in an Epidemic: One Approach.*

the poor male black widow spider, no one knew they could die from having sex. It did not require a science degree for me to observe, through obituaries, that in the early years of the AIDS epidemic, a large portion of the men who died from AIDS were in their late twenties or slightly older. I thought to myself, why so much older? Why not eighteen-year-olds? Or twenty-one-year-olds like me? How come we aren't dying from AIDS, too? This suggested to me the possibility of a long AIDS incubation period. I thought to myself that *if* a large portion of the men dying from AIDS in 1983 was in their late twenties or older, and *if* people generally became sexually active during their mid-to-late teenage years, *then* perhaps the incubation period for AIDS could be quite long, maybe five or even ten years.[16] But, if my unscientific theory were true, then it meant that everyone who had lived through and indulged during the 1970s sexual revolution potentially could be a metaphorical male black widow spider, a human ticking time bomb carrying the fatal AIDS virus, with no way of knowing it. Men, women, gay, straight, old, young. If people had been unwittingly transmitting the AIDS virus to each other for several years, then my unscientific theory might also explain the disease's already exponential growth by 1983. It also might mean that the known cases in 1983 were only the tip of a giant iceberg of AIDS diagnoses to come. AIDS cases ultimately might number in the thousands, or the tens of thousands, or the hundreds of thousands, or maybe even the millions. Again, terrifying. I hoped that my unscientific theory was wrong. In hindsight, it wasn't.

Gay men who were just becoming sexually active were lucky: we could take some precautions to protect ourselves in the face of the storm. Everyone else had the odds stacked overwhelmingly against them. These men may have felt perfectly healthy. But so does the post-coital male black widow spider.

As a result of all my reading of *Herald-Examiner* articles, theorizing and worrying, not only did I stop having unprotected sex in 1983, but I also quickly became a lifelong hypochondriac and germophobe.

In January 1984, one evening at The Athletic Club Gym in West Hollywood, about a week after I came out to my fraternity brothers, I was brushing my teeth after I finished my workout when a handsome and

---

16   Many years later, scientists determined that the median incubation period for AIDS was 9.8 years. Peter Bacchetti and Andrew R. Moss, "Incubation Period of AIDS in San Francisco," *Nature*, March 16, 1989, Volume 338, Pages 251–253.

muscular man with brown hair, piercing blue eyes, and a beautiful smile walked up to the bathroom sink next to me and said:

"It's nice to see someone in the gym taking such good care of his teeth."

I nodded and smiled at the man with my mouth full of toothpaste and continued brushing. I had seen him working out before at The Athletic Club.

"Hi, my name is Stephen," he said.

After I finished brushing, I introduced myself to Stephen with a proper handshake and we talked for a while. I learned some basics about him. He was born in New York City and raised in Washington, DC. An only child. He was an attorney and economist who had attended Yale University, the Massachusetts Institute of Technology (MIT), and Yale Law School. He spoke five languages in addition to English: French, Spanish, Italian, Latin, and ancient Greek. He was thirty-three years old, twelve years older than I was. He lived in the upscale Windsor Square/Hancock Park/Fremont Place neighborhood of Los Angeles, where he was renovating a house. He worked at one of Los Angeles's most prestigious law firms. I could tell instantly that Stephen was a brilliant man, and I have a special weakness for brilliance. Brilliance is my kryptonite.

When we finished our conversation, Stephen gave me his telephone number and I walked home from the gym. I had recently moved from Kings Road to an apartment on West Knoll Drive, just south of Santa Monica Boulevard and almost directly across the street from The Athletic Club—an apartment that had gorgeous views from its tiny third floor rear balcony: in one direction, a giant billboard of a pink Corvette occupied by Angelyne, who invented the idea of being famous for being famous, and in the other direction, the smelly trash bins behind the ultra-expensive L'Orangerie Restaurant on La Cienega Boulevard, a place where I could not even afford an appetizer. Instead of adding Stephen's phone number to the pile of phone numbers in the jar on my dresser, I set his phone number aside and decided that I would actually call it. I had just met the man who would sweep me off my feet, become the first love of my life, and be my life partner for the next seven and a half years.

Stephen and I had a whirlwind romance during the winter and spring of 1984. On our first date on January 27, 1984, Stephen cooked dinner for me at his house: grilled bacon-wrapped filet mignon. Although he was quite handsome, it was his high intelligence that made me fall head-over-heels for him. He was so impressive to be around. So young, and already so successful. So worldly, sophisticated, well-read, and well-traveled. He had everything going for him and had seemingly everything together. He could intelligently debate me on any subject, and sometimes even get me to concede. I had never met anyone like Stephen before in my life, and I found him irresistible. I admired him, and in many ways I wanted to be like him. Stephen was quite the catch, and he fell head-over-heels for me too. He told me that he loved my confidence, my sarcastic sense of humor, and the fact that I wasn't afraid to tackle the inherently risky career of writing.

With my academic schedule and his law firm job, we struggled to find times to date. We bonded over John Milton, whose literature I studied during winter quarter 1984. Even though he worked intense law-firm hours, Stephen actually bought his own copy of Milton's *Paradise Lost* so that he could read and discuss it with me. Who does such a thing for the person they are dating? He wanted to share Milton with me and that required serious effort! He often met me at Ben Frank's Coffee Shop on Sunset Boulevard or at Duke's Coffee Shop in the Tropicana Hotel across from The Athletic Club to read and critique my essays and term papers. He intensely proofread my capstone Milton paper, struggling to find anything to edit. He finally found one word in my paper that made sense to change.

We worked out together at The Athletic Club. Stephen took me to dinner at Chasen's and Jimmy's and The Palm. I took him to dinner at the much-less-expensive and lower-brow Hamburger Habit, the Greenery, Tail O' the Pup, and El Coyote. Or, when I could afford to splurge, I took him to the slightly-more-upscale-but-still-inexpensive French Market Place. We saw *Terms of Endearment*, the classic film and 1984 Best Picture winner about a mother who makes peace with her daughter who dies from cancer, and together we bawled our eyes out. We went to the Groundlings and saw the comedian Phil Hartman perform before his career launched into the stars. We went to Palm Springs for spring break, back when Palm Springs still allowed spring breakers. I was so infatuated with him that I actually wrote a poem pining for him when he went out of town on a business trip. Such an English literature major cliché! The songs from newcomer Madonna's first album served as the playlist for our romance.

Stephen and I enjoyed long conversations and debates about economics, politics, religion, literature, theater, and life. His intelligence was off the charts and acted like a drug for me. I learned that Stephen was a conservative Republican, both economically and socially. At the time, I also was a registered Republican, influenced heavily by my parents' Roman Catholic and conservative beliefs. In 1984, I was a fiscal conservative but socially quite liberal, and I certainly questioned all things political. Since political parties change over time, it's important to note that a Republican from 1984 would likely not be a Republican today—they would very possibly be a mainstream Democrat, or an Independent without a party, like me.

Stephen faithfully read conservative author William F. Buckley's *National Review* magazine, to which he subscribed, and I read each issue too so that I could point out Mr. Buckley's flawed logic and spark spirited debates. Stephen was quite religious, and attended St. James Episcopal Church on Wilshire Boulevard every Sunday and served on its vestry committee. In contrast, I stopped attending church immediately after my Roman Catholic confirmation. At twenty-one years old, I already mistrusted organized religions, and specifically my own, the Roman Catholic Church, even though I am spiritual and believe in God. I had listened intently in the catechism classes of my youth, but I asked too many questions and debated my teachers' answers. I disagreed and argued when I heard that my Jewish friends, classmates, and neighbors would not go to heaven because Catholicism was the "one true faith." I pondered how the Virgin Mary could get pregnant without having sex. I questioned how Mary's husband Joseph must have felt when he learned that God got her pregnant with Jesus, which sounded to me like adultery, an act specifically prohibited by the Ten Commandments. I wanted to know why Popes throughout history killed so many people in the name of the Roman Catholic Church when the Ten Commandments also prohibit killing. I asked how Jesus could hang around with Mary Magdalene, a prostitute, but now the Roman Catholic Church condemned prostitutes. I even questioned the Ten Commandments. Why just these ten? As my young mind grappled with the faulty logic of the Church, my curiosity drove my catechism teachers at Our Lady of Lourdes nuts and I spent a fair amount of time seated on a chair outside Monsignor Stroup's office, not for misbehaving in class, but for asking questions.

I admit that I am a smartass and enjoyed questioning my teachers to make them squirm. For example, I queried the obvious overpopulation problem of purgatory, the Church's designated "waiting room" between this earthly world and heaven, after one teacher explained how each one of our good deeds would shorten our time there by perhaps a few days, but each one of our bad deeds or sins, even minor ones, would add hundreds or thousands of years to our purgatory sentence: "I don't understand this math, does this mean that no one is in heaven today because everyone is still stuck waiting in purgatory?" Prior to my first communion, another teacher required everyone to conduct a practice first confession before making our first real confession with an actual priest behind the screen. For our homework, she asked us to think of some made-up sins that we could confess to her so that we could get the hang of the process. She acted as the priest behind the screen. I prepared thoroughly, and brought a list of ten sins, one from each of the Ten Commandments. I only got to confessing my fourth made-up sin before my teacher figured out what I was doing, lost her temper, and shouted at me from behind the screen, "Christopher Zyda, get out of this confessional right now! Your penance is 100 Our Fathers!" So much for the anonymity of the confessional booth!

I scrimped and saved to buy twenty-five-dollar tickets so that Stephen and I could attend a Joan Rivers comedy show at Studio One in West Hollywood on March 11, 1984. A fairly expensive ticket for me at the time, but her show raised much-needed money for the recently founded AIDS Project Los Angeles. Rivers took a huge career gamble in doing that show. In 1984, no other celebrity would lend their name to any sort of AIDS-related cause. But Joan Rivers did. She was the first trailblazer from the entertainment industry to help the gay community fight AIDS, even before Elizabeth Taylor, and for that Joan Rivers deserves eternal gay sainthood status. I knew that we had to support Rivers, her show, and most importantly the work of AIDS Project Los Angeles, and so I surprised Stephen with the tickets as my first birthday gift to him. I still have my receipt for the tickets. Robert, one of my closest friends from junior high and high school and also gay, joined Stephen and me, as did my sister, Joan, and we all arrived early so that we could sit in the front row of seats arranged on the disco's giant dance floor and hopefully be picked on by Ms. Rivers. It worked. She skewered us mercilessly, and then gave us the potted plants from the stage for being such good sports.

One night in those early weeks of dating Stephen, my friend Bryn showed up at my apartment door. When I met him, Bryn and I instantly became close friends, but we never dated. Bryn was the natural, effortless bright light of every room that he occupied. He hailed from Minneapolis, was my age, and worked as a waiter at the Hard Rock Cafe at the two-year-old Beverly Center shopping mall. The Hard Rock Cafe featured the iconic eye-catching rear-end of an old turquoise blue Cadillac sticking out of its roof, as if it had just crashed there, turn signal still blinking. I ate at the Hard Rock Cafe often after class so that I could hang out with Bryn during his breaks. Stephen and Bryn coincidentally shared the same, fairly uncommon, middle name: Barrett.

Bryn lived by himself in a large, nicely furnished one-bedroom apartment on Larrabee Street just north of Santa Monica Boulevard, quite an unusual living situation for someone of his age and occupation. Bryn did not seem to want for money. For his birthday party on New Year's Eve in 1983, Bryn hosted a lavish catered celebration at his apartment where we all watched a midnight screening on his large screen television of Michael Jackson's newly released blockbuster *Thriller* music video on MTV, the two-year-old Music Television Network cable channel. Because of Bryn's affluent lifestyle, I assumed that he came from a wealthy family since I met him through my former roommate Chris, the descendant of a family fortune minted during the Gilded Age. As soon as Bryn entered my apartment, I could tell that he had something on his mind.

After the usual niceties, Bryn said, "I've never told you where my money comes from."

I joked back, "You don't need to, I already know that you're a trust fund baby just like Chris."

"No, not a trust fund baby," Bryn replied. "Most of my money comes from doing something that's not legal." Bryn tested out the waters with me before proceeding further.

I squinted and asked, "Like drugs? Are you a drug dealer?" This would have shocked me because Bryn had been my friend for almost a year and I never once saw him use drugs, or even talk about drugs.

"No, not drugs," Bryn responded. Then a pause. "Chris, I'm a gay male prostitute. A call boy. A gigolo."

What a curveball. I never suspected for a minute that Bryn could have been a prostitute. He was so handsome, so tall, so blond-haired and blue-eyed, so muscular, so clean cut, so all-American. Then it dawned on me: so... marketable! No wonder Bryn had so much money at the age of twenty-one. Everything suddenly fell into focus for me.

32

In addition to my Milton course at UCLA, I was enrolled in a course in George Bernard Shaw's literature and I had recently finished reading Shaw's classic play about prostitution, *Mrs. Warren's Profession.*

I exclaimed, "You're Mrs. Warren!"

Bryn, looking confused, responded, "I'm who?"

"Mrs. Warren, the main character in George Bernard Shaw's play about prostitution," I said. I was excited to share my new knowledge about the world's oldest profession.

"Mrs. Warren is the heroine of the play! Mrs. Warren became a prostitute because she wanted to provide a good life for her daughter. Mrs. Warren became a successful businesswoman and made a ton of money and sent her daughter to Cambridge University, where she graduated with honors! Mrs. Warren was amazing!"

"Well, then, just call me Mrs. Warren," said Bryn. "Why does everything have to be a literary reference for you?" Bryn, who never attended college, liked to tease me about my tendency to connect the literature I studied at UCLA with real-life situations.

I had many questions for Bryn, and I listened with rapt attention while he explained the 1984 world of gay male prostitution to me:

"Every day at five p.m., I go to the pay phone in front of the Mayfair Market on Santa Monica Boulevard and from there I call David," said Bryn. "David is my trick master, and he tells me if and where I'm going to work that night."

"Sometimes I earn a few hundred dollars, sometimes it's thousands of dollars."

"My clients aren't who you might think. A lot of them are famous people. It's all very high-end and classy." Bryn never divulged the names of any of his famous clients, and I never asked. I never met David, his trick master, either.

At the end of my grilling, however, Bryn turned serious, and said, "I hope that you will still be my friend now that you know this, Chris."

I remembered from catechism that Jesus had hung out with Mary Magdalene. I figured that if Jesus could have a friend who was a prostitute, then I could do it too.

I replied, "Of course, Bryn. You and I are friends for life, and you can always count on me. I don't care one bit. You're now my own personal Mrs. Warren!"

"But don't call me Mrs. Warren in front of anyone else," admonished Bryn. "You are the only person that knows this about me besides David, my trick master."

Bryn and I were, in fact, friends for life. I wish I had a photo of him.

Through the spring of 1984 Stephen and I continued our romance and I fell more in love with him. I turned twenty-two in May 1984 and for my birthday Stephen threw a swimming pool party at his house. Several of my friends attended, including Bryn, and Stephen also invited some of his gay friends for me to meet. This was the first time that our respective friends ever mixed. Stephen's friends were all at least ten years older than me. All of them Ivy League college graduates. All quite established in their careers. One of them was Mark, an attractive UCLA economics professor whom I recognized from campus and also West Hollywood. Stephen's friends were all nice to me, but I felt quite uncomfortable being so much younger and less established than they were. I felt a bit like arm-candy and I didn't like it. Stephen assured me that no one cared. Joan and her wonderful partner, Jane, also attended my birthday party.

Yes, you read that correctly: my sister was a lesbian. Joan, ten years older than me, served as a second mom to me when I was growing up, and I admired her immensely. To me, she was larger than life. Since I'm describing her in the past tense, you can tell that she's not around anymore. I'll get to that.

First, a bit of my family background: I am the youngest of three children. My brother Michael is eight years older than me. When I first questioned my parents as to why my sister was ten years older than me and my brother was eight years older than me, my mom and dad explained to me that my birth was a "surprise." I later learned that I was the product of my parents practicing the unreliable Roman Catholic rhythm method of birth control. I grew up believing that I was not a welcome surprise, but instead an unfortunate Roman Catholic "accident."

My parents reinforced my belief by pointing out to me throughout my childhood that I was missing out on many experiences because our family had already done them before I was born, or as my parents called it, during the "BC period" (Before Christopher). My parents told me that the family wasn't going to repeat these experiences simply because I came along. As a result, scouting, national park visits, camping, and cross-country driving trips were all off-limits in my childhood. My parents somehow thought that it would be comforting to periodically show me their home movies of my BC family enjoying all of these experiences without me. Instead, it made me feel left out and reinforced to me that I wasn't such a happy surprise.

Joan and Michael, both brilliant, had an intense sibling rivalry that I never understood. This played out in unfortunate ways. When I was around five years old, one night at the dinner table, during a loud argument, Joan stabbed Michael in his stomach with her butter knife. Not a deep wound, but it did draw blood. I quietly ate my dinner while my parents, sister, and brother all screamed at each other over the ensuing bloody mess.

Screaming matches occurred often in my family's home, as our nearby neighbors could attest. My parents, my sister, and my brother were world-class screamers. As a result, I despise screaming to this day. I spent much of my childhood trying to be a perfect child, get straight A's in school, and not be screamed at, because deep down I believed the only reason I existed was due to an unreliable Roman Catholic birth control method. I felt that I really wasn't supposed to exist at all.

I dreaded when my parents had date nights and left Joan and Michael to babysit me. The moment that my parents' car left the driveway, the fights would start between my sister and brother and I would run to take cover in my bedroom with my door shut. On one of these date nights when I was six years old, I had left my set of building blocks in the hall outside my bedroom, and my blocks became projectiles that Joan and Michael threw at each other during a fight while I huddled in my room. Eventually, one of the blocks crashed against my door with a loud thud and that was the last straw for me. I threw open my door to see a dent in its hollow white wood veneer, and suddenly I became a fellow Zyda family screamer, too:

"Stop fighting right now! You are ruining my toys! And you broke my door!"

Then I made my sister and brother fix the dent in my bedroom door as best as they could before our parents came home from their date. It's the only time that I ever saw them work together as a team other than when they both slammed their bedroom doors in unison whenever I started to practice my piano lessons in the living room. I was six years old when the Building Block Battle happened. Joan was sixteen, and Michael was fourteen. Who was babysitting whom?

Joan was an incredibly talented writer, and blessed with the passion to become a newspaper reporter from childhood. We nicknamed her Brenda

Starr after the ace reporter in the well-known comic strip. Incredibly focused, full of energy, beautiful, popular, funny, the life of every party. Joan started college at California State University Northridge (until 1972, it was called San Fernando Valley State College) and wrote for the *Daily Sundial*, its student newspaper. My parents didn't really want her to go to college. They wanted her to marry her boyfriend Kevin, stay home, have children, and not work, much less pursue a journalism career.

Soon thereafter, Joan scored a coveted writing internship at the *Los Angeles Times*, which quickly turned into a full-time job offer because her writing was that good. Joan grabbed this opportunity and never looked back. She dropped out of college to write news stories, feature stories, and win journalism awards.

Joan convinced the reclusive queen of silent films, Mary Pickford, to grant her first interview to anyone in decades at her Pickfair estate in Beverly Hills. She attended and reported on a State dinner at the Nixon White House. Joan interviewed and got to know Ronald and Nancy Reagan while Ronald Reagan was still the governor of California, became their friend, and soon their daughter Maureen Reagan was at our house hanging out and swimming in our pool. Joan's articles gleamed from the front pages of the *Los Angeles Times*. She was only twenty years old. Just incredible.

Then, the *Denver Post* hired Joan away from the *Los Angeles Times* and her career thrived even more in Colorado. She broke up with Kevin. I spent the summer of 1974 living with Joan in Denver, where we climbed Pikes Peak, prospected in a gold mine in Idaho Springs, hitchhiked from Glenwood Springs to Aspen, rode the old wooden roller coaster at Elitch Gardens, and caught my first trout in Lake Evans using Velveeta cheese.

Then, in 1975, the *Chicago Tribune* knocked on Joan's door, and she moved to Illinois for an even bigger job. During the 1976 presidential election campaign, candidate Ronald Reagan and his wife Nancy gave their friend Joan a ride on their campaign plane from Chicago to Los Angeles so that she could scoop a one-on-one interview with the Reagans and also make a surprise visit to me and my parents. I spent the summer of 1978 with Joan in Chicago, where we sailed on Lake Michigan, danced the Hasapiko at a Greek restaurant while drunk on Ouzo, and visited the top of the five-year-old Sears Tower, which was then the world's tallest building. I met Joan's "best friend" Jane, whom I discovered several years later Joan had recently started dating.

Joan also taught me how to drive on the upper and lower streets of downtown Chicago's Loop, a crazy place to learn how to drive a car, and this explains a lot about my style of driving today.

At the *Tribune*, Joan covered some of Chicago's biggest news stories, including the grisly John Wayne Gacy murders in 1978 and the even more horrific American Airlines flight 191 DC-10 crash in 1979 that killed 273 people near a trailer park next to Chicago's O'Hare Airport. She became skilled at talking her way through police barricades. Her journalism career was on a meteoric rise. I knew that it was only a matter of time before she scored a job at one of the country's most prestigious newspapers, either the *New York Times* or the *Washington Post*. Her future seemed unbelievably bright in a career field overwhelmingly dominated by men.

Until early 1980. Joan's journalism career came to a crashing halt at the age of twenty-seven when she was fired by the *Chicago Tribune* for being a lesbian. Actually, she wasn't officially fired for being a lesbian, but Joan connected the dots and you can, too.

According to Joan, corroborated by a number of her *Chicago Tribune* colleagues, it all started with a purse.

A purse that was conveniently "forgotten" in the *Tribune*'s newsroom by one of Joan's female colleagues, who was known to have slept with several men in the newsroom. Well, this colleague called Joan and asked if she could bring her purse to her residence after work since they lived close to each other.

Red Flag #1: How many grown, educated, professional women do you know who would "accidentally" forget their purse at the office and ask you to bring it to their home after work? You know, the purse that also has their house keys in it?

When Joan showed up after work with the allegedly forgotten purse, her colleague answered the door wearing a negligee, holding a copy of the lesbian novel *Rubyfruit Jungle* in her hand, and said, "Oh, this book is so interesting," and then right on her front doorstep made a sexual pass at Joan. Joan declined the highly inappropriate overture, and then left as quickly as possible. That was Red Flag #2.

Shortly after this encounter and to Joan's horror, this female colleague then "outed" her to the entire *Tribune* newsroom. When my sister, crushed by this, asked her colleague, who she thought was a friend, why she had done this, the colleague replied, "Because it makes good gossip." That was Red Flag #3.

Then, trouble started for Joan. Remember, this was 1980, and it was difficult enough for any woman to be working in a male-dominated newsroom at a major metropolitan newspaper during that era, much less a lesbian woman who had been outed. Soon, whenever a new edition of the *Tribune* came off the printing presses, the editor, who typically distributed copies to all of the newsroom reporters, stopped giving Joan a copy, and she had to find her own copy of the newspaper elsewhere. That was a very bright Red Flag #4.

Overnight, the newsroom had become a hostile work environment for Joan because she was a lesbian. But it's important to remember that in 1980 in Chicago, none of this was illegal. Gays and lesbians had no workplace protections at all. Her boss was merely doing what he was allowed to do.

Then, one day Joan's editor boss called her into his office and accused her of sending inappropriate messages to a female coworker through her word-processing terminal. He shook a stack of papers of these alleged messages in her face, but he wouldn't let her see them. He berated and insulted her. He told her that she could resign on her own or she would be immediately fired. He wouldn't let her consult with an attorney before she made her decision. He wouldn't discuss a settlement agreement with a non-disparagement clause. He wanted her gone from the newsroom right then and there. Joan was terrified and crushed, but she knew exactly what was happening to her—it was all because she was a lesbian. This is what the red flags had led to—Joan being cowed and bullied by a man, her boss, a Roman Catholic by the way, who served as her executioner, jury, and judge.

Never mind that the newsroom's word processors weren't password-protected the way that email is secured today, so any one of Joan's colleagues could have typed messages from her terminal when she stepped away, which she did often throughout the work day. Perhaps someone thought that framing Joan for sending inappropriate messages to a female colleague would "make good gossip" and be a fun prank to play on the outed lesbian in the newsroom who now had a target on her back. Perhaps Joan's *Rubyfruit Jungle* colleague felt rejected by her and this was her revenge. We will never know.

Never mind that Joan's journalism work product was impeccable. You can read her articles yourself in the *Chicago Tribune* archives. Never mind that only a few years earlier, Rick Soll, a male *Tribune* colleague, was caught outright plagiarizing much of his column from another writer and received only a thirty-day suspension without pay as punishment—a slap on the wrist for an outrageous, inexcusable, intentional professional violation. In fact, it wasn't until Mr. Soll subsequently plagiarized a second column that he resigned/got fired. By contrast, these messages that Joan wasn't allowed to see, allegedly sent from her word-processing terminal, which could have been composed by anyone in the newsroom, after all of the exceptional work that she had done at the newspaper over five years, somehow rose to the level of requiring Joan's instant termination. No warning in her human resources file, no second chance or one-month suspension without pay like her male colleague had received, no investigation by the newspaper that prided itself on its investigative journalism and fairness. Instead, a rush to judgment and the immediate loss of her job. Her boss pressured her intensely to resign in his office, and in the biggest mistake of her life and without appropriate legal counsel, a terrified twenty-seven-year-old Joan agreed. After she left the building, a number of her colleagues heard him say, "Thank God that dyke is gone from the newsroom."

And, yes, I'm sure that all of this made "good gossip" for the newsroom for weeks.

Then, when Joan tried to collect unemployment benefits, her former boss told the unemployment investigator that she had resigned on her own free will, was never threatened with firing, and insisted that she receive no unemployment benefits. The investigator, who interviewed Joan's former boss over the phone while Joan sat in her office, slammed the phone down and exclaimed, "that man is lying," and then approved the unemployment benefits.

Unfortunately, it turned out that Joan's punishment was much, much more than losing her job at the *Tribune*. It meant the loss of her career. Her former boss blackballed Joan from ever working again at a top newspaper by continuing to give her a horrible, ominous, non-specific, but damning job reference to anyone who called him. Joan was smart enough to confirm this fact through friends who posed as potential employers and called him for a job reference. Joan's hundreds of published high-profile articles and long list of journalism awards no longer seemed to count for anything. Indeed, they worked against her, since her writing for the *Tribune* was so well-known that any potential employer eventually would call her former boss for a reference. Joan's firing devastated her. She had so much promise in her life, she was a talented writer with an ascending career, and one despicable homophobic man stole everything from her. This horrific experience completely altered the arc of her life.

Joan should have marched right to the nearest American Civil Liberties Union office and filed a wrongful termination lawsuit against the *Chicago Tribune*. If she had made this choice, the lawsuit would have been a groundbreaking public battle and a major news story. She would likely have won. But Joan didn't fight back. She didn't want to be the lesbian discrimination poster child. She didn't have the strength to come out publicly. Although she had come out of the closet with friends around 1978, she didn't tell me that she was a lesbian until the spring of 1983 when I had told her that I was gay myself. Even then, when Joan finally came out to me and shared with me the heartbreaking story of her firing by the *Tribune*, she swore me to secrecy to never tell anyone in our family about any of it. She never spoke of it to them. So, our mom and dad lived the rest of their lives never knowing the tragedy that happened to their daughter in Chicago, and why. Joan's horrible experience of being fired by the *Tribune*, however, made me worry about how my own future life and career would be impacted by my being gay. It underscored for me why many men and women from my generation chose to stay bolted in the closet so that they could live in society more easily and without the discrimination that my sister experienced. I vowed that if I ever encountered homophobia in my own life, I would fight back.

After a lengthy job search, Joan got hired as a reporter by the *Los Angeles Herald-Examiner* by an enlightened editor who said, "Who cares about that, you're a great writer," after she told him that her former boss at the *Chicago Tribune* would not give her a good reference because she was a lesbian. In fact, Joan is the one who told me about the part-time student job position in the *Herald-Examiner*'s library. Unfortunately, the *Herald-Examiner* had less of a reputation than the *Chicago Tribune*, and it represented the first in a string of successively worse jobs for her. Over the years, Joan's anger about being fired by the *Tribune* for being a lesbian and her choice in the moment to not fight back simmered and grew, and her life force weakened, and her career trended downward with each new job. Absolutely heartbreaking.

Even at the wonderful twenty-second birthday party that Stephen hosted for me at his house, I could tell that Joan's increasing bitterness toward life grated on him and that the two of them never would be close. By this time,

Joan had already been stewing for four years over her firing, and Stephen never fully appreciated the horrible pain that she had suffered.

Through the month of May 1984, Stephen and I continued our romance. To my chagrin, I learned that Stephen enjoyed WASP-y Los Angeles social events. Stephen was proud of his social registry listing in the *Los Angeles Blue Book*. I thought he meant the *Kelley Blue Book*, which helped people figure out the value of old cars, and I had no idea that this publication chronicled the "who's who" of Los Angeles high society. Stephen had many WASP-y friends involved in the Junior League and the Orphanage Guild, and friends who had memberships in the Los Angeles Country Club, and the Beach Club, and the Valley Hunt Club, and the California Club, and the California Yacht Club, and the Jonathan Club, and the Bel-Air Bay Club, and friends who had summer homes in Montecito, Newport Beach, Rancho Santa Fe, and St. Malo. Stephen himself was a proud member of the Metropolitan Club of Washington, DC, a private men's club. He also was a member of the Yale Club of New York City. Stephen loved to talk about all of these private clubs and how he knew so many people in what I nicknamed Blue Book Society. So many clubs, and I had no interest at all in private clubs. His interest in Blue Book Society made me wonder what he got from knowing these people. He enjoyed their company, but he seemed to enjoy more the fact that they had a high social standing. There's a nuance here. Stephen was a social climber. From my perspective, he pursued these people for the wrong reasons, and this highlighted an insecurity in him. It showed me that even with his Yale degrees and stellar legal career, which should have been enough for anyone to accept him as their friend and, more importantly, for him to accept himself— Stephen still had insecurities about his place in the world that caused him to socially climb and aspire to join private clubs. Where did these insecurities come from in this man who seemed to have everything in life going for him? His seeming perfection had a few cracks.

Stephen insisted on introducing me to some of his Blue Book Society friends, but I quickly concluded that these people were shallow and that I had nothing in common with them. What did a simple middle-class kid like me from the San Fernando Valley have in common with a woman from San Marino who gushed in a pseudo-British accent about the exclusivity of the Valley Hunt Club and her family's summer home in St. Malo that is so much better than other beachfront homes because it is gated off from the unwashed masses? Yuck. I didn't want to know any of these people. One of his Blue Book Society friends, however, a spry seventy-eight-year-old woman named Jessie, a newspaper heiress and a grand dame of Los Angeles society, oddly bonded with me. Jessie occupied one of the higher rungs in Blue Book Society, but she was as down to earth as any person could be. I adored Jessie's unpretentiousness.

These cracks, and the differences between Stephen and me, started to flash for me like warning lights. As my UCLA graduation approached in June 1984, our young relationship increasingly made no sense to me. I focused more on Stephen's and my differences than the qualities that drew us together. My heart loved Stephen, but my brain told me that our relationship faced too many insurmountable obstacles. I could tell that his interest in Blue Book Society would drive me nuts in our future together, and it also would require a ridiculous "keeping up with the Joneses" mentality and a great deal of money that I was unlikely to have for a very long time, or ever, given my writing career. Even if I had the money, I couldn't imagine myself ever seeking out friends to improve my social standing, joining any sort of private club, or owning a home in an exclusive gated community on the ocean that shunned the unwashed masses. I was also not thrilled with his positions on social issues, such as women's reproductive rights. I am for a woman's right to make her own health decisions, and he was against it "for religious reasons." We had already debated this topic extensively, and I could see that he would never change his mind. Stephen also had intense shame about being gay. I had some shame about being gay, too, but I was grappling with my sexual orientation and working through it far better than he was. He certainly didn't want anyone in Blue Book Society to know that he was gay. He was definitely far more Republican than I was, because even in 1984 I already rejected the party's increasingly regressive social platform. In retrospect, Stephen possessed some of the qualities of a highly conflicted Log Cabin Republican from today.[17]

---

17   Log Cabin Republicans is an organization of lesbian, gay, bisexual, and transgender (LGBT) Republicans founded in California after the 1978 defeat of California's Proposition 6, known as the Briggs Initiative, which would have prevented gays and lesbians from teaching in public schools. Interestingly, former California Governor Ronald Reagan, then preparing for his second Presidential election campaign, strongly opposed the Briggs Initiative and was instrumental in its defeat. "Log Cabin" is a reference to the first Republican US President, Abraham Lincoln, who was born in a log cabin, who championed the principles of liberty and equality, and who also is rumored to have been gay or bisexual. A Log Cabin Republican member today, in my opinion, is highly conflicted because today the Republican Party actively seeks to inflict significant harm on the LGBT community.

Stephen also was twelve years older than me. When you are twenty-two years old, a twelve-year age difference is a chasm. He already was well established in his career, and I hadn't even graduated college. I could not contribute equally to our finances, potentially for many years while I established myself as a writer, and maybe not ever. How could our relationship ever possibly work? My heart was no match for my brain, and so my brain overruled my heart. I decided that the sooner I ended it, the better. In early June, just before my final exams, I drove to Stephen's house to call it off.

"Let's be honest, Steve, we can't be together long-term and you know it," I began.

Then, I went through my list of reasons why it made no logical sense for us to be together.

"Steve, I can't keep up with you financially. You are thirty-four and I am twenty-two. We are in such different places in our lives. I don't know when I'll be able to contribute on an equal financial basis, if ever."

"So, what?" he replied. "That's fine with me."

"It's not fine with me, though. I don't want to feel pressure to make money. I don't want to be a kept man. I want to be a starving writer and make money in my own good time, or not, without worrying about any pressures from you."

"There won't be pressures," Stephen insisted.

"You can't promise that, Steve. Let's imagine that it's fifteen years from today, and I'm still trying to break into the writing field, and I've sold nothing, and you still are supporting me. By then I'll be a thirty-seven-year-old struggling writer. How will you feel? You will feel resentful. I know it. It would be entirely fair for you to feel that way. I'll feel terrible too, because I won't be pulling my weight. That will make it harder for me to write. At the age of thirty-seven, if I give up writing at that point it will be virtually impossible for me to break into another career. How is that for our future, Steve? That could, in fact, be our future."

Stephen was at a disadvantage in this conversation because I had already thought of every angle and every answer to each counterpoint that he might make. He listened. I continued pushing him away.

"You and I are different on so many levels. You seek out your Blue Book Society friends and you dream about joining the Los Angeles Country Club, and I never would set foot in there because it discriminates against

African Americans, Jewish people, women, and who knows who else. I'm not interested in people who validate their self-worth by being members of a private club that discriminates against other people. I am not a social climber, and I don't want to become one. You and I are so different on this score."

Stephen kept quiet. He already knew that when it came to social justice issues he could never win an argument with me. Plus, my Los Angeles Country Club comment made a particular point with him because he really did dream of becoming a member there someday. When Stephen had first told me this aspiration, I shared with him the little-known and long-buried story of how in 1973 the Los Angeles Country Club, which historically granted a membership to each Mayor of the City of Los Angeles, eliminated this courtesy membership when Tom Bradley, the city's first African American mayor, won his election.[18] They offered a free membership for the Mayor, as long as he was a white man. This is discrimination that one would expect in Alabama, but not in Los Angeles, California. Certainly not by 1973. The best part of this story: around 1975, the oil tycoon George Getty II donated his family mansion to serve as the residence for the Mayor of the City of Los Angeles. The Getty family mansion was located at 605 South Irving Boulevard—right in the middle of Windsor Square, Los Angeles's most WASP-y neighborhood, and a few blocks from Stephen's house. The Windsor Square/Hancock Park/ Fremont Place neighborhood was home to many members of the Los Angeles Country Club. Whether intended or not, the Getty family's donation turned out to be a subtle fuck-you to the bigoted Los Angeles Country Club and its Blue Book Society members. These people wouldn't see Mayor Bradley golfing at their precious golf course, but he ended up "ruining the neighborhood" (or, from my perspective, improving it). I have always loved this wonderful, mostly forgotten footnote of Los Angeles history.

I concluded by saying, "Being a starving writer is probably good for my character anyway. You and I can't be together for many reasons, and you know it."

Stephen listened as I spoke, and he made fewer and fewer counter-arguments. He became quiet. He could tell that my mind was made up. He understood what I was saying, and even though he did not agree with my logic, he accepted my decision, and we broke up.

---

18   The Los Angeles Country Club finally allowed its first African American member, former San Francisco Forty Niners football player Gene Washington, to join in 1991.

Stephen did not attend my UCLA graduation two weeks later, nor my graduation party. I did not invite him.

In hindsight, I can see the pattern for how I have dated men my entire life. Kevin, one night, and then I was done. Marty, barely half a summer, and then I ended it. Stephen, five months, and then I broke up. For the other men, their phone numbers either languished in the jar on top of my dresser, or they never made it past the first few dates with me. I am a hard one to lasso. I never make the first move, but I'm an expert at making the last one. Time and again, my brain rules my heart.

Immediately after graduating, I started a job as a personal assistant for a small-time creepy producer in Hollywood whose career was going nowhere and I quit after five days.

Then, I worked as a chauffeur for the 1984 Los Angeles Olympic Organizing Committee. I drove and accompanied Raoul Mollet, the President of the Belgium National Olympic Committee, and his wonderful wife Marie-Louise, to almost every major Olympic event, to dinners at fancy restaurants, and even to Disneyland. Nearly every Los Angeles resident either left town or stayed home during the 1984 Olympics because of the threat of gridlock, and as a result in those remarkable weeks you could drive from the Olympic Village at UCLA in Westwood to the Los Angeles Memorial Coliseum, on the Santa Monica Freeway and the Harbor Freeway, with an entire lane all to yourself, in under fifteen minutes! You also could find a parking spot on the streets of Los Angeles everywhere you looked! What an amazing life experience for me to see so many memorable Olympic moments, including the incredible opening and closing ceremonies produced by the famous showman David Wolper, all from some of the best seats in the house. The Mollets gave me all of the gifts they received as Olympic dignitaries, and they invited me to come visit them in Belgium and stay with them. The 1984 Olympics were a special moment in time in Los Angeles history and in my life.

Then, with no full-time job after the Olympics, I moved back home to Porter Ranch to live with my mom and dad until I could get on my feet. Moving home was a difficult decision because it gave my parents power over me, and the chance for them to gloat a bit at my expense.

You see, my parents and I had already waged three significant battles by the time that I turned twenty-two. I won all of them.

Round 1: The Smoking Battle. My mom, a registered operating room nurse who knew better, smoked cigarettes since high school. Throughout my childhood, she chain-smoked, in the house, with the windows closed and air conditioning running, and I suffered from nearly endless second-hand smoke. When I turned twelve, I mounted a campaign to make my mom quit smoking. With my allowance money, I took the bus from our home to California State University Northridge, located three miles away. In the university's Oviatt Library, I researched articles on the dangers of smoking. Using the library's Xerox machine, at ten cents per page, I photocopied the scariest articles I could find. Then, each morning I placed an article on our brown Sears refrigerator door underneath a magnet that my mom had received at an American Cancer Society medical conference. Each morning, my mom would see the newly posted article on the refrigerator, read it, crumple it up and throw it in the trash, and yell at me. When I ran low on scary articles, I took the bus back to the Oviatt Library, armed with more allowance money, and repeated the cycle. I kept this up for about six weeks. Finally, my mom cracked, and one morning she quit smoking cold turkey in the kitchen right in front of me, after yelling at me one last time, "God damn it, Chris!" My mom never smoked another cigarette. Victory Chris.

Round 2: The Private School Battle. My parents, without my knowledge or prior approval, applied for me to attend a private high school so that they could pull me out of the Los Angeles Unified School District. The reason: my parents feared school desegregation, and specifically they feared that I would be bused from Porter Ranch to an inner-city school. In 1976 and 1977, in Los Angeles there was a bit of talk about desegregating the public schools with busing, but no one really believed that it ever would happen (and it didn't happen). This fear of possible busing also helped spawn a 1977 effort for the entire San Fernando Valley to secede from the City of Los Angeles, which also didn't happen. In the midst of this white suburban sociopolitical turmoil, my parents succumbed to racially based fearmongering and freaked out, secretly submitted an admissions application for me, and then announced to me at my fifteenth birthday dinner that I would attend the Roman Catholic Chaminade College Preparatory School in Woodland Hills in the fall. This was their big "birthday present" for me. I lost my temper and a heated discussion ensued.

"I'm not going to Chaminade," I insisted.

"You have to go, you are our son, you are living under our roof, and you have to do what we say," my dad eloquently pointed out.

Dad had made a good point. I needed to raise the stakes.

"Only until I turn sixteen, Dad," I replied. "You see, at age sixteen, I can take the high school proficiency test. If you send me to Chaminade, I will take the high school proficiency test the moment that I turn sixteen, and I will pass it, and I will go straight to college, probably on scholarship, and I will never come home again."

"Are you serious?"

"Yes."

I stunned my parents. See, I had done my research. Skipping most of high school was a real possibility for me, particularly since I earned good grades in the honors track at school. I continued:

"I don't want to have to make an entire new set of friends when I start high school. Switching schools now makes no sense."

"It makes no sense for you to go to public high school in Watts, either," my dad argued back. Dad always invoked "Watts" as his scary proxy for the unsafe inner-city of Los Angeles. He believed that anything south of Mulholland Drive was Watts, including Century City, Beverly Hills, Bel-Air, Holmby Hills, Brentwood, Hollywood, Pacific Palisades, Venice, Marina del Rey, and Santa Monica. He always conveniently forgot that Charles Manson, one of Los Angeles's most notorious murderers and his dangerous "family" of murderous cult followers had lived at the Spahn Movie Ranch in Chatsworth, a mere two miles from our home in Porter Ranch.

"That's never going to happen, Dad. No one believes that except for you and Mom. I'm going to Granada Hills High School, and not Chaminade. Just think of all the private school tuition money that you will save by keeping me in public school. We can take better vacations. Let's go to Hawai'i!"

Then my dad said, "You could get killed if you stay in public school, Chris."

To which I replied, "Then you'll save even more money by not having to pay anything for my college. Again, better vacations. Think of the upside."

I admit that I was a smartass fifteen-year-old teenager. My parents and I stalemated over private school. Over the ensuing weeks, my parents proposed various strategies to convince me to attend Chaminade, including the promise of giving me my own car when I turned sixteen. I didn't budge.

Finally, my parents proposed a compromise: if I attended an informational session with one of the Roman Catholic priests at Chaminade and still didn't want to go there afterward, then they would let me attend public high school. I went to the session, I met with the priest, and I listened to what he had to say. He looked like a monk and wore a dark brown religious robe. He assured me that I would not need to dress this way if I attended Chaminade, although I would need to wear a uniform and cut the length of my hair. The priest emphasized, as though it were a good thing, how each student received extra attention from teachers because the school only had 400 students. Four hundred students? My elementary school had over 600 students, my junior high school had over 2,500 students, and my hoped-for high school had over 3,500 students. I liked fading into the crowd. With only 400 students at Chaminade, how could I possibly hide? In our drive home from the meeting, my parents capitulated, and in the fall I attended Granada Hills High School as planned. That summer, my parents and I vacationed in Hawai'i, paid for with the private school tuition money I saved them. Again, victory Chris.

Round 3: The College Major Battle. My parents desperately wanted me to go to medical school and become a doctor. Even though my heart already was focused on working in Hollywood, I humored my parents and entered UCLA as a chemistry major and briefly looked into medicine. During my first year, I took several math and science courses, but I really excelled in, and loved, my English literature and composition courses. So, at the end of my freshman year, I informed my parents that I was switching my major from chemistry to English literature. Mom and Dad were not happy. In addition to destroying the medical doctor dream that my parents had for me, I had selected a college major that they deemed to be useless and completely unemployable. Another series of heated discussions between us ensued, but I stood my ground and remained an English literature major. I pointed out to them, "At least I am not switching my major to music," a college major that I knew terrified my parents to their very core (they had already drawn their line in the sand over my majoring in music while I was still in high school, and I let them win that skirmish). I insisted, "I will still have a great career, you both have always told me that I can do anything if I work hard enough." At the end of these conversations, my dad admonished me, "Remember, you can't move back home after graduation." Again, victory Chris.

Now, here I was three months after graduation from college moving back home to live with my parents. Victory Mom and Dad.

I sent out résumés and went on job interviews during the day, and I wrote voraciously in my bedroom upstairs at night. I found a full-time job at UCLA as an administrative assistant to Margaret, a high-level administrator. Margaret had attended Stanford University in the late 1940s and was its Associated Women's Student Body President (women were not allowed yet to be president of Stanford's entire student body). A trailblazer and a tremendously classy woman. She had majored in English literature, too. I credit Margaret with cultivating all of my good management abilities, for reining in my worst ones, and for teaching me about the importance of "beach days." I worked for Margaret during the day, and I wrote at night. The rhythm worked.

Then, I received a postcard from Stephen in early September 1984. He had thoughtfully mailed the postcard inside an envelope so that my parents couldn't read it, since I hadn't yet come out to them. The envelope was postmarked from Southwest Harbor, Maine. The photo on the postcard featured a seagull, alighted on a pier in a Maine fishing village, looking out over the ocean and into a beautiful sunrise in the distance. On the other side of the postcard, he wrote:

"I miss you and I am lonely without you. Please let me see you again. Stephen."

This postcard touched my heart, and I relented. I missed him too. Stephen and I started dating again after he returned to Los Angeles. With the music of Prince, Tina Turner, the Culture Club, Cyndi Lauper, Madonna, and the Pointer Sisters in the playlist of my life, we discussed how to bridge our differences and stations in life. Stephen compromised, and I compromised. Actually, Stephen mostly compromised because I insisted that we live primarily at my economic level. Blue Book Society wasn't banned outright, but he accepted that I wouldn't have any part in it. We agreed to try to make our relationship work, together. This completed our bond, and then I fell fully in love with Stephen and I gave him my heart. By the holidays, we were a serious couple, around the same time that voters approved the incorporation of West Hollywood as its own city. Upon its incorporation, West Hollywood made double history by simultaneously electing a majority of openly gay city council members and the country's first openly gay mayor, Valerie Terrigno. Gay Camelot had officially arrived.

Unfortunately, the clouds had arrived, too. The world for me started to go off the rails in December 1984, and it started with Ryan White.

In December 1984, Ryan White, a thirteen-year old hemophiliac boy in Kokomo, Indiana, was diagnosed with AIDS after he was exposed to the virus by a contaminated blood treatment. Ryan White instantly changed the discussion in America about AIDS and proved that the mushrooming epidemic would touch everyone—regardless of sex, age, and sexual orientation. You would think that a thirteen-year-old boy who contracted the AIDS virus by accident would have unleashed an outpouring of unconditional love from the largely Christian community in which Ryan White's family lived, but instead the exact opposite happened. Even though the Center for Disease Control and Prevention had already ruled out the possibility of casual transmission for AIDS in 1983 making quarantines and masks unnecessary, a group of parents in Kokomo opposed Ryan's efforts to attend public school.[19] The ensuing battles and lawsuits, covered extensively in the news media, between his courageous family, that group of Kokomo parents, and the Kokomo school system, highlighted the worst of America's irrational fear of AIDS, the height of human ignorance, and the failure of Christians to respond with love. The White family received death threats from their neighbors. At one point, someone fired a bullet through the living room window of the White family house, which forced them to flee the town and ultimately move away.[20] Some Christian values!

On a parallel track to Ryan White's heartbreaking saga, by December 1984, AIDS had fully breached the walls of West Hollywood's Camelot. I remember the AIDS virus changing the world so quickly, in an instant. I felt as though a giant black hole opened up and started swallowing people into it. During a time of what should have been youth, optimism, possibilities, and happiness, instead death and dying suddenly surrounded me as friends fell sick and died from the AIDS virus. A surreal and horrifying insanity. It all

---

19   Centers for Disease Control and Prevention, September 9, 1983, "Current Trends Update: Acquired Immunodeficiency Syndrome (AIDS)—United States," *Morbidity and Mortality Weekly Report*, Volume 32, Number 35, Pages 465–467.

20   Alex Witchel, September 24, 1992, "At Home with Jeanne White-Ginder; A Son's AIDS, and a Legacy," *The New York Times*.

happened as if someone had flipped a switch to teleport the world into a new reality. The Athletic Club started to post the AIDS obituaries of its members on a bulletin board right next to the gym's front desk. It traumatized me to see this chronicle of death each time I went to the gym. Articles and photos of vibrant young men, whom I knew, who now were dead. A macabre scorecard. But a necessary one, because people were disappearing every day.

This was the devastating backdrop to my growing relationship with Stephen. Although the world had turned upside down, by February 1985, we had fallen madly in love with each other and I moved into his house in Hancock Park on South Arden Boulevard, near Third Street and the Marlborough School for Girls. To commemorate this milestone, I purchased my first piano, an upright made by Tokai, and financed it with an outrageously high-interest rate loan from Household Finance. Since Stephen and I also wore the same size clothes and size 11 shoes, we both instantly doubled our wardrobes, too. Stephen soon left his high-powered law firm job to join California Federal Savings and Loan as a senior counsel to oversee the firm's fledgling mortgage-backed securities efforts, a great new opportunity for him. To save money, I built a writing desk for my new home office out of an unfinished solid door and four 4"x4" posts that I used for legs, all purchased at Anawalt Lumber. I called it "construction chic."

But other than my happiness from moving in and living with Stephen, I remember 1985, the year that I turned twenty-three, as a year full of increasing sadness and devastation. It was a year of sobering firsts as the AIDS crisis mushroomed. The Broadway theater produced the first plays about AIDS: *As Is* in March, and *The Normal Heart* in April. Also in April, the Food and Drug Administration started using the first AIDS test, an ELISA test for IgG antibody to HIV-1, not to diagnose people because of its high false positive test results, but instead to screen the nation's blood supply.[21] AIDS Project Los Angeles held its first AIDS Walk in Los Angeles in July. In August, the AIDS virus made the cover of *Time Magazine* with the headline, "AIDS: The Growing Threat, What's Being Done." The US Public Health Service had already "recommended" that gay and bisexual men not donate blood since March 1983, but in September 1985, the Food and Drug Administration upgraded that recommendation into a formal lifetime ban. Also in September, the actress and icon Elizabeth Taylor joined the fight

---

21   Merrill Fabry, June 27, 2016, "This is How the HIV Test Was Invented," *Time Magazine*.

against AIDS, helping establish the American Foundation for AIDS Research (amfAR) along with powerhouse cofounders Mathilde Krim, PhD, Joseph Sonnabend, MD, Michael S. Gottlieb, MD, and Michael Callen. Elizabeth Taylor then became a tireless and lifelong fundraiser for AIDS research and support.

On October 2, 1985, Rock Hudson became the first major celebrity to die from AIDS, having long hidden but finally publicly disclosed his diagnosis only two months earlier.[22] Hudson would be one of many talented people from the world's entertainment and arts communities who would lose their lives in the AIDS epidemic and provide an important and much-needed public face to it. The NBC network broadcast *An Early Frost*, the first television movie about a man dying from AIDS, in November. My parents watched *An Early Frost*, and my conservative Roman Catholic mom telephoned me afterward with her review: "He should have never been born." Gulp. Also in November, Dionne Warwick released her emotional hit "That's What Friends Are For" to raise money for AIDS research—a truly beautiful song, at the top of the music charts for months, but an unfriendly ghost from the playlist of my life. To this day, I still have trouble listening to it because of the memories that it evokes.

Rather than offer love and support, religious fundamentalists seized on the opportunity to preach that AIDS was a punishment from God for the "sin" of being gay. Lyndon H. LaRouche Jr. launched a nationwide campaign to institute mandatory quarantines for all people with AIDS.[23] Opportunistic conservative politicians aligned themselves with LaRouche and injected the fear of AIDS to win votes and gain advantage in the culture wars between religious fundamentalists and the rest of American society. Why on earth did a virus that kills innocent Americans need to be politicized? Delta Airlines changed its contract of carriage to exclude people with HIV and AIDS from its flights.[24] Doctors, nurses, hospitals, and even mortuaries refused to work with "AIDS victims," a stigma-filled term used for years by the media. Trained nurses refused to hold or care for infants born with AIDS, dooming

---

22   Throughout this memoir, I reference the AIDS-related deaths of people from the entertainment and arts communities. These deaths are fused with my memories of the time as important public historical markers, and by including them it helped me remember my story.

23   Barbara Vobejda, October 9, 1985, "LaRouche Unit Asks AIDS Quarantine," *The Washington Post*.

24   Jack Anderson and Dale Van Atta, November 6, 1987, "Delta's Puzzling Policies on AIDS," *The Washington Post*.

these innocent babies to die alone with no love whatsoever. AIDS hysteria and discrimination abounded. Melrose, the always jovial African American woman who worked at The Athletic Club, now frequently cried at the front desk while the gym's membership died. I had increasing difficulty pursuing my creative writing with all the death and sadness around me. I didn't give up, but the process became writing molasses. The playlist of my life, as this loss mounted around me, featured the hopeful, uplifting songs from Whitney Houston's first album, including "How Will I Know" and "Saving All My Love For You." For me, Houston's early music is the playlist for the onslaught of AIDS, and her beautiful voice makes me think of death.

Stigmatism and ostracism ran wild. In 1985, when it came to ostracism Los Angeles wasn't really all that different from Kokomo. Much of humanity missed the opportunity to do the right thing in the face of the AIDS epidemic. Many of our friends, upon their AIDS diagnoses, simply chose to ostracize themselves and disappear from public out of shame. We would only see them again in hospitals or, all too often, never hear from or about them again—until their obituary appeared on The Athletic Club's gym bulletin board or in *Frontiers*, West Hollywood's gay community news magazine, or maybe never again at all. I became obsessed with searching for and reading obituaries, an obsession that continues to this day. Beginning in 1985, our friends started to leave Los Angeles to scatter everywhere because of the virus. This particularly pained me since it went against my craving for complete order in my life. I couldn't keep track of where people went. Was he dead? Was he dying in a hospital somewhere? Did he move back to his hometown to be with family? Did he go on disability and move to Palm Springs to die alone in a $10,000 condominium? Did he go back into the closet? Did he go into hiding to ride out the storm? The answer was "all of the above." As people scattered because of AIDS, so did my life. There could be no order when life itself could not be counted on. I aged much more than a year in 1985. I was only twenty-three years old.

That year, I started to spend evenings and weekends visiting friends in hospitals: Sherman Oaks Hospital, UCLA Medical Center, Cedars-Sinai Hospital, Century City Hospital, and Midway Hospital. I came to know them all, their convoluted hallways, AIDS wards, cafeterias and vending machines, pay telephone booths, and waiting rooms. Try to imagine the insanity of visiting one friend in the hospital, and then discovering that one or more other friends were hospitalized there too, fighting the same illness. I remember seeing worried, grieving partners and friends, sitting stone-faced in hospital waiting rooms alongside me, all of us trying to comprehend the reality of our reality: what do we do now? The AIDS virus has turned the whole world against us.

The number of funerals and memorial services that I attended beginning in 1985 eventually made me numb. I stopped crying at them because I had nothing left inside. My AIDS grief was a constant process, like watching a repeating slow-motion film unfolding right in front of me over and over, and knowing how the film ended: always in death. In 1985, AIDS treatments only delayed the inevitable, because at that time the treatments were worthless.

The sun was gone, dark clouds now blanketed the sky, and rain started falling all around me. Welcome, Chris, to the storm.

I took comfort that I was not single and dating, but partnered and living with Stephen as AIDS devastated the world all around us. In February 1985, when I moved in with him, he and I had agreed to be a monogamous couple, and so I made an exception to my safe-sex rule. We promised each other that we would make it through the storm, together. The one ray of sunshine throughout 1985: Stephen was the picture of perfect health.

CHAPTER 3
RAIN

T HE RAIN CONTINUED, THE storm got worse, and sheer terror gripped the world's gay communities throughout 1985 and 1986. AIDS literally exploded. Try to imagine that you were a gay man living in San Francisco in the 1980s and that you faithfully read its weekly gay newspaper, the *Bay Area Reporter*. Below is how the newspaper's obituary section transformed (remember, I am obsessed with obituaries):

Total Number of Obituaries Published[25]

1980	1981	1982	1983	1984	1985	1986
0	4	10	11	92	212	479

These sobering statistics are from a relatively youthful segment of just *one city in America*.

In August 1985, with our friends getting sick all around us, Stephen and I took our first vacation together. We flew to New York City, then drove to New Haven, then to Boston, and finally to Southwest Harbor, Maine, where his parents had a house on the ocean. Stephen wanted me to meet his parents and some of his friends from Yale University.

This was my first trip to New York City. Stephen and I flew on People Express Airlines, a low-cost airline formed in the wake of airline deregulation, from Los Angeles to Newark, New Jersey. I drove our rental car from Newark

---

25   GLBT Historical Society's Online Searchable Obituary Database for the *Bay Area Reporter*, http://obit.glbthistory.org/olo/index.jsp. Note that these statistics are the total number of obituaries published, some of which were not AIDS-related, but the overwhelming majority were from AIDS. In addition, not everyone in San Francisco who died from AIDS had an obituary published in the *Bay Area Reporter*.

Airport into Manhattan through the Holland Tunnel. My introduction to New York City was swift and harsh, as everyone's introduction to that metropolis really should be. When we emerged from the tunnel into the sharp curve in what I now know to be TriBeCa, I saw pedestrians crossing the street in front of me. So, I did what every good California driver would do in this situation: I stopped for them. Well, I learned in that instant that New York City drivers don't stop for pedestrians, and they don't care much for drivers who do. The screeching of car tires behind us, followed by car horns blaring, and a few middle fingers and choice expletives hurled at us brought the lesson home. Stephen turned to me with a smirk and said:

"You're not supposed to stop for pedestrians in New York City. Didn't you know that?"

I responded, "No, Steve, I did not know that, but thanks for the tip."

Stephen and I stayed at the Yale Club on Vanderbilt Avenue next to Grand Central Station. You had to wear a coat and tie to walk through the front door. So ridiculous and un-Californian. Stephen, who knew the city fairly well, took me on a full tour. We ate lunch at the Plaza Hotel, walked through Central Park, and visited the Tavern on the Green. We walked down Fifth Avenue. I saw a barefoot homeless man standing in the middle of the street in front of the two-year-old Trump Tower, staring at an empty candy wrapper in his hand and muttering to himself, while cars and pedestrians passed him by without even noticing him.

Stephen introduced me to David, his best friend from Yale University, who also was gay and lived and worked in the city. David was tall and thin, with curly brown hair, and wore circular wire-rimmed glasses. Bookish. Stephen and David briefly had dated when they were roommates at Yale, and they were still the best of friends. David was delightful and intelligent, and we bonded instantly. I could immediately see that he and Stephen had a deep friendship, but in many ways they were polar opposites. David rolled his eyes when Stephen mentioned private clubs. I liked that. Since David had met Stephen on their first day at Yale, they had a shared history that allowed David to make playful comments such as, "Don't forget, I know where you came from," which got under Stephen's skin and provided an interesting clue for me. David was single, perpetually so, according to Stephen. He was an artist at heart, but worked for a consulting firm that designed retail store layouts to make it difficult for customers to find their way around, thereby hopefully making them shop longer and buy more. David joined Stephen and me for our tour of the city.

Although I had already seen roadshows of *A Chorus Line*, *Annie*, *Evita*, and *Dreamgirls* at the Shubert Theater in Century City, in New York City I saw my first-ever bona fide Broadway show. Tickets to the seven Tony award-winning blockbuster Broadway musical *Cats* at the Winter Garden Theater were out of our price range, so we opted for *Sunday in the Park with George*, at the Booth Theater, starring Bernadette Peters and Mandy Patinkin. David and I loved the show, but Stephen hated it and left at intermission to meet us for dinner afterward. I will never forget my sense of awe upon leaving the Booth Theater to see the bustle of Times Square, the *New York Times* building with its delivery trucks lined up outside, and the neon lights and crush of people. Exhilarating. The three of us had a post-theater dinner at Cafe Un Deux Trois, and then we took a tour of the gay neighborhood of Greenwich Village, including a visit to the famous Stonewall Inn.

The next day, Stephen, David, and I drove up I-95 to New Haven singing along with the car radio blaring the latest 1985 pop hits, including Wham's "Wake Me Up Before You Go-Go," Chaka Khan's "I Feel for You," Huey Lewis and the News's "The Power of Love," and USA for Africa's "We Are The World." In New Haven, I met Carl and Janie, two of Stephen and David's close friends from their days at Yale. Carl and Janie were married and lived in a multiunit residence that they co-owned and had renovated with David. Carl and Janie's home looked beautiful, and they were kind and welcoming to me. Carl, Janie, and David reminisced about the Yale class of 1972, and I observed the conversation among these four longtime friends with fascination. Stephen and David took me on a personalized tour of the beautiful Yale campus, and I learned more about their early history together.

From New Haven, we drove to Boston, and then to Maine with a stop at the L.L. Bean store in Freeport to take our photo in front of its famous canoe, and finally to Southwest Harbor, a small coastal community located on Mount Desert Island near Bar Harbor. As we drove across the bridge that connects Mount Desert Island to the rest of Maine, Stephen reviewed the rules of the visit with me:

"Remember, my mom knows that I'm gay but my dad doesn't."

"Yes, I remember," I replied, mildly annoyed. We had already practiced this drill so many times. "I promise that I will just be a friend who rents a bedroom in your house, who happens to be twelve years younger than you, and whom you mysteriously decided to bring on your summer vacation to meet your parents. Your dad will never suspect a thing. When he leaves the room, I will kiss you. Sounds perfectly simple and innocent to me."

Stephen gave me a raised eyebrow.

Ah, the complicated and sometimes very heavy secrets that some gays and lesbians from my generation had to keep in order to live our lives, to keep our jobs, to keep our families, to keep our friends, to keep the peace, to keep the world from unraveling around us. So many, many secrets. I have always thought that gay people would make the best undercover CIA agents since we learn how to master secret-keeping from such a young age. Keeping secrets takes so much energy, though. Constant work. Debilitating after a while, really. My twenties were full of many secrets, and, in retrospect, stupidly so. This was just one more.

I was excited to finally meet Stephen's parents and get to know them. He had not spoken much to me about them so I knew only tidbits of information. His father was a retired psychologist who had worked for the US Army, and his mother was a retired schoolteacher. His parents were originally from the Bronx in New York City, and had lived for many years in Washington, DC, where they had raised Stephen, but they now lived in Yorktown, Virginia. Stephen told me that he had moved to Los Angeles in part to place some distance between himself and them. I wondered why he needed the distance.

Stephen's mother regularly called his home telephone line and left stream-of-consciousness voice messages on his answering machine tape. Stephen never answered his phone. He always screened calls through the machine to identify the caller before deciding whether to answer. When his mother called, he wouldn't pick up the phone to speak to her. He wouldn't even listen to her message as she recorded it. He would walk away from the machine and listen to her message later. He called his mother back about one out of every five of her calls to him. Phone calls with his mother caused anxiety for him, and he spent time gearing himself up before calling her back. Sometimes I overheard her messages as she left them. To me, she sounded like a nice mom, someone genuinely interested in her son. She had a heavy Bronx accent. Nothing she said on her messages sounded upsetting, at least to me. It just sounded like she missed him, her only child. His father never called at all. When I asked him about this, Stephen told me that his weekly psychotherapist appointments were partly to help him manage his relationship with his parents.

I loved our trip to Southwest Harbor. Their house was huge and it was located right on the water, so I figured that Stephen's parents had a lot of money. What a beautiful place to have a second home. Stephen's parents were kind to me, although his father was a bit standoffish, soft-spoken, and difficult to engage in conversation. I wondered if he suspected the truth about my relationship with Stephen. I wondered if he noticed that I wasn't really sleeping in the bedroom next door to Stephen's, even though we had carefully arranged the room to make it appear that I slept there. I wondered how Stephen's mother managed to keep her son's sexual orientation a secret from her own husband and how that made her feel. Oh, the draining energy of secrets! As for his mother, it was impossible not to notice the collection of religious crosses that she wore on a gold chain necklace, with some of them being quite large. When she, Stephen, David, and I were alone together, the conversation took a different tone since she was in on our secret. She had an outgoing personality, and seemed open-minded and accepting of gays and lesbians. I liked her, and I hoped that she liked me, too. It was clear that Stephen felt much closer to his mother than his father.

Several conversations with his parents revolved around how proud they were of him, especially of his Yale and MIT educations, his success, and how he, and they, knew all these important people. Some of this sounded to me like typical parental doting on their prodigal son. My parents could do the same thing to me in front of their friends, even though it irritated me. Stephen's father talked about how he had worked with four-star US Army generals, and his mother spoke about their active DC social life even though they now lived in Yorktown. In these conversations, there was an undercurrent that conveyed to me that they felt they were better than other people, something my parents never did. The entire concept of "knowing people" was a big deal to his parents, and a yawning head-scratcher for me. I thought to myself, "This probably is what all wealthy East Coast people do in the comfort of their own homes." At the time, my only other "wealthy East Coast person" data point consisted of a brunch at Joe Allen's with my former roommate Chris's East Coast mother, whom I watched in awe as she swallowed Bloody Marys as if they were water at 10:00 a.m. on a Sunday. In contrast to Stephen's parents, in my family's world *everyone* was equal. I imagined that Stephen's parents lived in a vast estate in Yorktown, Virginia, that looked like Jefferson's Monticello, and I looked forward to seeing it someday. When I asked Stephen about his parents' doting, he told me that his mother smothered him. When I inquired if he ever asked her to smother him less, he looked at me like I was an alien from Mars. Aha: confident Stephen was afraid to confront his mother.

In Southwest Harbor, I ate my first-ever lobster and crab, and I visited the beautiful Acadia National Park, Echo Lake, the big yellow Claremont Hotel, and the Bass Harbor Head Lighthouse. I took everyone to dinner at the Asticou Inn in Northeast Harbor to thank Stephen's parents for their generosity in hosting me. I left Southwest Harbor hoping that I had made a good first impression on his parents, albeit as Stephen's "renter." It was hard for me to know for sure, since Stephen, David, and I did so much sightseeing on our own during our three-day visit that we only saw them at dinnertime. Regardless, I thought that Stephen's parents were nice, and I looked forward to seeing them again.

By 1985, Stephen also had met my parents. I wasn't out of the closet yet with them, so more secrets. I told my parents that Stephen was my landlord and friend. If they had ever asked me if I was gay, I would have told them the truth, but they never asked. My parents were smart enough to know what was going on, but they didn't want to know, so they didn't ask. Keeping this secret saved my parents from having their strict Roman Catholic worldviews challenged and it kept the peace in my family. My sister constantly admonished me, "Even if you ever tell Mom and Dad that you are gay, don't you dare tell them anything about Jane and me." So, we kept the secrets. This secret-keeping may seem absurd today, but this was my world in the 1980s as a for-the-most-part-still-closeted young gay man, and certainly closeted with most of my family.

My parents adored Stephen. They easily adopted him into our family, regularly inviting us over to visit. My parents also invited Joan and her "roommate" Jane, and the six of us would eat meals, play board games, and have a great time together. Four of the six of us in the room knew the secrets, and two of us allegedly were in the dark. Energy-draining secrets. This all seems so ridiculous today but that's what we did. The six of us spent virtually every holiday together at my parents' house, too. My parents gave Stephen Christmas presents, a sign they really cared for him. When my parents called me on my home telephone line, Stephen would wrestle the handset away from me so he could talk to them, too. Shortly after Stephen and I returned from Maine, Joan and Jane hosted a surprise sixtieth birthday party for my dad at their home. My mom and Stephen danced as though they were old friends.

My brother Michael did not attend the party. I'm fairly sure that Joan did not invite him. By 1985, Michael was estranged from my parents and Joan. His estrangement began almost as soon as he left home in 1972 to attend college at the University of California San Diego to study computer science. In his sophomore year, Michael met a female student named Tyerin and quickly moved in with her. Our conservative Roman Catholic parents did not approve of premarital cohabitation. This created a rift between my parents and Michael. Joan, who carried her sibling rivalry with Michael into adulthood, combined with her simmering anger from being fired by the *Chicago Tribune*, fanned the flames of dissent and accelerated the growing divide between my parents and brother.

This resulted in my parents and sister driving Michael and Tyerin away from our family. I stayed out of their arguments as I had done throughout my childhood, but I longed for my family to get along. By 1985, at the age of thirty-one, Michael had already earned his PhD in computer science, landed a position as an assistant professor at the Naval Postgraduate School in Monterey, married Tyerin, had a three-year-old son and a newborn daughter, and owned a home in Carmel, one of California's most beautiful coastal cities. There was so much for my parents to be proud of about my brother, and his wife and young family, but instead they obsessed over his premarital cohabitation. Joan egged them on. So incredibly stupid, disappointing, and lamentable. Sadly, this led to my parents never really getting to know either of their only two grandchildren. My parents also missed out on spending time with my brother and his intelligent and interesting wife. And guess what? Michael and Tyerin are still married today.

Why were my family dynamics so screwed up? This requires a detour into our history to understand why, like a modern-day Tevye and Golde from *Fiddler on the Roof*, my mom and dad resisted the changing society around them to their own detriment.

They each grew up poor, and each was the first person in their respective families to attend college: engineering for my dad, and nursing for my mom. My dad was a first-generation American. His father, my grandfather Sigmund, known as Ziggy, immigrated to America in 1910 as a single man from a small town in Bohemia called Trebic, at that time still part of the Austro-Hungarian Empire before the creation of Czechoslovakia. Two of Ziggy's brothers, August and Russell, immigrated with him. August emerged from Ellis Island with his last name correctly spelled "Zeida" by the immigration officer. Ziggy and Russell, however, processed by a different immigration officer, emerged from Ellis Island with their last names misspelled as "Zyda."

Upon concluding that American women were too independent, Ziggy placed an advertisement for a mail-order bride in a Bohemian newspaper. His brother August did the same. Russell, the third brother, did not place an ad for a wife, and lived his entire life as an unmarried bachelor in a room in my grandparents' house. I am fairly sure that my great uncle Russell was gay.

My dad's mother—my grandmother Anna—along with her sister Bessie, from their farming village outside Prague, answered Ziggy's and August's mail-order bride advertisements, initially as a joke. But then the two sisters seized the opportunity to leave the old country. Anna married Ziggy and Bessie married August, and then they all jumped on a ship to sail to America. The two new married couples and my bachelor great uncle all settled in the poor Vauxhall neighborhood in Union, New Jersey, at 57 Maple Avenue.

My grandfather Ziggy worked as a laborer for Krementz and Co. Jewelry in Newark, New Jersey, and my grandmother Anna worked as a maid, cleaning houses. Ziggy and Anna, both devout Roman Catholics, barely spoke English when they arrived in America. But they learned English quickly, and emphasized the importance of education and cultural assimilation to my dad and his younger sister, also named Anna. My dad became high-school valedictorian, and earned a ticket out of the Vauxhall neighborhood with a scholarship from the US government to study electrical engineering during World War II at the Newark College of Engineering, and then at the Stevens Institute of Technology for his master's degree. He had a military deferment during World War II while he studied how to design weapons and radar systems for the US war effort.

My mom's ancestors had immigrated to America mostly from Ireland, but also England, France, and Switzerland, in the mid-1800s. They began their American journey in the tenement slums of Water Street, in New York City's lower east side. Eventually, they crossed the Hudson River to settle in a small radius of northern New Jersey towns. Three generations after immigrating to America, however, the American Dream had still eluded them because of discrimination against Irish immigrants and their descendants.[26] "No Irish Need Apply," "Protestants only," or "Americans only" appeared at the bottom of countless job postings during that era, evidence that America has nearly always been anti-immigrant. The occupations of my mom's ancestors demonstrated their struggles on the bottom rung of American society: laborer, another laborer, worker in a woolen mill, barber, shoemaker, pipefitter, painter, truck driver.

One of my great-grandfathers on my mom's side of the family, Thomas, died in 1919 during the Spanish Flu pandemic of 1918–1920, a virus that killed more than fifty million people worldwide. Thomas's wife Mary had died five years earlier shortly after giving birth, leaving Thomas to raise six very young children all by himself. He is buried in a pauper's grave, next to his wife, and along with two strangers, in East Orange, New Jersey, without even a headstone to mark the spot. Thomas's death created six young orphans, all of whom miraculously survived the deadly flu pandemic. This left my fifteen-year-old grandfather Edward as the oldest of the six orphans to raise his siblings to adulthood practically all by himself with little money.

When he turned twenty years old, Edward married my grandmother Mildred, and then they had five children including my mom. Edward worked as a truck driver, but he possessed a talent for art and could paint Mickey Mouse as well as any animator at The Walt Disney Company. Mildred was a stay-at-home spouse. They were both devout Roman Catholics, too. Edward and Mildred settled their family in the poor Vauxhall neighborhood in Union, New Jersey, at 2796 Vauxhall Road, just two blocks away from my dad's family at 57 Maple Avenue. My mom and dad met each other in elementary school, and played together in childhood. My mom graduated high school as valedictorian one year after my father did, and she earned her ticket out of the neighborhood with a scholarship to the Jersey City Medical Center School of Nursing, courtesy of the US Army's Nurse Corps program during World War II. By the time my mom graduated, however, the war ended, so she never served actively in the army, although she was technically a veteran.

My parents, each the smartest person in each other's orbit, married in 1948, and made the leap from their poor childhood roots into the American Dream of middle-class careers in northern New Jersey. All because of their higher education, thanks to the US government and the war effort. This

---

26   Dermot Quinn, *The Irish in New Jersey,* Rutgers University Press, copyright 2004, pages 54–126.

explains why my parents constantly stressed the importance of good grades and higher education to their three children…at any school *except* the University of California Berkeley because it was, in my parents' words, "a hotbed of liberal pinko communism."

In 1956, Dad received a work promotion that required the family to relocate from New Jersey to Los Angeles, where he continued to design weapons of mass destruction for the US military and later electrical and radar systems for the Space Shuttle program. Mom worked as a tough-as-nails operating room nurse. They settled in the San Fernando Valley suburbs, where I was born, as the proverbial surprise, in 1962. Although my parents had bootstrapped themselves first into the American Dream, and then lucked into the miraculous California Dream and Los Angeles Dream, their worldviews always were only one small step away from their poor, rigid, conservative Roman Catholic childhood roots in Vauxhall, New Jersey. Because of this, my parents could only see the world around them through a harsh black-and-white religious lens, and not the shades and colors in between, where most of life actually occurs.

As for me, although I am mostly a laid-back Angeleno Californian who loves the ocean, white sandy beaches, the sun, and good weather, I also have the added seasoning of a no-nonsense, take-no-prisoners, smartass New Jerseyan. Completely bicoastal.

Now you can understand why it was so difficult for my mom and dad to accept Michael living with his girlfriend Tyerin "in sin" while he attended college. But Michael's premarital cohabitation would be the least of my parents' challenges as the world changed around them. They were destined to live through a painful American twist on *Fiddler on the Roof*, in which Joan, Michael, and I successively trampled on their rigid Roman Catholic worldviews simply by living our lives differently than they had predetermined for us. Michael, with his scandalous premarital cohabitation, simply was the first of us to test them, and he paid the price.

◆◆◆

IN THE MIDDLE OF January 1986, Stephen developed a large, painful, and itchy red rash on his back. He couldn't reach his back, so I rubbed calamine lotion on it to dull the pain and itchiness. Two days later, when the rash had not improved, he went to the doctor and learned that he had shingles. His case of shingles was the first indication that his immune system was compromised by the AIDS virus. Most of the time, but not always, shingles strikes older people or people with weakened immune systems. Stephen was only thirty-five years old.

At the time, I read about shingles and learned that it is caused by the same virus that causes the chicken pox, and it can infect a person who had never had chicken pox. My inner hypochondriac instantly worried. In my elementary school, when the chicken pox made its rounds through the classrooms, I was one of the few students who did not come down with the disease. I made it safely to adulthood without experiencing it. Now, I knew that I had been directly exposed to the chicken pox virus. In addition, I learned that getting the chicken pox as an adult is a very serious medical situation.

Sure enough, I came down with the chicken pox around two weeks later on January 28, 1986, the same day that the Space Shuttle Challenger exploded in mid-flight. I saw the news footage of the disaster playing on a television in a restaurant near my office at UCLA when I started to feel hot flashes. Then I started to break out, and I rushed home to bed. For the next several days, I stayed in bed with a nearly constant high fever, the sickest that I have ever felt in my life. While delirious with fever, I watched dozens of old episodes of *The Gumby Show*, which strangely played on one Los Angeles television channel nearly all day long in February 1986. I missed work for three entire weeks.

Stephen and I both recovered from our illnesses, but the Space Shuttle Challenger disaster serves as a marker for when rain from the storm first fell on my immediate world.

In the months after Stephen recovered from shingles, I noticed a steady decline in his energy. On March 9, 1986, Los Angeles hosted its first marathon, trying to build on the success of the 1984 Olympics, but he was too tired to cheer the marathoners on with me when they ran right down Rossmore Avenue past Third Street, only one block from our house. Or maybe he just thought watching marathoners run by our house was boring. After all, he wasn't interested in sports. Yes, that made sense. By April 1986, around the same time as the Chernobyl nuclear disaster and the massive Los Angeles Central Library fire that destroyed more than one million books, Stephen's energy had declined such that he took frequent naps on weekends, began to fall asleep too early at night, and had difficulty waking up in the mornings to go to work. But he had always struggled with insomnia, and he definitely was not a morning person, and his new job at California Federal Savings certainly was challenging since mortgage-backed securities are complicated structures. I told myself that these factors likely explained his tiredness. Wouldn't they? He and I went to Palm Springs for Memorial Weekend, and Stephen was too tired to participate in the Hands Across America celebration with me even though the route went right down the middle of the street in front of our hotel. But it was well over 100 degrees outside, and he said that he wasn't a fan of Hands Across America, so it made sense that he rested indoors with air conditioning while I held hands with strangers in the street underneath the blazing sun. Didn't it? But I started to worry that something was wrong with him. Five days after Hands Across America, Perry Ellis, the well-known American fashion designer, died from AIDS on May 30. AIDS was mushrooming everywhere, and by the end of 1986, according to amfAR, AIDS cases reported to date in the US would be 28,712 with 24,559 deaths, a mortality rate higher than 85 percent, and the Centers for Disease Control and Prevention (CDC) would estimate that approximately 493,000 Americans were living with HIV.[11, 27]

In the spring of 1986, Stephen also started to become disorganized. He still brought work home from the office but he did not work on it after dinner as he used to do. I told myself that his relatively new job probably was overwhelming him. New jobs can be overwhelming at first; in fact, all the really worthwhile jobs are like that. Right? He also started to neglect paying his bills on time, and piles of invoices and mail soon covered our dining room table. He lost most of his sex drive, too. Stephen's declining energy and increasing disorganization started to prevent him from doing his share of our household chores. We were a team, so I picked up the slack for him, but deep down I worried—no, dreaded—that something serious was wrong.

As Stephen's energy declined, soon he began to consume an unhealthy amount of alcohol. Far more than one drink per day. He also became a heavy chain smoker. Still in denial, I wondered if these developments could be the source of his low energy level and disorganization. I theorized that his budding addiction problems might be caused by work stress since his job created a great deal of anxiety for him. But his banking work hours were much better than his former law firm hours, and mortgage-backed securities

---

27   Centers for Disease Control and Prevention, "HIV and AIDS Timeline," https://npin.cdc.gov/pages/hiv-and-aids-timeline. AIDS statistics from this same source are cited throughout this memoir.

shouldn't have been difficult to comprehend for someone brilliant like him. Stephen's anxiety continued to grow, as did his heavy drinking and smoking, and his tiredness. His office was close to our house, and he started to come home for lunch to take naps, but he would drink while at home and sleep beyond lunchtime and sometimes not go back into the office. He started to get into trouble because of his inconsistent work attendance.

I descended more into denial, trying to convince myself that Stephen's growing addictions were the cause of everything going wrong with him, because a person can recover from addiction. You couldn't recover from AIDS in 1986. As close as Stephen and I were, I couldn't yet bring myself to ask him about AIDS because I was still deep in denial and terror about what was happening. After all, if Stephen had AIDS, then I had it, too.

Then, Stephen was asked to give a speech at a retirement lunch for his boss at California Federal Savings. This freaked him out. He couldn't focus on the speech; he couldn't write a single word. He was in big trouble. So, I wrote his speech for him, to say goodbye and good luck to Ed, a retiring man I didn't even know. We practiced his speech delivery over and over so he wouldn't be nervous. The retirement speech was a huge hit. If I hadn't written it, he might have been fired.

Within a matter of only a few months, this brilliant man whom I loved deeply, with his seemingly perfect life, wasn't so perfect anymore. Stephen's cracks had turned into fissures. It all happened right in front of my eyes, like a fairy tale run in reverse. Instead of the classic frog turning into a prince, my prince charming was looking more frog-like. In addition to worrying about his health status, I felt cheated, frustrated, and increasingly concerned about our relationship, and I kept living in denial, with ever-increasing dread, telling myself, hoping, lying, that his addictions were the source of everything going wrong with him. I thought about how we had only two good years together, and now he was falling apart. I worried that if he actually had AIDS, then abusing alcohol and cigarettes were the worst things that he could do for his health.

In early June, I found a bottle of Valium pills in our bathroom, with Stephen's mother's name listed on the prescription bottle. What?

"Steve, what's going on here?" I asked him. "Why is your mother sending you her Valium pills? If you need a prescription for Valium, then you should get it from your doctor, not from your mother."

"I have so much anxiety at work, Chris," Stephen replied.

"Please go see your doctor about your anxiety and why you are so tired," I said. "You are napping and sleeping a lot, and you are drinking a lot of alcohol, and if you are mixing alcohol with your mother's Valium pills, that is not good. This all might be the cause of your tiredness and anxiety. Plus it is affecting your work."

I was so close to asking him outright if he had AIDS after I discovered the Valium, but my own deep denial prevented me. If Stephen actually had AIDS, I would know soon enough. I wasn't ready yet to face it.

Despite my repeated insistence, Stephen refused to go to see his doctor about his tiredness and anxiety.

In hindsight, it's clear that the AIDS virus was progressing in his body, making it difficult for him to work, concentrate, and think. Stephen turned to alcohol, cigarettes, and now Valium to deal with his growing anxiety— not primarily about his job, but about the fact that he knew something was seriously wrong with his health, and he suspected what it was, and this understandably terrified him.

Stephen, like many other gay men of that time, didn't want to go to the doctor only to learn that he had AIDS-related complex, the precursor to full-blown AIDS, when in 1986 AIDS was a death sentence. But by early summer 1986, Stephen also started to have intestinal problems, including bouts of diarrhea, coughing, and night sweats. It was abundantly clear to me that something very serious was going on with his health.

By this time, I was fairly sure that Stephen had AIDS. My campaign of denial over the past few months had shattered. This was upsetting in itself because I loved him very much and it broke my heart to think about him dying. But it surely meant that I had AIDS too because Stephen and I had engaged in unprotected sex. A lot of it.

Sheer terror gripped me as I absorbed and finally faced this reality.

And anger.

And guilt.

And shame.

I was also overcome by an incredible wave of sadness and grief. Sadness and grief for Stephen whom I loved deeply, for me, and for us. Sadness and grief for realizing that our lives would be cut short, we would not achieve our dreams, and it would all end in the horror of AIDS.

As I wrestled with my sobering new reality, I drove to Santa Monica State Beach and walked along Palisades Park and to the end of the pier. I stared past the dark blue swells of waves that gently lapped the pier's wooden pylons below and into the horizon at the occasional boat that passed by on the ocean while seagulls dove for fish around me, and I inhaled the fresh, saltwater-tinged air. Never before did I contemplate life, the meaning of life, the searing pain of life, the complete and total unfairness of life, and my own now-looming mortality on such a deep level. Seemingly everyone around me was dying from AIDS, and now Stephen, and even me, too. At twenty-four years old, my life had barely even started, but now I was thinking about how my life would end. My life and dreams and future were falling apart. I thought about Diane, a classmate of mine who died from cancer when we were in junior high school and only fourteen years old. So young; too young. She was my dancing partner at my sixth grade graduation from Beckford Avenue Elementary School. She was so brave as she battled disease. She came to school on crutches after the doctors amputated one of her legs. She never lived long enough to even formulate her own dreams and future, much less briefly pursue them, as I had a chance to do. But Diane sure fought a great fight, I do remember that.

Putting myself into Stephen's shoes, I could tell he also saw his life crumbling, his grand dreams being slowly extinguished, his aura of success being chipped away, and the grim reality of his own death appearing on the not-too-distant horizon. I was devastated, sad, and angry as I realized that our first two years together were likely the best ones of our relationship, and, in fact, the best years of any relationship that I would ever have in my own life since I would soon die, too.

As life unraveled, one night shortly after the Valium incident, Stephen attended a charity dinner with some of his Blue Book Society friends. I stayed home. I was awoken by the phone at around 2:00 am. It was Stephen. He was in downtown Los Angeles, in jail, after being arrested for driving under the influence, and his car had been impounded and towed away. As I drove downtown to bail him out, I decided that it was time for a serious talk in the morning about his drinking, declining health, and the possibility of AIDS. We were both going to tell the truth to each other today.

That morning, I started off with, "Steve, your drinking is out of control. But I worry that something else also is going on with your health besides your drinking and we need to talk about it."

"AIDS," he responded. "Chris, I think that I have AIDS." Stephen got to the central issue now that I finally was confronting him. Then, he immediately said, "Please don't break up with me."

"Are you crazy, Steve? I love you, and you are my partner, and the last thing on my mind right now is breaking up with you. I have been so worried about you these past few months. You are not taking care of yourself. Should you go get tested?"

"No, I don't want a test, not now. What good is it for me to know? There is nothing to be done, no treatments. I'm trying to keep it together at work, my energy level is so bad."

"Whatever it is, Steve, we will get through it together. But if you do have AIDS, the alcohol, Valium, and cigarettes aren't helping matters. Please take better care of yourself and preserve the health that you still have."

"Chris, I am so sorry if I have given AIDS to you," he said.

Then, Stephen and I hugged, and we cried together for a long time. The truth finally out, at least between the two of us. In our family, we were no longer going to be secret-keepers.

Now, you might be thinking, why didn't we just both go and get AIDS tests to know for sure? The answer is simple: it was 1986.

Ah, the dilemmas in 1986 of choosing to know, or not know, if you had AIDS. Dilemmas on several levels. In 1986, you could get an AIDS test—the same HIV ELISA test used by authorities to screen the nation's blood supply. The HIV ELISA test, however, produces a high false-positive result, which means that a lot of people test positive for AIDS with the HIV ELISA test when, in fact, they don't have AIDS. So, step one in the AIDS test dilemma was to determine whether the high false-positive results and inaccuracy of the HIV ELISA test was worth the risk. Can you imagine testing positive for AIDS only to have the doctor then say something along the lines of "take comfort in the fact that a large percentage of positive test results actually are wrong"? Where is the peace of mind in that? I struggled to understand the benefit of taking the HIV ELISA test.

To add more stress to this dilemma, anonymous AIDS tests didn't exist yet in 1986, so the mere act of getting tested for AIDS was itself a high-risk activity. To get tested, you needed to request one from your doctor because tests were tightly controlled. The doctor would draw your blood, and it would take between seven to ten days for the results to come back. The doctor would report your AIDS test, and its results, to your health insurance company, and this would go on your permanent health record. If you had an AIDS test on your health record, with either a negative or positive test result, it then would be used by health insurance companies to discriminate against you and deny you the ability to purchase an individual health insurance policy if you ever needed one, and you also could have your current health insurance policy canceled. C. Everett Koop, President Ronald Reagan's Surgeon General, went off the Republican Party script and advocated anonymous AIDS testing and also safer sex practices in 1986, and he incurred the full wrath of religious conservatives and the health insurance industry.

Twisted irony, I know. Knowledge about their health status should empower people, but not with health insurance companies champing at the bit to deny people healthcare. If you were self-employed, the last thing you would want to do in 1986 was get tested for AIDS because your health insurance company might then cancel your individual policy, regardless of your AIDS test result. If you were lucky and your health insurance company didn't cancel your policy, then you could never switch your health insurance policy to another company because that AIDS test on your health record would mark you as forever uninsurable. If you worked for an employer that provided a group health insurance plan, and you dreamed of starting your own business someday, that same AIDS test on your health record would keep you from obtaining a health insurance policy in your own name, thereby preventing you from starting your business. You could easily end up trapped in your job because of its group health insurance plan.

So, in 1986, if you had AIDS or suspected that you had AIDS, these AIDS testing dilemmas quickly condemned you to what I call "health insurance prison." In health insurance prison, you must find a job with a good group health insurance plan so that you have good health insurance when you get sick. In health insurance prison, even if you dislike your job you can't quit in order to preserve that good health insurance for when you eventually do get sick. In health insurance prison, you pay many medical costs yourself without submitting insurance reimbursement claims because you don't want your health insurance company to know about these treatments and then cancel your policy.

During the 1980s, more and more Americans found themselves in health insurance prison, thanks to a combination of AIDS, greedy health insurance companies, and powerful insurance company lobbyists. A nationwide, powerful, supermax prison that still exists today. A simple business model fosters health insurance prison: health insurance companies collect ever-increasing health insurance premiums from customers, but every year they cover fewer health insurance claims and pay out less money. The result: huge industry profits. Health insurance company stockholders win. Health insurance company executives win. Americans lose.

Since the 1980s, the number of inmates in health insurance prison has increased to a staggering population as the health insurance industry pursued a range of punitive strategies. It perfected the art of canceling individual health insurance policies with fine print "gotcha" language buried in their appendices. Unfair. It devised the technique of purging insurance rolls by selectively exiting health insurance markets so that customers with medical conditions would lose their health insurance, even after dutifully paying premiums for years, and then be rendered unable to obtain new health insurance because of their now "preexisting conditions." Evil. It convinced regulators to allow health insurance premium increases at rates significantly higher than inflation, thereby putting the financial screws to all Americans. Greedy. It then created high-deductible health insurance policies under the guise of helping customers save money on high premiums, only to simultaneously shift significantly more medical costs to customers. Deceitful. Even that wasn't enough: eventually the industry came back to gouge high-deductible policy holders with exorbitant premium increases, too. Corrupt. It twisted the fine print buried in insurance policies to deny covering a drug that was approved by the Food and Drug Administration if a doctor prescribed that drug for a purpose other than its official approved use. Cruel. I lived through all of this.

Today, even with the Affordable Care Act's (ACA) protections for preexisting conditions, health insurance prison applies not just to Americans with AIDS, but also to those with cancer, diabetes, high blood pressure, heart disease, and all sorts of other chronic diseases that health insurance companies don't want to cover. All so that health insurance company stockholders can make more money, and company executives can buy more houses and yachts. Make no mistake: insurance companies thoroughly despise the ACA's preexisting condition protections, and their well-heeled lobbyists will do everything in their power to repeal the act, including bribing politicians and judges. What's frustrating to me is that we, the American voters, allowed this to happen by not voting our interests for the past forty-plus years. In my opinion, the health insurance industry is a devastating cancer upon American freedom.

Of course, the final dilemma in getting tested for AIDS in 1986 was to decide whether or not you wanted to know if you were going to die, since this is what an AIDS diagnosis meant. A simple fact. In 1986, even though Stephen's health already was faltering, I still felt completely healthy, even though I was a hypochondriac and germophobe and ran to the doctor over every sniffle. Despite my fear from knowing that Stephen likely had AIDS, and that I likely had AIDS too, at the age of twenty-four years old I did not yet want to officially confirm that I was going to die from the virus. Almost as important to me given my fear of health insurance prison, I did not want to hinder my ability to obtain health insurance in any way. So, in 1986, I chose, as Stephen did, to not get tested for AIDS—yet.

But since I knew that I likely had the AIDS virus too, I needed to come up with a contingency plan. Unfortunately, that contingency plan meant an immediate death—not of me, yet, but rather the death of my writing career and dreams.

This is when the storm completely changed the course of my young life.

It had become increasingly hard for me to summon the concentration and energy needed to conquer the writing world, and to take the risks that writing requires, when the whole world seemed to be dying around me—now including Stephen and me, too. I believed that AIDS would not show up in me possibly for several years given its long incubation period, but it eventually would. I decided to use my next few years of good health to find a more stable career that would provide me with the good health insurance plan that I was certain I would need someday. Plus, I knew that I would need to make a lot of money to pay for Stephen's upcoming medical care, and someday my own. Certainly much more money than a struggling writer could earn. Health insurance prison had me within its walls. I needed to make some focused decisions based on my reality, and out of a limited set of choices I made the best choices that I could make.

All of this led me to apply for admission to graduate business school.

I made this choice because while working for the UCLA administration, I had learned a great deal about finance and accounting from my boss

Margaret, and our wonderful colleagues Liz and Cid. All four of us had become good friends. I realized I had a strong aptitude for finance, and my three smart women mentors encouraged me. By 1986, personal computers had made their way into the workplace, and I became proficient at Lotus 1-2-3, the popular spreadsheet program at that time, before Microsoft Excel even existed. Margaret, Liz, and Cid inspired me to apply to graduate business school and pursue a finance career.

Toward the end of the summer of 1986, I took the Graduate Management Admissions Test (GMAT) and scored quite well. With my GMAT score and my strong college GPA, I knew that I would be admitted to a top graduate business school program. Sandy, a close friend from college, and I wrote our respective business school applications together at Barney's Beanery in West Hollywood, where only two years earlier West Hollywood's first mayor, Valerie Terrigno, had torn down the restaurant's infamous longstanding sign, "Fagots (sic) Stay Out." I applied to five of the alleged top-ten graduate business school programs at the time: The Wharton School at the University of Pennsylvania, Columbia University Business School, New York University School of Business, the Yale School of Management, and the UCLA Graduate School of Management.

Of course, I would only be able to attend business school if California's Proposition 64, a ballot initiative sponsored by fundamentalist religious conservatives that advocated labeling AIDS as a communicable disease and requiring the mandatory reporting and quarantining of all people with AIDS, didn't pass in the November 1986 election. The media referred to it as the "AIDS quarantine initiative." Fortunately, it didn't pass. Otherwise, I suppose Stephen and I would have been carted off to live in a prison camp somewhere in the California desert. Or perhaps instead Stephen and I would be forcibly tattooed with "AIDS" on our upper forearms and buttocks, a reprehensible idea championed by conservative icon William F. Buckley in 1986.

I wrote my business school applications with deep sadness. I was killing my writing dream and taking a different road. I was figuratively "jumping from the H," just as the actress Peg Entwistle did in 1932 when she climbed to the top of the "H" of the iconic Hollywood Sign and jumped forty-four feet to her death, her Hollywood dream broken at twenty-four—the same age that I was. I was being inherently practical and planning for what I believed to be my inevitable death from AIDS. Madonna, Cyndi Lauper, and the newcomer

Janet Jackson battled with Whitney Houston over who would claim the title of Queen of Pop in the playlist of my life through the restaurant's sound system while I agonized over my bleak future.

My friend Sandy wrote her business school applications across the leatherette booth from me from a perspective of sincere hope and excitement for her own future. Sandy, who knew me well, didn't understand my decision to apply to business school. I hadn't shared with her anything about Stephen having AIDS or my belief that I had AIDS, too.

"You're so creative, Chris," she said. "You don't belong in business school."

I tried to spin for her a positive twist on my business school applications, while every word that I wrote hammered another nail into my writing dream's coffin.

"Well, Sandy, I'm not making much progress on my writing career," I replied.

She shot back, "It's only been two years, Chris! It takes time."

"It won't be the worst thing for me to get a master's degree in business," I argued. "Maybe then I can work in the entertainment industry in some other capacity. I can always keep up my writing, and you never know how things might play out. Lots of writers didn't publish anything until they were thirty, forty, fifty, or even sixty years old. In the meantime, I'll have a good backup plan for a career."

My spin-doctoring to Sandy was 100 percent bullshit, but eventually she accepted it. I couldn't let her, or anyone else for that matter, in on Stephen's and my dark secrets about our health.

Barney's Beanery remains to this day a very unfriendly ghost from my past: the location where, at age twenty-four, the storm killed my writing career and dreams and I formulated my contingency plan to prepare for my own death.

At home, I put all of my creative writing projects away and into a box—all of my scripts, stories, partly written novels, papers, index cards, notes, and the 5 1/4" floppy disks that stored all of them—and then I pushed the box into a dark corner in the back of one of our closets and I shut the door on my writing career.

On Halloween in 1986, my friend Bryn and I enjoyed a wild night of fun in West Hollywood. I needed it. It was still one year before the city would inaugurate its official Halloween Carnival, which then grew into today's giant annual street party on Santa Monica Boulevard that stretches all the way from Doheny Drive to La Cienega Boulevard. But even back then, thousands of costumed partiers, including the two of us, overflowed from the clubs and from the sidewalks and into the street. Groups of costumed revelers paraded along the boulevard's wide grassy median. The median was the best place to view the scene, if you could get there. People with drinks in their hands darted across Santa Monica Boulevard through the crawling traffic to get to the median and back again. Music blared into the street from the bars and clubs along the boulevard. Los Angeles County Sheriff's Department deputies tried to keep some semblance of order. With Los Angeles as the world's entertainment capital, and with so many creative gays and lesbians working in the entertainment industry as makeup artists, hair stylists, and costume designers, the Halloween costumes were incredible, outrageous, detailed, impeccable, and over-the-top. Bryn and I had a blast drinking, running around, and hunting down our friends to see which costumes they had donned for the occasion. He knew that I was working on my business school applications and said at one point, "Maybe I should choose a new line of work, too."

In the midst of all of this partying and celebrating in the middle of Santa Monica Boulevard, it occurred to me that everyone at this raucous Halloween celebration *needed* to be there, just as I did. Our friends were dying all around us. Our hearts all were breaking. We feared for our own lives and futures. But life still needed to be lived. So we would party and dance and enjoy this moment as a big "fuck you" to the storm bearing down on us.

I finished and mailed all my business school applications in November 1986, just after California voters soundly rejected Proposition 64, and around the same time that Cleve Jones and others made the first AIDS Memorial Quilt panels in San Francisco for what eventually would grow into the NAMES Project.

With my graduate school plan in action, Stephen and I spent the first part of the week of Thanksgiving 1986 in his hometown of Washington, DC. One night he took me to dinner at the Metropolitan Club, the elite private men's club that he loved where you had to wear a coat and tie to set foot in the building. So pretentious and un-Californian. We visited some national monuments and museums, and he introduced me to some of his Washington, DC, friends, including a gay Roman Catholic priest who lived with his partner(!), a doctor. Before I met them, Stephen admonished me, "Don't mention that I've told you this secret. Since he's a priest, he doesn't want anyone to know that he's gay and living with a partner."

I responded, "I'm not surprised he feels that way. That's sort of like being a bank robber and then working at a bank."

The closeted priest ended up serving us a lunch that included a delicious cold cucumber soup, and when I asked him for the recipe, he refused to give it to me. Can you imagine? Such an excellent secret-keeper, even down to his recipes.

Then, on Thanksgiving Day, Stephen and I drove four hours to his parents' home in Yorktown, Virginia, the city where George Washington secured America's independence in 1781. Their home wasn't Monticello as I imagined it would be, but it was a lovely four-bedroom house that sprawled across five acres. In Los Angeles, a house like this in 1986 would have cost millions of dollars, if you could even find one that had that much land. In Yorktown, however, it cost around $100,000. Perhaps I had misjudged Stephen's parents' wealth, not that it mattered one bit, except for the fact that his parents still acted as though they were better than other people, which perplexed me. I wondered how, then, could they own a large waterfront second home in Southwest Harbor, Maine? The answer, clarified by Stephen: the waterfront house in Maine had been rented.

I started to see a picture form of two parents with more modest means than my own parents who likely spent their life savings to send their only son to Yale and MIT so that he could realize his and their American Dream. Obviously, there's nothing wrong with this; lots of parents make sacrifices for their children to give them the best advantages in life. But why, then, would Stephen's parents act like they were better than everyone else around them? What makes a person do that? Insecurity! The potential motivation for Stephen's social climbing in Blue Book Society started to fall more into focus for me. Maybe it was to make his parents proud of him? Maybe he wanted to get as far away as possible from his family's humble roots, but he was doing it in a misguided way? Maybe because of his insecurities he overcompensated by focusing on external validations? Even though our lives already were derailed by AIDS, I wondered why Stephen couldn't simply have been happy to be the brilliant man from humble beginnings who went to Yale and MIT and had a stellar legal career. After all, that's pretty darn fantastic all by itself. It should have been enough. Now with AIDS in the center of our lives, the insecurities that I increasingly saw in Stephen made more sense. But these insecurities had formed cracks that now had grown into fissures as life continued to beat both of us down and push us into the unknown challenges ahead that would determine whom we would both eventually become. The lyrics of Missing Persons's hit song, "Destination Unknown," aptly described our situation: "Life is so strange when you don't know, how can you tell where you're going to, you can't be sure of any situation, something could change and then you won't know."

Stephen's best friend, David, flew in from New York City and met us at Stephen's parents' house in Yorktown. It was a nice Thanksgiving celebration, and over the three days we were there I got to know Stephen's parents a little bit more, but Stephen insisted that he, David, and I do so much sightseeing in the area that again we didn't spend much time at home with them. Stephen's father thought I was still his son's renter. He thought I was still sleeping in the bedroom next to Stephen's. Ugh, secrets. Nearly three years into my relationship with Stephen, and I had only spent a total of six days with his parents, while in contrast, Stephen had spent time with my parents nearly every week for over two years. I still didn't really know Stephen's parents very well. Not very well at all.

CHAPTER 4
DELUGE

AFTER I MAILED MY GRADUATE school applications, the world around me spiraled even more out of control. Stephen. My sister. My friend Bryn. The storm unleashed a deluge of torrential rain on me while I tried to maintain some degree of control over my life and plan for my own bleak future.

First, near the end of 1986, Stephen lost his job at California Federal Savings and Loan. A scary blow for him given his health status. Luckily, Stephen received a generous severance package, including health insurance coverage, so we would be fine financially for twelve months. But he needed to find a new job even as his health declined in order to secure good health insurance for the rest of his life.

Unfortunately, all of the free time that Stephen now had on his hands accelerated his alcohol and prescription drug abuse. He stayed at home all day watching television, sleeping, drinking, smoking, and taking Valium or Xanax—the prescriptions still in his mother's name—all while his health worsened. He made a complete mess of his life on nearly every level during this time period. One day, I walked in on Stephen in our bedroom snorting lines of cocaine off a small mirror. Instantly infuriated, I lost my temper.

"Steve, what in the hell are you doing?" I yelled. "You have a compromised immune system and you are doing drugs. Are you trying to commit suicide? Everyone else who we know with AIDS is doing everything he can to stay alive, and you are trying to kill yourself."

Stephen obviously had no good answers for me. I continued:

"If you want to die as a drug addict, then you can do it alone because I will move out and break up with you. I can't make it any clearer than this."

Eventually, I didn't perform so much of an intervention as deliver an ultimatum:

"When your severance package runs out, you will be working in a new job. You also will not be abusing drugs, effective immediately. Otherwise, our relationship is over. I will not be a party to suicide, and I will not stand by and watch you destroy whatever remaining life you have left while all the rest of our friends with AIDS are taking care of their health and fighting for their lives. Imagine if you kill yourself from your drug abuse and then the following week they discover the cure or vaccine for AIDS? Is that sliver of hope worth nothing to you?"

My comment about a possible cure or vaccine was delusional and I knew it when I said it. Occasionally, a news story or a government official would declare that an AIDS vaccine could exist within "two years," but given the length of time required for vaccine development, these statements only offered false hope. Plus, I hadn't even attended one day of business school yet, but I already knew that the healthcare and health insurance industries and their powerful lobbyists likely would never allow an AIDS cure or vaccine to see the light of day because it would decimate their industry profits. Ronald Reagan, now in his second term as president, didn't even seem interested in fighting or curing AIDS for Americans. He could barely even utter the word "AIDS," and members of his White House staff such as Press Secretary Larry Speakes publicly joked about the disease and gay men. The best that any of us probably could hope for were drugs and treatments that made the disease "manageable" so that healthcare industry profits could continue to skyrocket.

But I meant everything else I said, and I was angry that my partner could not summon a fighting spirit, so I grabbed the cocaine and mirror from Stephen and flushed all the cocaine down the toilet. Then, I went through our medicine cabinet and I also flushed the pills in every bottle that had his mother's name on it. Stephen lost his temper. He grabbed the mirror back and threw it at me. It missed my head and crashed against the wall behind me, and a small shard of its glass splintered off and flew into my eye. More yelling ensued. After I pulled the shard out of my eye (fortunately no real damage was done), I turned to Stephen and said, "No more drugs from your mother. Your mother is not a doctor. Your mother doesn't know that you have AIDS. If you want Valium or Xanax, go to your own doctor and tell him what is going on and then have him prescribe it for you. That way, he can monitor your usage and help keep you healthy. And no more drugs—period! If you can't comply with my request, then I'm out of here and our relationship is over." Then I added, "You're also quitting smoking! It's a horrible habit. Quit!"

Fuck, fuck, fuck, fuck, fuck!!! The central relationship of my life was on the brink.

Over the ensuing weeks, I insisted to Stephen that there was something still worth living and fighting for. My classmate Diane, a fourteen-year-old from Nobel Junior High School, did it, so clearly he could do it and I could do it too. But that's me, I'm a fighter, and I guess I have always been one. Perhaps it's the New Jersey in me. During this period, our relationship descended into a disaster, with endless conflict, stress, and arguments as Pat Benatar's angry hit "Love is a Battlefield" underscored our life. We were perilously close to breaking up. At Stephen's insistence, we went to a joint counseling session with Michael, his psychotherapist. After I explained to Michael what was going on between us, he took my side in the debate with Stephen and chastised him for not being more open with him about what was going on in his life (seriously, how can a therapist ever possibly help you when you don't tell him what is going on?). At the end of our session, Michael flat-out said to Stephen, "You need to take better care of your health, and find a job." That was our one and only joint counseling session.

Then, Joan lost her job at the *Herald-Examiner* when the financially struggling newspaper downsized. For about six months, she worked at the gay newsmagazine, *The Advocate*, as its National News Editor under the pseudonym Joan Cort because she was not publicly out as a lesbian. She did not tell our parents that she even worked there or even list the job on her résumé. Good God, still more secrets!

Then, Joan found a job at a magazine called *Pool and Spa News*. No other newspaper would hire her because of that despicable *Chicago Tribune* editor who fired her, who by that time had left the *Tribune* to serve as an editor at the *Chicago Sun-Times* but six years later still was discriminating against her with his horrible job reference. Here she was, at the age of thirty-four, with her incredible intelligence and journalism experience, working at Pool-and-Fucking-Spa-News, writing articles about chlorine levels, pH tests, which types of leaves clogged up pool filters the most, and the latest trends in swimming pool floats. It made me furious. She was miserable with her job, but needed to work to help her wonderful and patient partner Jane pay their bills. A heartbreaking descent from her career heights. Joan's energy, like Stephen's, was waning while her storm in life slowly flooded her soul. She needed help.

I staged a one-man intervention. Joan loved *The Golden Girls* television series, so I obtained two tickets for us to see a winter taping of an episode one Friday night at the Sunset-Gower Studios in Hollywood. There's something to be said for escapism when you have a lot to escape. At dinner afterward, I intervened. Joan listened.

"Joan, I love pools and spas, but you know that you cannot continue to work at *Pool and Spa News*," I began. "Your writing talents are too good to spend them writing about chlorinated water. You and I both know that the world has changed over the past sixteen years since you graduated from high school. All the really good jobs, including the ones in journalism, now require college degrees. Plus, you are a woman so you have to be twice as good as a man to get half as far. You dropped out of college to write for the *Los Angeles Times*, but now you are thirty-four years old, and regardless of what that asshole homophobic editor from the *Chicago Tribune* says about you, employers today will expect you to have a college degree. You need to go back and earn that degree. You can do it in under two years, and then you can reset your career."

Joan, my sister who once brimmed with energy, did not put up any fight. Life had beaten her down. I could see it in her eyes. Her only substantive comment was a question: "How do I do it?"

"I have a plan," I responded. I already knew exactly what to do.

I filled out Joan's admissions application to transfer into UCLA. All she had to do was sign her name. I ordered her high school and college transcripts, too. She got accepted to UCLA as a junior transfer student history major for the fall of 1987. I wrote all Joan's letters to the UCLA registrar to ensure that she received the maximum transfer credits from her prior coursework. All she had to do was show up for class at UCLA, study, and take the exams.

"How will I pay for college?" Joan asked me.

"Don't worry, we will figure it out," I replied. "I have a plan, and I will help pay."

For part one of my plan, I convinced my parents to pay for Joan's UCLA tuition under the logic that they had already paid for four years of college for both my brother and me, but only two years for Joan, and so out of fairness they really should pay for her final two years at UCLA. Otherwise, this would amount to shameful parental discrimination against Joan for being a woman, and how would my parents ever be able to live with that for the rest of their lives? If there was one subject I had mastered in my Our Lady of Lourdes Catholic Church catechism classes, it was the usefulness and power of Roman Catholic guilt. My parents agreed to pay Joan's tuition. Victory Chris, once again.

Part two of my plan required Joan to work in various journalism jobs part-time around her UCLA class schedule, which she agreed to do.

The final part of my plan was to pay for her textbooks with my own money.

I felt relieved to know that she would be back in college, and if my plan worked she would earn her bachelor's degree by 1989. Then she could start fresh with a new career. I so much wanted for her to get her career back on track and regain her life spirit. Her wonderful partner Jane was on board and was incredibly supportive. Regardless, I still worried a great deal about Joan. She was following the plan, but I didn't know how much she was owning it. She was my big sister, ten years older than me, but I increasingly started to feel like her big brother.

Joan's escalating life challenges underscored for me how I sometimes felt like I was the only adult in my family. I had been guiding my mom and dad, my sister, and, to some extent, my brother for almost as long as I could remember, and I was by far the youngest of all of them. I felt like I carried so much weight for my family members. Now, by helping Joan get accepted to UCLA so she could earn her college degree and get her life back in order, I was adding an extra layer of stress to my life, like one more stone added to my shoulders. But I had to intervene because I could see my sister starting to circle a drain to nowhere. This highlights another personality trait of mine: I micromanage the lives of everyone around me whom I care about.

Then, in early 1987, my friend Bryn moved into one of our spare bedrooms. He had quit his work as a prostitute after he had been diagnosed with AIDS. Yes, Bryn too. Bryn now had no income, so he moved out of his beautiful apartment and sold all of his possessions except his clothes. He needed a safe place to live while he figured out the next steps in what remained of his life, and he worried about whether anyone in his family would take care of him, particularly at the end of his life. Of course Stephen and I welcomed him into our home with open arms.

Stephen, Joan, and Bryn. Each fighting for their lives. Each of their life struggles made even more difficult because of what I call "negative tapes" programmed into their subconscious. Negative tapes are programmed into all of our minds as we grow up—by parents, siblings, schoolteachers, mentors, insensitive classmates, neighborhood bullies, and organized religions—and can cripple us later in life when our subconscious minds can't reconcile these deeply buried negative messages with the real world around us. Every one of us, gay or straight, young or old, male or female, every single race, has negative tapes. But these tapes can particularly be problematic for gays and lesbians, since from a young age we are conditioned to feel like the alien "other."

We periodically see the harmful effects of negative tapes in the news when a public figure engages in destructive behavior. Negative tapes can be about anything: not feeling smart enough, not feeling good enough, not feeling pretty or handsome enough, not feeling loved or wanted, feelings of abandonment, fear of failure, fear of success, and yes, shame about being gay or lesbian.

Where do I begin with my own negative tapes? There are so many. Some of them lead directly back to the Roman Catholic Church and its skill at instilling its members with shame and guilt: about being gay, about sex, about being damned to hell or to millions of years in purgatory for doing just about everything. Most people who are raised Roman Catholic, like me, eventually learn to laugh about and reject *some* of the illogic and corruption of this organized religion even though it also contains some wonderful spirituality at its core. But through our laughter, we know that our Roman Catholic childhoods scarred us with negative tapes that keep playing in our adult minds.

Some of my negative tapes come from elementary school and junior high school when I was bullied. At my junior high school graduation at Devonshire Downs, in an almost *Carrie*-like moment, as I walked back to my seat after receiving my diploma, a fellow classmate jumped to her feet and screamed at me at the top of her lungs, "Burn in Hell, Zyda!" I barely knew her. I was more friends with her twin brother and his girlfriend, but clearly she was angry at me about something, and felt that she had to get it off her chest right in the middle of graduation. Perhaps it was the tacky blue polyester leisure suit that I wore to graduation? I admit that it was a poor fashion choice, even though polyester leisure suits were all the rage in 1977. The painful sting of my classmate's curse to my fifteen-year-old self-abated somewhat when everyone within earshot looked at her like she was a crazy person and yelled at her to sit down and shut up. But it hurt and it's a negative tape for me.

My mom and dad programmed me with some additional negative tapes, but also some quite strong positive ones. Positive tapes that would serve me well through the storm and in my life. My parents constantly reminded me that I was smart, that my natural curiosity about learning was a good thing, and that I could achieve anything that I wanted through hard work. They also instilled in me a healthy and sarcastic sense of humor, cultivated further by a *Mad Magazine* subscription they maintained for me throughout my childhood and teenage years, and because of this, I can laugh at and find sarcasm in any situation. They also emphasized to me "what other people say about you doesn't matter," the best positive tape for childhood bullying such as my classmate's. They encouraged me to think for myself, to stand my ground in an argument, to do the right thing, and to live a principled life, even though they may have regretted it when I disagreed with them. Again, all positive tapes for me. In my life, I have always chosen to focus on my positive tapes and mute the volume on my negative ones.

But Stephen, Joan, and Bryn—all fighting their own storms—couldn't seem to tap into any positive tapes that might be buried in their subconscious minds to help them cope. Because I loved each of them deeply, this caused a deluge of additional stress for me. All as I planned for my own bleak future.

I was under so much stress that I canceled my membership at The Athletic Club in mid-1987. With the increasing stress in my life, and with more members of the gym and our other friends dying from AIDS, I didn't want to go there, or to any other gym. Depression was taking hold in me. Exercising fell by the wayside. I didn't want to go anywhere near West Hollywood anymore. "True Colors," from the playlist of my life, underscored my sadness as life beat down everyone around me, and me, too.

Sometime during 1987, when I was twenty-five years old, the American Psychiatric Association completely removed "homosexuality" as a diagnosis in its Diagnostic and Statistical Manual of Mental Disorders, the DSM-II (many references to homosexuality as an illness had already been removed in 1973). As a result, gays and lesbians were no longer considered mentally ill in any way, shape, or form. I felt exactly the same as I did before these expert psychiatrists reclassified me as not mentally ill. It's crazy to think that I lived twenty-five years of my life with a respected profession believing that it was sick to be who I was.

On February 4, 1987, the famous piano entertainer and showman Liberace died in Palm Springs, allegedly from a combination of anemia, emphysema, and heart disease. As a fellow piano player since I was age seven, I adored Liberace and his death broke my heart. The Riverside County Coroner then ordered an autopsy, which determined that Liberace instead had died from pneumonia due to complications from AIDS. At the time, I thought the coroner had engaged in a tabloid sideshow, and I fumed about how gay people had become political footballs in the culture wars and the AIDS crisis. But it was important for the world to know that Liberace had died from AIDS because it gave yet another public and beloved face to the AIDS pandemic. Like Liberace, each subsequent person from the entertainment and arts communities who either died from AIDS or turned HIV positive helped raise the profile of the pandemic to the world, and this spawned more action, a good thing.

In March 1987, Stephen's best friend David visited us from New York City to deliver the news that he had been diagnosed with AIDS. Now David, too. Stephen took David's news hard, but did not share his own AIDS news with his friend—yet. He still hadn't been tested. More secrets. The Food and Drug Administration had recently approved the first antiretroviral drug to treat AIDS, Zidovudine/Azidothymidine, more commonly known as AZT. David told us that he would be taking AZT to fight his disease. Even with this hopeful AIDS drug becoming available, Stephen still refused to go see his doctor about his declining health, particularly now because he still was in between jobs and he didn't want any black marks on his health insurance record. He was threading a dangerous needle.

Also in March, I heard back from graduate business schools. Columbia University Business School, the New York University School of Business, and the UCLA Graduate School of Management all accepted me. The Wharton School at the University of Pennsylvania and the Yale School of Management rejected me. My acceptance to three out of five of the allegedly top-ten graduate business schools at the time felt amazing. A glimmer of sun momentarily poked through the storm clouds above me, and my eyes squinted from the glare. The universe had sent me a sliver of encouragement, and I savored it.

Given the rocky state of my relationship with Stephen, I considered—for a moment—breaking up with him and attending business school at Columbia or NYU. If I attended graduate school in New York City, there was no way that Stephen would be able to join me. The long distance would make for an explainable breakup, if I wanted one. I could escape his drug and alcohol abuse. I thought to myself that if he was intent on killing himself with alcohol and drugs before AIDS could do it, then maybe I should let him. As tempting as my breakup idea seemed, it only was a momentary fantasy. I still loved Stephen deeply. He was trying very hard to stop his substance abuse—not perfect yet, but he was making some progress in getting his life under control since my ultimatum a few months earlier. He also had mostly given up smoking in favor of wearing endless Nicorette patches. He was busy looking for a new job, too. I had introduced him to Bob, a legal headhunter I had met at the gym, who agreed to help with his job search. I updated and typed Stephen's résumé for him. With Bob helping, we had some hope. I knew that I could never live with myself if I broke up with Stephen knowing that he had AIDS. I had promised him that we would make it through the storm together. But I increasingly felt like the more experienced adult in our relationship even though I was twelve years his junior. I was telling him what to do, when to do it, and how to do it. At least he was listening to me, and starting to get his life back in order. My emotions alternated between anger at him over the fragile state of our relationship, and sadness and worry over his progressing illness while mine still waited in the wings. I was in way over my head at this point. I was living both of our lives, carrying him. Carrying my sister, too. Worrying about my friend Bryn, too. Sometimes I wondered if I was carrying myself.

The UCLA Graduate School of Management ranked the lowest of the three business schools that accepted me. But it also was the least expensive, so I would incur significantly less student loan debt there. Also, UCLA was the closest school to Hollywood, the world's entertainment capital, and I still wanted to work in that industry before I died, even if not as a writer. I would not have to move to attend UCLA either. So I chose UCLA. Stephen was incredibly relieved at my decision. He knew that our relationship was in deep trouble. My attending UCLA might give us a chance to save it.

On July 2, 1987, as I prepared to attend graduate school, Michael Bennett, the talented choreographer of *A Chorus Line* and *Dreamgirls*, two of my favorite Broadway musicals, died from AIDS. I was so sad that I would not see any more of this man's amazing work. The AIDS epidemic, now a global pandemic, continued to expand exponentially all around us. By the end of 1987, according to amfAR, AIDS cases reported to date in the US would grow to 50,378 with 40,849 deaths, a mortality rate higher than 81 percent.[11] The CDC also would hold its first national conference on HIV and Communities of Color in New York in August 1987 as AIDS increasingly became an epidemic of non-white populations.[27]

In September 1987, at the age of twenty-five, I started in the UCLA MBA program, shortly after Pope John Paul II made his historic pilgrimage to the city of Los Angeles, even as he sought to cover up the mushrooming priest pedophilia scandal engulfing the Roman Catholic Church. On the first day of my orientation, the dean of the school announced that the faculty had changed the curriculum by adding several more required courses in an effort to emulate the Harvard Business School. The dean also announced that the school would eliminate grading on a curve. Scores of 90 percent or higher would receive an A, scores between 80–89 percent would receive a B, and so forth. If everyone scored at 50 percent, then we would all fail. These unexpected changes to the curriculum increased my stress level significantly before school even started.

The school occupied one of the ugliest buildings on the UCLA campus. I would spend much of the next two years of my life in this bleak building. The few windows it had were covered with exterior aluminum sunshades that had mostly rusted in place due to lack of maintenance. Hardly any light of day seemed to reach us in our classrooms. On October 1, 1987, toward the end of my first week of classes, something happened that made the building even uglier: the Whittier Narrows earthquake, a moderate quake of 5.9 on the Richter scale, which struck at 7:42 a.m. just as I headed to my 8:00 a.m. statistics lecture. As I stood in the doorway of a stairwell during those twenty heart-stopping seconds, with the dilapidated building rocking back and forth and fissures appearing in the walls next to me, I thought, "Look at the bright side, Chris, maybe you're not going to die from AIDS after all."

Given my undergraduate English literature degree, I knew that I would have to work twice as hard as my business school classmates, most of whom had majored in economics or engineering, to keep pace. To boost my lagging confidence, I overcompensated and committed myself to be at the top of my class academically so that I would have the best career options (and company health insurance options, too) after graduation. I took copious notes in my classes, and I studied long into the nights, every single night after Stephen fell asleep. It's amazing how little sleep I could get by with in those days. I was on a mission.

Two weeks after I started classes, on October 11, 1987, the first public display of the NAMES Project AIDS Memorial Quilt panels occurred on the National Mall in Washington, DC, as part of the Second National March on Washington for Lesbian and Gay Rights. I so wanted to attend this march and see the quilt in person, but school made it impossible. I watched television news footage of the historic march, attended by an estimated 300,000 people, almost four times larger than the first March on Washington for Lesbian and Gay Rights held in 1979. Even though the first AIDS quilt panels had only been created less than one year before, the NAMES Project Quilt already covered an area of the Mall larger than a football field and included 1,920 panels.

In another business school twist, on Monday, October 19, 1987, less than three weeks after the earthquake, the Standard and Poor's 500 stock index suddenly plummeted 20.47 percent in *one day*, still to this day the largest one-day stock market crash in history, even greater than the crash of 1929 that began the Great Depression. The media named the crash "Black Monday." The stock market had already struggled for much of October 1987, but Black Monday drove a momentary nail in the coffin of the US economy and instantly chilled summer internship recruiting at business schools. My classmates and I now would have a much harder time finding summer internships between our first and second year. All of us worried for our careers after that crash, and for good reason. More stress.

For me, even as the economy and the equity markets faltered, I loved being in business school. It served as an escape from the storm around me. I could pretend that my life was somewhat "normal" when I was in the cocoon of class. No one in business school was sick and dying. This was my chance to take some control of my life and find a good job before becoming sick myself. Except for a small and closeted group of fellow gay and lesbian students, no one during my first year of business school even knew that I was gay and had a partner. Absolutely no one at school knew that I had a partner who had AIDS.

Then the strangest thing happened. Many of my classmates struggled with the business school curriculum, but for me the coursework was actually easy, especially the accounting, economics, finance, and statistics courses—way easier than my undergraduate English literature coursework. It was all basic math and common sense. I earned straight A's in my first quarter, and was elected to Beta Gamma Sigma, the MBA honor society. This English literature major was at the top of my business school class! My confidence soared. Another glint of sun through the dark clouds, and I basked in it.

While I studied my ass off at UCLA, a more energized Stephen worked to find a new job before his severance package from California Federal Savings ended. Stephen's health had improved somewhat now that he was taking better care of himself and had stopped abusing alcohol and drugs. His hard work paid off, too, as, thanks to the help from my friend Bob the headhunter, he got hired as a senior legal counsel for Imperial Savings and Loan, starting in January 1988. Just one problem with Stephen's new job: the company was located in San Diego, approximately 145 miles away from Los Angeles.

This threw another wrench into our life. I was planning on targeting jobs in the entertainment industry in Hollywood, and now Stephen needed to live and work in San Diego, at least during the week. I did not relish this, especially when our relationship still was on fragile terms. But he needed to start working again for the income, and in order to have good health insurance when he would become more seriously ill. What's more, he had no other job prospects, so we decided he should take the job. Stephen agreed to do most of the commuting in our new long-distance relationship so that I could focus on business school and look for jobs in Los Angeles. He also would continue to look for a job in LA. He moved into his corporate-provided housing in La Jolla on New Year's Day, 1988. At our home in Los Angeles, it was now just me, Bryn, and our three cats. Yes, Stephen and I had adopted three cats, all of which he had rescued from precarious situations. He loved cats. He even trained one of our cats, Edith, to do tricks on a makeshift trampoline. Yes, a trampoline. This was hilarious to watch, because that cat was truly fearless and crazy.

When it came time for me to find a summer MBA internship, however, few companies wanted to interview me, even with my top grades. The rocky US economy and stock market crash took its toll and eliminated many job opportunities. MBA recruiters looked down on my English literature degree, and the negative tapes inside me whispered, "See, Chris? Your parents warned you not to major in English literature." In the few interviews that I did obtain, recruiters berated me for my choice of undergraduate degree and my prior work experience in the UCLA administration instead of in a "real business." Just brutal. Furthermore, I had zero family connections for internships.

By early 1988, with zero leads, I realized that I needed to create my own summer job opportunity. If I was going to be dead soon, I vowed to at least first work for a while in the entertainment industry and I set my sights on the pinnacle. The world's best entertainment company at that time was, and in fact still is, The Walt Disney Company. I decided that come hell or high water, my summer internship would be at Disney. I was, in the words of Bon Jovi's 1988 song, "Livin' on a Prayer."

I found a copy of Disney's annual report in the business school library and called the office of every executive listed in it, asking about summer internships. I struck out. Everyone I spoke to referred me to the Human Resources department. All right, people, so I'll call the Human Resources department.

I reached a woman in HR named Debby. She was nice and sweet to me and said, "Well, we don't have any summer internships available right now, but you can always check back later to see if one opens up."

I asked Debby, "How often should I check back?"

She responded, "Well, things can change rapidly around here, so you should check in around once a week."

I thanked Debby. Then I called her every Monday morning for the next three months. She continued to be nice and sweet to me each and every time I called, and each time she politely told me that nothing was available. By April 1988, my desperation for a summer job became extreme, and I feared that I might not find anything at all. But in early May, Debby told me that yes, finally, Disney had an opening for a summer finance internship, and that if I could meet with her quickly, she would place me at the top of the list of candidates.

I responded, "How about right now?"

I made it to Debby's office at the Disney Studios lot in Burbank an hour later, something I never could have done if I had attended business school in New York City.

Debby and I clicked instantly. The internship would have me working for the Finance Director and Chief Financial Officer of Disney's Consumer Products division to prepare the company's 1989 fiscal year budget, which for the very first time would be completed on personal computers with Lotus 1-2-3 instead of a giant mainframe computer. I cheered to myself because I was proficient at Lotus 1-2-3 thanks to all the finance work I had done for my three UCLA mentors Margaret, Liz, and Cid. Debby told me that the internship didn't pay very much. I could live with that because I would be working for the greatest entertainment company in the world before I died. Debby told me that the internship needed to start immediately, at least on a part-time basis, even before I finished my final exams. I could live with that, too.

Debby advanced me to the next level, where I interviewed with Linda, Mark, Susan, Al, Joanne, and Tim, all of whom would be my bosses and colleagues for the summer. Everyone apparently liked me, and then The Walt Disney Company hired me.

This twenty-six-year-old English literature major, whom almost no one even wanted to interview for a summer internship, was now working for The Walt Disney Company! To say that I was over the moon with excitement about this would be a huge understatement. I was in the door—a Disney cast member (Disney calls all of its employees cast members). I cried from happiness and relief. Stephen was ecstatic for me, too. We celebrated at our house with Bryn. I fell asleep afterward still clutching my Disney offer letter while Stephen tucked me in.

Disney paid me $400 per week in the summer of 1988, significantly less than I made at UCLA before entering business school. I still have my offer letter and first paystub in a scrapbook in my bedroom closet.

Here's the crazy kicker: I had "suicided" my summer job prospects on Disney. There was no Plan B. In my make-it-work job search I never even sent one letter or résumé or made one phone call to any other entertainment company. Yes, I know that my come hell-or-high-water approach was not the smartest job strategy. But in my case, it worked, and to this day, it's the craziest roll of the dice of my life. I lived on a prayer and it came true. I went to business school because of AIDS, and then I got hired by the greatest entertainment company in the world. Yet another ray of sun from the universe broke through and shined on me, and I celebrated my good fortune.

But there was still a deluge all around me. It was about to get worse. Much, much, worse.

CHAPTER 5
THUNDER, LIGHTNING, RAIN, AND HAIL

O<small>N THE</small> F<small>OURTH OF</small> July weekend in 1988, my friend Erika married the love of her life, Rick, in San Francisco. I was a chuppah holder in the wedding, and my friend Robert was an usher. Stephen did not join me because he was working at his new job in San Diego. Erika and Robert are my two closest friends. Erika and I met in elementary school, and we both met Robert in junior high school. The three of us were virtually inseparable through high school. We went our separate ways during college, but we have always remained close and have periodic reunions to this day, which we call our "chills." The friendship of a longtime friend who knew you before you were anybody is something to cherish in this world.

By 1988, Erika, Robert, and I hadn't been together for nearly five years, so the wedding was a reunion for the three of us. It also served as a bon voyage party for Robert, who soon would move to New York City for his blossoming design career. We had all just turned twenty-six years old. Erika's wedding was a welcome celebration of life, and a distraction from my worries about Stephen and my future. I hadn't yet told either of them anything about Stephen's and my health secrets.

Shortly before Erika's wedding, my friend Bryn announced that he was moving out of our home and going back to Minnesota to live with his sister for the rest of his life. She had promised to take care of him. I knew that I would never see him again. A heart-wrenching goodbye. Bryn—my friend, my sidekick, my fun partner in crime—was scattering, too. Bryn assured me that he would stay in touch with me. But in 1988, we had no email or Facebook to make staying in touch an easy thing to do. The worst mistake

I made in that emotional moment of goodbye was forgetting to ask Bryn for his sister's contact information. I simply assumed that he would call or write to me once he got to Minnesota safely.

Erika's wedding weekend also was a moment for me to savor the early success of my summer internship at Disney. I worked in the basement of the Roy O. Disney building on the Disney Studios lot, on the corner of Mickey Avenue and Dopey Drive, on the same floor as the Disney University (the name of Disney's HR department) and the Disney Archives. I was making progress on organizing the Consumer Products Division's annual budget, thanks to my proficiency with Lotus 1-2-3. My bosses and colleagues seemed pleased with my performance. I felt as though I had a chance to secure a full-time job at the company after graduation from business school. Fingers crossed. There was a sense that I was finally controlling a little bit of my life, underscored for me by Janet Jackson's 1988 hit song "Control."

But after that bright Fourth of July weekend in San Francisco, the storm ominously darkened my skies, portending so much worse to come. From that moment forward, the dramas and villains of the literature that I studied in college started to leap off the pages of my *Norton Anthologies of English Literature* and into my life. The three witches in the opening scene of William Shakespeare's *Macbeth* prophesied and cursed Macbeth's future, but their words foreshadowed my future, too:

> *When shall we three meet again?*
> *In thunder, lightning, or in rain?*
> *When the hurlyburly's done,*
> *When the battle's lost and won.*
> *That will be ere the set of sun.*
>
> —Act One, Scene One, Lines 1–5, *Macbeth*,
> by William Shakespeare[28]

Indeed, thunder, lightning, rain, hurlyburlies, and battles all awaited my future. In the process, this twenty-six-year-old would learn firsthand, as those three witches also prophesied, that sometimes in life "fair is foul, and foul is fair."

The week after the wedding, Stephen started feeling terrible. I was at work in Burbank, and he stayed home sick at his apartment in La Jolla. I checked

---

28   *William Shakespeare: The Complete Works*, Alfred Harbage, editor, copyright 1981, page 1,110.

in with him regularly, a few times each day. He had a fever, but he felt better when he took Tylenol. He felt worse with each passing day. One afternoon, I telephoned to check in on him and he was totally out of it, incoherent. He sounded delirious and short of breath. Something bad was happening, and it terrified me. Stephen needed to get to the hospital quickly, but we didn't know anyone in La Jolla who could drive him, and I was 145 miles away. He suddenly dropped his phone, I heard it bounce on the floor, and I could hear him coughing in the background. He didn't come back on the line. Oh, no.

I called 911. The operator could only dispatch paramedics in Los Angeles, not in La Jolla. I begged her to figure out a way to patch my call into the 911 system in San Diego. She put me on hold. I waited, and waited, and waited. Finally, she came back on the line to say that she had found a way to get me through. I gave Stephen's address and apartment number to the San Diego 911 operator. Wondrously, she gave me her direct number so that I could follow up with her.

The paramedics arrived at Stephen's apartment within minutes. They found him still conscious on the floor, but in bad shape. They took him to nearby Scripps Memorial Hospital. He was admitted immediately to the Intensive Care Unit (ICU). I called there for a report, and the nurse told me, "Stephen has pneumocystis carinii pneumonia from AIDS. He also has overdosed on Tylenol. His liver is not functioning properly right now because of the Tylenol. You should come to the hospital right away if you want to say goodbye. The prognosis is not good."

Oh, my God.

I hung up the phone and ran to my boss's office. He was out at a meeting. I told his executive assistant that I had a family emergency in San Diego and needed to leave work immediately. I didn't know when I would be back. Then I jumped into my car and drove straight to Scripps Memorial Hospital. The longest three-hour drive of my life. All I thought through my tears as I drove was "Please don't die, please don't die, please don't die." I parked and ran to the ICU. The doctors and nurses filled me in on the dire situation. Because Stephen had pneumocystis carinii pneumonia, it meant that he had what is called "full-blown" AIDS. In 1988, the vast majority of people with AIDS contracted pneumocystis carinii pneumonia as one of their AIDS-related afflictions. Several of our friends, in fact, had already died from this very fast-moving illness. In addition, I learned from the doctors that high doses of

Tylenol can damage a person's liver, as it did to Stephen. His liver was already likely damaged from his earlier alcohol abuse.

Stephen was unconscious in his hospital bed and pumped full of drugs through intravenous tubes. I couldn't even mouth words to him. I sat next to his bed and held his hand, worried sick, and I cried. The doctors and nurses told me that he most likely would not make it through the night.

I was devastated. "Where Do Broken Hearts Go," Whitney Houston's emotional 1988 ballad, underscored this horrible moment of my life.

Stephen's parents needed to know this terrible news, so I called them at their home in Virginia. It was late at night East Coast time. His mother answered the phone and his father got on the line too, and then I said, "Stephen is in intensive care at Scripps Memorial Hospital in La Jolla, and the situation is grave. He has AIDS. The two of you should get here as quickly as possible."

In that short phone call, Stephen's mother had just learned that he had AIDS. In addition, Stephen's father learned that his son was gay, had AIDS, and that I was his partner. A ton of bricks had dropped on them, thanks to me. But the time for secret-keeping had run out. There was no gentle way for me to convey this unfolding dire medical situation to his parents. They needed to get from Virginia to La Jolla, and quickly, if they wanted to see him alive. Bricks were required.

I stayed with Stephen all night long. The ICU nurses didn't make me leave. At one point in the middle of the night, I took a short break, walked outside the hospital, and paced around the virtually empty parking lot. Suddenly, I saw a couple of rabbits. Then some more rabbits. The rabbits hopped around me in the moonlight in the parking lot and around the nearby bushes. It made me think of Stephen's pet nickname for me: Rabbit. At that moment, I didn't believe in signs, but I desperately hoped those rabbits were some sort of message from the universe that he somehow would survive.

I went back to the ICU, and a while later Stephen started to stir. He opened his eyes for a bit, mustered a smile at me, and then drifted back to sleep. Then, I totally lost it and sobbed uncontrollably.

He miraculously made it through the night, and we started to see improvement. When he became more conscious, I told him that his parents were on their way to California.

Also that morning, I called my mom and dad. The time for secret-keeping had run out for my parents, too. They were leaving later that day for a two-week trip to Ireland to celebrate their upcoming fortieth wedding anniversary and would be unreachable, so I decided to tell them—everything. From the pay telephone booth in the lobby of Scripps Memorial Hospital, I called them: "Stephen is in the hospital very ill, and he has AIDS. I'm not Stephen's roommate, I'm his partner."

A ton of bricks dropped on my mom and dad, too. The previous twenty-four hours crystallized for me that it was time to stop lying to my family or anyone else close to me regarding Stephen's AIDS diagnosis or the fact that I was gay. I didn't want to spend one more ounce of energy keeping these secrets.

My mom and dad did not take this news well at all. Compared to my brother Michael, who had devastated them merely by living with his girlfriend before he married her, my news about Stephen's AIDS diagnosis while simultaneously coming out of the closet to them—over the telephone, no less—was the veritable quadruple axel of how to instantly crush the hopes, dreams, and worldviews of conservative Roman Catholic parents. I could not have come out to them in a worse way, even if I tried. Oh, wait, actually there was one way for me to make everything worse: eventually in that call, my mom asked me, "Do you have AIDS, too?"

"Probably," I answered.

The call was brief, certainly under ten minutes. I did not want to get into debates or arguments, so I wrapped it up as quickly as I could by saying, "You have a plane to catch, and I need to get back to the intensive care unit. We can all talk about everything when you get back from Ireland. Have a good trip."

Then I hung up.

I had just delivered one hell of a bon voyage present to my parents. In the span of about twelve hours, I had thoroughly crushed both Stephen's parents and my parents with secret-busting bricks. These bricks were crushing me too, but I had more than two years to prepare for them.

My parents did not speak to me again for the next four months.

The universe now crashed around me with thunder, lightning, rain, and hail.

Stephen's mother arrived at the hospital later that day. But his father stayed home in Virginia. This went unexplained, and I found it very odd and sad. His best friend David also arrived that same day from New York City.

Thankfully, Stephen's health steadily improved, and he moved from the ICU into a regular hospital room. His liver had suffered some damage from his Tylenol overdose, but it was functioning again, enough for him to live. Stephen's mother, David, and I stayed with him during the day, and at night the three of us slept at the apartment. Stephen's father never came to see his son who had almost died.

Stephen, shaken to his core by his near-death experience, while still in his hospital bed, asked a Roman Catholic Trappist monk named Basil to convert him from an Episcopalian to a Roman Catholic. Basil was a friend of a friend of Stephen's mother who serendipitously happened to be visiting San Diego at that time, had an angelic presence about him, and I am convinced that he had clairvoyant powers, too. Basil subsequently became our good friend, and he was not your typical Roman Catholic priest. He had authored several books about spirituality, including a journal about living in a remote religious area of Greece called Mount Athos.

Stephen continued to improve and was released from the hospital after a week. We all celebrated his release by going to see *Who Framed Roger Rabbit*, a Disney film that led the box office in the summer of 1988. *Roger Rabbit* was the first Disney film to combine live action photography with animation since Disney's 1964 groundbreaking and award-winning *Mary Poppins*. The film's plot included a clever fantasy backstory of how the Los Angeles Pacific Electric Railway Company's Red Car transit system came to be dismantled in the mid-twentieth century in favor of freeways and traffic jams. This gave Stephen a personal connection to the film's premise, since one of his Blue Book Society friends, Alexandra, was the great-granddaughter of one of the founders of the Pacific Electric Railway Company. *Roger Rabbit* delivered the uplifting Disney movie ending that the four of us sorely needed. All of us loved the film—except Stephen's mother.

"Disney movies are so stupid," she pronounced. Then she went on to add that there was nothing redeeming about Disney because it was *only* an entertainment company.

Whoa. She knew that I was working at The Walt Disney Company in what I considered to be my dream job, and she just threw down the gauntlet by insulting its very essence right in front of me. But, rather than engage her in a debate right then and there, I let it go unchallenged. I figured that she was still in shock from the trauma she had just lived through, so maybe her politeness filters were out of whack. She deserved a break.

After that, Stephen went on permanent disability from Imperial Savings and Loan, and his mother and David went home. I returned to my summer job at Disney. My bosses were incredibly understanding and didn't pry. They could tell that I was shaken to my core by whatever had happened. Stephen moved back to our home in Los Angeles. We tried to resume as normal of a life as we could. But what really can possibly be normal after surviving a near-death experience, and with death still waiting in the wings? His disability income was not enough for us to live on long-term, but after I graduated from business school I hoped that my salary would allow us to be on a better financial footing. At least Stephen had good health insurance. Between Stephen's disability income and good health insurance, we were very lucky. Even so, the increasing financial pressure in our lives from his illness worried me.

Now that we knew for sure that Stephen had AIDS, and his secret was out to our families, I decided that it was time for me to find out about my HIV status, too, even though this terrified me. But I was ready. Ready, finally, to know the truth. Just as I had ended secrets with my family, I needed to end secrets with myself.

In the summer of 1988, the UCLA Student Health Center started offering anonymous AIDS tests for students, so I would be able to determine my HIV status without the test or its result going on my health record and jeopardizing my health insurance options after business school. If the health insurance industry was going to try to fuck with me and deny me insurance over getting an AIDS test, then I was going to fuck right back with the health insurance industry by not letting it know that I even took one and make Surgeon General Koop proud.

So, in August 1988, I took an anonymous AIDS test at the Health Center. I waited the required week for the results to come in. A very long, anxious week. Then I went back. The UCLA Student Health HIV test counselor, a registered nurse, ushered me into a windowless exam room to discuss the findings. I braced myself. As much as I had made peace with everything, and was ready for her confirmation that I had the AIDS virus, my heart was still racing as probability was about to become certainty. She sat down and rustled through the papers in her hands that had my anonymous results coded with a number. I held my breath.

And then she said, "You are negative."

Time suddenly stopped. The universe came to a grinding halt. I sat in front of her, stunned. I squinted my eyes at her. I tilted my head in disbelief. I must have misheard her, or perhaps I had gone crazy and was hearing voices. After a pause, I said:

"Can you repeat that, please?"

"You are HIV negative," she answered.

Her lips were moving and the sounds coming out were in sync. Apparently, I had heard her correctly.

"That can't be right," I replied. "I had unsafe sex for a very long time with my partner who has AIDS. He and I even sometimes accidentally shared toothbrushes and razors. The test has to be wrong."

"The test is right."

I asked her, "Did you do the Western Blot test?"

In early 1987, the Food and Drug Administration had licensed the new Western Blot test for AIDS, developed by Stanford University. This was much more accurate than the HIV ELISA test, which had a high false positive rate. The test counselor answered:

"We did both the HIV ELISA test and the Western Blot test. We did each test twice. That's why we drew two separate vials of blood from you last week, and we sent the vials to two separate testing labs. That's four separate AIDS tests. All of them came back negative."

None of this was computing for me. I suddenly thought of my mom, the tough-as-nails operating room nurse, who had always warned me, "Never trust anyone in the medical profession. No one knows what they are doing. Always get multiple second opinions." This reinforced my skepticism.

I continued: "But how can I possibly be HIV negative when I had unsafe sex for such a long time with someone who has AIDS? I don't understand this. Is this because AIDS has a long incubation period? Please explain to me how these AIDS tests work. How accurate are they? Can they be trusted?"

Then I grilled the test counselor regarding everything about these tests. She explained to me the test methodologies, their accuracies, and their probabilities of being right and wrong. We did the statistical math together on a sheet of white paper. T-statistics. Z-scores. Hypothesis testing. The statistical probability of a false negative reading for these two tests was zero. The HIV ELISA test was known to deliver a high false *positive* result, meaning that you could be HIV negative but it might incorrectly indicate you were positive. But the HIV ELISA test didn't deliver a high false *negative* result. That's why the HIV ELISA test worked so well for screening the nation's blood supply. The new Western Blot test was even more accurate. That's why UCLA used both AIDS tests, she explained. If the HIV ELISA test result came back positive, then as a verification the Western Blot test result would have come into play to determine if this was accurate. If the HIV ELISA test was positive but the Western Blot test was negative, then you were HIV negative. But then, just to be certain, in that case they would evaluate the two test results from the second vial of drawn blood, which had been sent to a separate testing lab, and then cross-reference the second test's two results with the results from the first two tests. In my case, all four of my tests—two HIV ELISA and two Western Blots, from two different testing labs—were negative. There could be absolutely no other answer than that I was negative for the AIDS virus.

I took all of this in, and I followed and understood the math thanks to my business school statistics courses. I knew that the test counselor had to be right. She was extraordinarily patient with me as I cross-examined her with questions about how the AIDS tests worked.

Then she said, "Usually, when I tell people that they are HIV negative they don't argue with me."

Now, my heart was beating through my chest. Time started to move forward again. My life was returning. I had a future again.

I didn't have the AIDS virus after all! This was real. This was happening. Slowly but surely, I began owning this miraculous new reality.

I had lived the past two years of my life in constant fear that I had AIDS when I didn't have it, all because of the fucking health insurance industry and its health insurance prison. The sun broke through the storm clouds above and shined on me once again. Then I said, "I need to hug someone right now. Can I hug you?"

Now, everyone who knows me knows that for me to ask someone for a hug is a huge, huge deal. I'm not a hugger. It's an unfortunate byproduct of my hypochondriac and germophobic nature. But suddenly the urge to hug the UCLA Student Health HIV test counselor, a person whom I didn't even know, overwhelmed me.

"Of course you can hug me," she replied.

Then I jumped to my feet and I hugged her. The test counselor's hug was amazing. No hug in my life has ever felt so good to me as that hug from that woman I didn't know in that small, windowless exam room in the UCLA Medical Center.

As I hugged her, I did not cry but I was deluged with emotions. Elation, happiness, and relief. Anger, embarrassment, shame, and guilt for living more than two years with the false certainty that I had the AIDS virus. Disbelief. All at the same time. The textbook definition of confusion. I had never before felt so confused at such a deep level, to my very core.

After I finished my hug with the test counselor, I said:

"We have to do it again."

"Another hug?"

"No, another test. We have to make sure."

"We *are* sure."

"But I want another test."

"Have you had unsafe sex with your partner or anyone else in the past six months?"

"No."

"Then you're fine, you're HIV negative. Besides, you can't have another HIV test here for thirty days. Come back in six months."

"Fine. Then I will see you again in thirty days."

My mom had always warned me to get multiple second medical opinions, and so I would do just that. Throughout my second year of business school, I would take several additional anonymous AIDS tests at the UCLA Student Health Center—all of them would confirm that I still was HIV negative.

I profusely thanked the test counselor and walked to a nearby UCLA restaurant named the Bombshelter for lunch. I sat at one of its tables and thought about the future that had just been returned to me. I now had a completely different time horizon. Those countless lightning bolts from the storm that had struck nearly everyone all around me, including Stephen, didn't strike me too. Somehow, the universe sheltered me from the worst part of the storm. But why? How? Why? How? Why? How?

To this very day, these remain the great unanswered questions of my life.

Then I thought about Stephen, who had AIDS and who, absent a miracle drug or treatment, would die from it. I thought about how I would now survive him, how I would still be here after he was gone from this planet.

I would be the "longtime companion" referenced in his obituary someday (since gays and lesbians in 1988 could not marry, this is how newspapers at that time referred to the surviving partner of someone who died from AIDS). I would have a future life someday without Stephen, and hopefully a long one.

And I felt guilty.

Later that day, I arrived home and told Stephen my news. He hugged me. As we held each other tightly, we cried together. We both knew what this meant. Although it was good news for me, it didn't change Stephen's reality. Now our lives were on different paths. This was the kind of poignant, dramatic moment that I have seen in many films but never thought would occur in my life: the emotional scene where the couple realizes their ultimate destiny when only one seat remains on the rescue helicopter, or the crashing airplane has only one parachute, or a floating door serves as a lifeboat to protect only one person from certain death in icy waters.

"I want you to have a great life after I'm gone," Stephen finally said.

That was one of many exceptional things about him. He was always my biggest cheerleader, even at a heartbreaking moment like this. At least now that I knew I was healthy, I would be able to take care of him for the rest of his life.

But I still felt guilty.

After Stephen's near-death experience, literally everything in his life was stripped away: his job, his legal career, his dreams of being in Blue Book Society. Everything external completely gone, for sure. His life was now on a different and much shorter path. Given his history, he could have easily curled up into a ball, returned to his drug and alcohol abuse, and died in anger and despair. Part of me dreaded that this would happen. But instead, right after he told me that he wanted me to have a great life after he was gone, he added, "I'm going to have a great life too, whatever is left of it."

Out of seemingly nowhere, a stronger and more resilient character emerged in him. Then he said, "I'm going to research new possible treatments that might extend my life. There are experimental AIDS treatments out there, and one of them is bound to work. I'm sure of it."

After all our tense arguments and wrangling in 1986 and even into 1987 that had pushed our relationship to the brink, I was surprised and thrilled to hear him adopt a fighting spirit and show some hope. Without me even prodding him or encouraging him. Here was the confident, hopeful Stephen whom I had met in early 1984. He was back. Then, he added, "I'm going to enroll in UCLA to earn a Doctor of Philosophy in Classics, with an emphasis on religion and philosophy. I have always wanted to study the classics. I'll become a classics professor!"

Now that everything he once valued had been stripped away from him, Stephen seemed to get clarity on what he really valued as he took control of his life again. Wow. Most importantly, he did it when the chips were down and no one would have been surprised if he had simply given up on life. Stephen's new fighting spirit was the flicker of a lone candle in the vast darkness of our lives at that time.

That's the moment when Stephen and I adopted *carpe diem* as our joint life motto: "seize the day," the Latin battle cry of all English literature majors. Nothing underscores the brevity of life more than a terminal illness and a near-death experience. One is left with two choices: sit at home and wait to die, or make the most of the time you have left with carpe diem. It was inspiring to see Stephen take the latter path. Carpe diem spoke to me too since I had just lived two years of my life falsely believing that I had the AIDS virus. Once he settled back in our home in Los Angeles, Stephen applied to UCLA's classics doctoral program. UCLA had an unexpected opening in the classics graduate department and accepted him readily. He already could read and speak Latin and ancient Greek, and spirituality and religion also were crucial life questions for him, as evidenced by his recent conversion to the Roman Catholic faith. He stopped talking about Blue Book Society and instead focused on his health; in fact, he started to take great care of his health. Stephen became truly happy and centered, maybe for the first time in his entire life, as he looked forward to pursuing his PhD, even while death loomed in his future.

Stephen and I made a pact to carpe diem the hell out of everything. Our theme for everything we did every day was seize the day, even menial chores like taking clothes to the cleaners.

We didn't have much money, but Stephen and I decided that travel would be part of our carpe diem plan. For our first destination we chose Hawai'i. We went there in September 1988, after I finished my summer internship at Disney, and before I started my second year of business school and he started his graduate studies. Hawai'i at that time was an inexpensive destination from Los Angeles. I had been there once before in the summer of 1977, with my mom and dad after our battle over private school, and the state's *aloha* charm had already placed its spell on me.

Stephen and I both fell in love with Hawai'i, and, more importantly, we fell in love with each other all over again. We traveled on a shoestring budget, stayed in inexpensive hotels and condominiums, and mostly cooked for ourselves. Hawai'i was paradise, and especially paradise for us. We visited and explored every accessible island: O'ahu, Kaua'i, Maui, Lāna'i, Moloka'i, and the Big Island of Hawai'i. We visited ancient Hawai'i burial grounds, hiked Hawaiian trails, and searched for petroglyphs. We climbed Diamond Head on O'ahu. We drove the winding road to Hana on Maui, and stopped at practically every pool and waterfall to swim. We rode in a Zodiac boat along the Nā Pali Coast on Kaua'i, explored sea caves, and saw dolphins spinning out of the sea. We went to a luau at Tahiti Nui on Kaua'i in the middle of a pouring rainstorm underneath a corrugated metal roof, getting splashed with mist but didn't care, and the staff there gave us a bottle of champagne after learning we were a couple. We visited Kīlauea, the erupting volcano. We hiked around Lāna'i when the island was undeveloped for tourists and full of pineapples and sugar cane. We bodysurfed at Hulopo'e Beach on Lāna'i in waves that were full of silver fish that crashed and flopped all over us. We visited the former leper colony on Moloka'i. We stayed in a low-budget condominium on Kaua'i next door to a restaurant owned by Charo, the Spanish-American flamenco guitarist and actress. We listened to Bobby McFerrin's "Don't Worry, Be Happy" and "Kokomo" by the Beach Boys over and over. Both were hits in 1988. They became our Hawai'i theme songs.

Hawai'i was heaven for us. Stephen's health was quite good and I could almost pretend that the sword of Damocles hanging over his life wasn't there. He shed the last remnants of his East Coast upbringing as we soaked up the sun, swam in the eighty-plus-degree ocean water, ranked the different beaches we visited, and communed with nature. But, most importantly, he and I reignited our relationship. We called this Hawai'i trip our delayed honeymoon, since Father Bob from St. James Episcopal Church had secretly married us in our Hancock Park backyard more than two years earlier.

At the end of our Hawai'i trip, we decided that our two favorite white sand beaches were Ke'e Beach on Kaua'i, and Hulopo'e Beach on Lāna'i, and that our two favorite black sand beaches were Punalu'u Beach on the Big

Island, and Wai'anapanapa Beach on Maui. We agreed that Wai'anapanapa Beach was our favorite and the most beautiful Hawaiian beach of all.

"Wai'anapanapa Beach is where I want my ashes scattered," I told Stephen.

My comment led to a discussion with him for the first time about his wishes for his own funeral arrangements. He told me that he wanted a Roman Catholic mass and to be buried in a cemetery, not cremated. He also said that he wanted a plaque in his name in the Memorial Hall at the Basilica of the National Shrine of the Immaculate Conception at Catholic University in Washington, DC.

"Well, you had better write all of this down in a will or directive," I said. "Otherwise, your parents will not know what to do for you. Remember, I'm not legally married to you. So, when you die, if you don't have your wishes written down your parents will decide all your arrangements for you, and I won't have any say in the matter."

"I will write this all down, and also tell my parents what I want," Stephen replied.

Then, our conversation shifted into his estate planning. It was a bit of a moot discussion because Stephen already was in significant debt from his hospitalization and treatments. He had no savings, no 401(k) plan, pension plan, or individual retirement account. He just had a small life insurance policy. The only real asset that Stephen "had" was our house, but even that didn't belong to him. I owned eight percent of the house, having purchased that minority position when he bought out his original coinvestor in the property. On my low UCLA salary, eight percent of an expensive house in Hancock Park was all I felt comfortable acquiring at that time, particularly given my plan to attend business school the following year. Because Stephen was unemployed when he bought out his coinvestor's interest, however, he couldn't qualify for a mortgage. So, at that time, his parents bought the other 92 percent of the house. They were listed on the mortgage note with me. Stephen and I paid all of the mortgage and tax payments, but he wasn't on the deed for the house at all. This ownership structure would prove fortuitous. First, it shielded the house from his creditors. This would come in handy for us from 1988 onward because it protected the home's equity from any liens from Stephen's mounting debts from hospital bills and medical treatments. Second, my small ownership percentage one day would prove to be invaluable in unexpected ways.

"I'm going to die with nothing, I have a negative net worth," Stephen said.

"Even though you're going to die with only debts, you should still make a will," I said. "If you want anything done with whatever is left and if you want your burial wishes followed, you need to specify them in a will. Otherwise, everyone will be guessing what you wanted. The time to get all of this in order is now, but I'm not going to badger you about it."

Then we changed the subject.

Stephen and I had so much fun in Hawai'i that we made plans to return in December for Christmas after we finished our final exams.

When we returned to Los Angeles, I started my second year at the UCLA business school and Stephen started his classics PhD program. I told one person, Martha, the Associate Dean of the MBA program, what was going on in my personal life in case I ever needed to rearrange my academic schedule for Stephen's medical care or in an emergency. She told me that UCLA would help in any way possible. I didn't want anyone else in business school to know about Stephen's illness.

Stephen and I settled into his routine of AIDS treatments and drugs. We amassed a veritable pharmacy in our bathroom. We soon learned the names and purposes of a long list of drugs: AZT, Trimetrexate, Interferon Alfa/Intron-A/Roferon-A, Ganciclovir, aerosolized Pentamidine/NebuPent, Diflucan/Fluconazole, Acyclovir/Zovirax, Bactrim/Septra/Sulfamethoxazole/Trimethoprim, Azithromycin/Zithromax, Rifabutin, Clarithromycin, and on and on. Just no more Tylenol! I banned it from our home.

We discovered an underground pharmacy in the mid-Wilshire area where we could buy Stephen's drugs without any insurance copayments. That saved us a lot of money. This same pharmacy also recycled unused drugs from people who had died from AIDS and gave them for free to people who had no health insurance. But it was all underground, and the pharmacist took a huge risk with his license in running that business. I hope he never got caught.

Stephen's AIDS drugs caused him headaches, nausea, muscle soreness, and tiredness. His nausea was a big problem, and quite unpredictable and could happen anywhere, so we traveled with plastic bags that I could whip out of my pocket at a moment's notice. The AZT regimen knocked his red and white blood counts down so much that every two to three weeks he needed to get a blood transfusion to fight anemia. I went with him to his treatments at Midway Hospital, as well as Century City Hospital, located right next door to

Beverly Hills High School's on-campus oil well. I studied my business school coursework while Stephen received his blood transfusions. At the same time as his blood transfusions, he also typically received an aerosolized treatment that helped prevent pneumocystis carinii pneumonia. For courage and fun, as part of our carpe diem strategy, Stephen wore a Batman T-shirt and a Batman pin to each of his blood transfusions. First AZT, then blood transfusions and some aerosol, with Batman pin and T-shirt, rinse and repeat. Over and over. I still have the Batman pin.

After one particularly grueling episode of nausea for Stephen that required a trip for us to the emergency room, I missed my business school classes for a day. When I returned to school and asked the woman who sat next to me in one class if she would share her notes from the missed session with me, she turned to me and said, "No. You are responsible for showing up to class and taking your own notes." My overly competitive and non-team-oriented classmate had no idea that my partner was at home dying from AIDS, and I couldn't tell her.

At home, I took over the feeding, grooming, and litterbox cleaning for our three cats because cat feces can transmit a disease called toxoplasmosis to a person with AIDS. To further reduce the risk for Stephen, I bathed all three cats every week. Of course, the cats hated the baths and I named the weekly ritual carpe diem cat wrestling. Adding to the insanity, I had developed an allergy to cats and had to take Benadryl every time that I touched them. But Stephen loved them very much, so it was all worth it.

Stephen and I also followed emerging AIDS research in medical journals and looked into several possible experimental AIDS treatments. Sometimes, we knew more about developing treatments than his own doctors did. David helped us, too, from New York City. We shared medical information back and forth with him, over the phone and through the mail—no Google or email existed yet to make this easy to do. We leveraged off medical information provided by the AIDS Coalition to Unleash Power (ACT UP), a group of AIDS political activists that formed in New York City around March, 1987, to literally fight for their lives. The members of ACT UP, led by founder Larry Kramer and many others much more brave than I could ever be, heroically fought to change the way that new drugs are approved in the United States, helping all Americans, not just people with AIDS.

In the fall of 1988, Stephen and David both got accepted into an experimental AIDS drug study at the UCLA Medical Center. The Amgen Company, at that time relatively small, had two promising potential new drugs pending government approval, Erythropoietin (also called Epogen or EPO), and Neupogen (also called Filgrastim). These two drugs stimulated the human body to produce red and white blood cells to fight the anemia caused by AZT (EPO is one of the drugs that Lance Armstrong later took to tilt the scales in his favor in cycling competitions). These drugs, administered by injection twice per day, needed constant refrigeration. I became skilled at providing the injections. Amazingly, these two new drugs worked. Stephen's and David's blood counts improved enormously, their energy levels rallied, and they needed fewer blood transfusions. The UCLA/Amgen study gave Stephen and David nearly two additional relatively healthy years of life. A real blessing. Along the way, Stephen, David, and I became good friends with one of the study's nurses, Nenna, and her husband, Al.

Since David was in the study too, he frequently visited from New York City and stayed with us so that he could complete his required medical checkups at UCLA. Because of this, Stephen and David got to spend a lot of time together at the end of their lives, which was great for these two longtime friends who shared so much history together. A real gift.

David, the perpetually single man who even admitted himself that he always struggled to find love, finally found a bit of romance very late in his life, in Los Angeles, with Jeff, an architect who had met David in New York City in the 1970s. It was wonderful to see these two men together, and I was so happy that David finally found someone to love, even if only for a short time before the storm claimed him. Another gift.

So starting with the fall of 1988, Stephen, my sister, and I all attended school at UCLA simultaneously. One classics major, one history major, and one business major. We would run into each other on campus occasionally, and we met for lunch sometimes. By 1988, Joan was a senior, on track to graduate with her Bachelor's Degree in history in June 1989, the same time that I would graduate with my MBA.

I had encouraged Joan to seek an appointment to UCLA's Communications Board in the hope that she would make some good connections for restarting her journalism career after college. My plan backfired horribly. She won the appointment, but instead of using the Communications Board to cultivate networking opportunities, she turned into a terror. Networking was the last thing on her mind. She transferred her long-simmering anger from her firing by the *Chicago Tribune* onto the UCLA administration, and she fought with everyone around her on this prestigious campus board that had launched many of its members into post-college big league media careers. Joan's storm was dragging her down, and the storm was winning. I couldn't do anything to stop it. The universe was teaching me the painful lesson that one person cannot fight another person's life challenges for them, no matter how much I prided myself on helpfully micromanaging the lives of others.

Stephen and I started to learn that the more his illness progressed, the more the world turned against us. As Shakespeare's witches predicted, "fair is foul and foul is fair." Stephen's health insurance company's constant denials of medical claims caused me endless stress, and taught me to loathe the health insurance industry even more than I already did. I learned another insidious strategy in the industry's business model: delay paying claims and wear sick patients down until they give up and die so that claims don't have to be paid. Fucking assholes. I don't know how the people running these companies can sleep at night. Mounds of insurance company paperwork and requests for additional information to justify Stephen's treatments deemed "potentially experimental" (health insurance industry code words for "we just don't want to pay for anything") covered our dining room table. I spent my evenings writing endless explanations for his health insurance claims. I memorized every provision of his health insurance policy. I was determined to wear his health insurance company down, and did. During my class breaks, from payphones (cell phones were a rare item, looked like bricks, and were only for the rich) I battled health claims adjusters until they caved in and covered many of his treatments. I wondered to myself, "How do sick people with AIDS fight these heinous insurance companies over medical claims if they have no family members like me to help them?" Of course, the answer is they don't. They just die. Stephen and I started to amass a sizeable amount of debt from the uncovered portions of his care, more and more of which we were required to pay in advance of his treatments. Given the never-ending claims battles with his health insurance company, I hardly even noticed that the Los Angeles Dodgers beat the Oakland Athletics to win the 1988 World Series. I missed the first National Coming Out Day on October 11, 1988, too.

From Stephen's near-death in July through Thanksgiving 1988, my mom and dad still hadn't contacted me. I knew that they were still angry with me because Joan and her partner Jane periodically conveyed news reports to me. First, my parents canceled a fortieth anniversary party that Joan and Jane had planned for them that summer. Then my parents told all of their friends that their party was canceled because I had ruined their lives. Drama, drama, drama. I was actually glad that my mom and dad weren't calling me. I didn't need their negativity. But shortly after Thanksgiving, my mom finally telephoned, and she began the call by asking, "What did I do to make you gay?"

"You probably didn't do anything," I replied. "But maybe you shouldn't have chain-smoked and consumed alcohol during your pregnancy with me. Or maybe it's because of my piano lessons. Maybe it's because you took me to see *A Chorus Line*. Or maybe it's because you and Dad never took me camping at Yosemite. Who really knows?"

She didn't appreciate my joking, but I often joke out of anger. It's a great coping strategy. At least my parents and I were back in contact again. Maybe we could repair our strained relationship. That telephone call opened our lines of communication again.

As I looked back, I thought about how the last six months of 1988 played out for Stephen and me like a Shakespearean tragedy as the harrowing storm gained more intensity, and its thunder, lightning, rain, and hail attacked us from every angle. We had been through so much together, but more was still to come. The hurlyburlies and battles, as foreshadowed by the three witches in *Macbeth*, hadn't even arrived yet. But they would, and soon.

In early December 1988, the Chief Financial Officer of Disney's Consumer Products division invited me to lunch at the executive dining room on the top floor of the Disney Animation Building at the studio lot. Even though I had completed my summer internship, my second-year master's thesis project focused on a new business opportunity in Disney's Consumer Products division, so I was still in regular contact with him. He delivered some fantastic news to me. Disney was going to hire me full-time after I graduated. The company didn't have a specific department in mind for me yet, but I would be hired into a finance role. He told me everything would be figured out in spring 1989 when they had a better handle on staffing needs. I jumped for joy inside. My post-MBA job search, which had barely begun, had already ended in the best possible way. Another ray of sun for me. I breathed a huge sigh of relief.

After we finished our fall quarter final exams, Stephen and I took our second trip to Hawai'i and had so much to celebrate: an experimental drug trial that seemed to be working miracles for him and a full-time job after business school for me at Disney. Against all odds, we were both ending 1988 with hope, and if those experimental Amgen drugs continued to work, well, then perhaps we even had a long-term future together.

So, in December 1988, both Stephen and I had a very *Mele Kalikimaka*. This means "Merry Christmas" in Hawaiian. On Christmas Day, we celebrated reading books while wriggling our feet in the white sand in front of our low-budget condo near Ke'e Beach on the north shore of the island of Kaua'i, no Christmas presents needed at all, while crystal clear waves gently crashed in front of us. Heaven. Then, Stephen reached into his pocket and pulled out a small ceramic white rabbit that he had purchased at a local drugstore and handed it to me as my Christmas gift. "A rabbit for my beloved rabbit," he said, and I smiled and kissed him. A gift that would become priceless to me. For once, the phrase Mele Kalikimaka wasn't just a mindless cliché, but was brimming with meaning for us as, amid the storm, we relished a break that we thought might last.

CHAPTER 6
HURRICANE WINDS

Kaposi's sarcoma, also known as KS, is a cancer that commonly affected people with AIDS in 1989. It usually appears as a series of tumors on the skin or inside the mouth. KS tumors, called lesions, are purple, red, and sometimes brown. They most commonly appear on the legs or face and look dreadful, but they typically cause no symptoms. Sometimes, they appear in the extremities, stomach, lungs, liver, or intestines.

Stephen's KS lesions grew inside his mouth, mostly on the roof. They were purple. They appeared just as President George H. W. Bush assumed office as the forty-first president of the United States. After Stephen's first lesions appeared, I regularly inspected the inside of Stephen's mouth with a small flashlight to track their growth.

Nothing really needed to be done about this, but Stephen insisted on treating them through one of the several unorthodox treatments that he pursued. Through the UCLA/Amgen study, he had discovered an oral surgeon at the UCLA School of Dentistry who operated on the insides of patients' mouths to remove these lesions, and he signed up for multiple lesion-removal sessions. These treatments seemed barbaric to me, but he wanted them, even though the surgeries caused him a great deal of pain while he healed.

Inside his mouth, he also battled candidiasis, also known as thrush. This is another opportunistic illness, caused by the yeast, or fungus, Candida. Most human bodies have Candida, but it causes no problems for people with healthy immune systems. Thrush looks like white spots or patches, sometimes a bit bumpy, and usually appears toward the back of the mouth. It can cause a sore throat, pain when swallowing, and can alter the sense of taste. As I inspected the KS lesions inside Stephen's mouth, and the scars from his lesion-removal surgeries, I also saw the effects of thrush.

In March 1989, around the time that the Exxon Valdez oil tanker devastated Prince William Sound in Alaska by spilling an estimated eleven million gallons of crude oil, Imperial Savings and Loan terminated Stephen's employment. I was surprised that the company hadn't terminated him much earlier. Luckily, my ongoing appeals to Barbara, the company's compassionate head of Human Resources, had delayed his termination for many months. However, the Savings and Loan Crisis had engulfed much of the country's financial industry, and Imperial Savings and Loan struggled under the weight of the souring junk bond portfolio that it had purchased from Drexel Burnham Lambert, the firm led by Michael Milken. By March 1989, the company needed to do everything possible to cut costs in order to avoid being seized by the government. I thanked Barbara for keeping Stephen on the company's payroll for as long as she did. She was a godsend to us.

Fortunately, Stephen's employment termination did not affect his disability income. But it did start the ominous countdown clock for his health insurance coverage. The Consolidated Omnibus Budget Reconciliation Act of 1985, more commonly known as COBRA, signed into law four years earlier by President Ronald Reagan, allowed workers who lost their jobs to continue, at their own expense, the health benefits provided by their former employer's group health plan for up to twenty-nine months. This meant Stephen's COBRA health insurance coverage would end in August 1991. After that, he would have no health insurance at all. August 1991 became branded into my brain as the date after which I had better be making a boatload of money to pay for my partner's medical care. I could feel the stress from the hurricane winds gaining strength.

In the spring of 1989, Stephen continued his classics studies and his quest for all things spiritual. By this time, he had left St. James Episcopal Church and joined Saint Andrew Russian Greek Catholic Church in El Segundo. Saint Andrew Church is an Eastern Catholic church that somehow falls under the jurisdiction of the Roman Catholic Church through a religious treaty forged long ago, even though Eastern Catholicism is a very different and much better religion than Roman Catholicism.

Stephen made many friends there, including the priest, Father Alexei. Stephen loved this church and begged me to come with him, so I joined him. The elaborate service went on for nearly two hours, followed by a huge potluck lunch for everyone. The people of Saint Andrew Church were welcoming to Stephen and me, even knowing that he was fighting AIDS and that I was his partner. No judgment whatsoever. Without question, these people had something very rare in the Roman Catholic Church: community. The universe was beginning to teach me the lesson that red is black, and black is red.

Around this time some of our friends began to ostracize Stephen and me because of his illness, and this hurt both of us a great deal. We were instantly deleted. His Washington, DC, friends dropped us first, led by the gay Roman Catholic priest and his live-in gay partner, the doctor. Irony, right? But I suppose that a priest who had trouble following the Church's vow of celibacy also would have trouble being a friend to someone when the chips are down. One of my best friends from college suddenly didn't want to see me anymore or return my telephone calls. One of Stephen's Yale classmates, a writer, abruptly ended his friendship with us and, after Stephen's passing, posted a disrespectful memorial on a Yale alumni website in which he went so far as to say that Stephen spent all his time in Los Angeles hanging out with drug dealers, and added that I had also died from AIDS. When I contacted this classmate to ask him to take down the post and to inform him that I was still very much alive, he responded, "I won't take anything down, that's how I remember it." Stephen and I were ignored by some friends one night at dinner at the Sizzler restaurant on Highland Avenue. A similar experience happened to us with other friends one Sunday morning while we ate breakfast at the Carnation restaurant on Wilshire Boulevard. One of my business school professors and his partner, who had developed a friendship with us during my first year of business school, dropped us like hot potatoes after they learned Stephen had been hospitalized. Other friends simply stopped calling us. Try to imagine the pain for Stephen of fighting a terminal illness, and then being rejected like this. It infuriated me. This was yet another curse for people with AIDS in 1989 because of the disease's stigma. Red was black, and black was red.

This progressive ostracism taught me an important lesson about friendship. Finding a true friend equates to finding a special grain of sand on a vast sandy beach: it's very difficult to do, but worth the effort. Authentic friendship can be quite ironic, too. First, you never know your true friends until you're in a really tough spot. Second, when you most need help in your life, you will be shocked and surprised at who actually steps up to help you. This was a true *Alice's Adventures in Wonderland* experience for me as I kept learning that red is black, and black is red. Sadly, I lost several friends during this period, not due to their death from AIDS, but due to their outright abandonment of Stephen and me. Fortunately, most of these people had the good sense to not try to contact me ever again.

Contrast this terrible treatment by some of our friends with the wonderful treatment we sometimes experienced at the hands of complete strangers. For example, one night I splurged to take Stephen out for a romantic dinner at Lawry's The Prime Rib restaurant on La Cienega Boulevard, and in the middle of our dinner Stephen suddenly felt nauseous and vomited all over the table before I could reach inside my pocket for the plastic vomit bags I carried with me. We were seated prominently in the restaurant's large dining room, and thankfully none of the nearby diners saw what happened, but our waiter saw and he immediately came over to help us. I said to him, "Please, go get some gloves," and without missing a beat he responded, "Don't you worry, I've got this." He cleaned up everything without drawing any attention to our table, and then he kindly helped us out of the restaurant, his arm around Stephen, and comped the bill. He turned out to be "family" too, a complete stranger who treated us better than some of our friends did. Red was black, and black was red.

As these abandonments occurred, in other corners we made surprising new friendships. Stephen's new friends at Saint Andrew Church were a wonderful comfort for us, notably Noel and Chris, and their teenage daughter Jenise. Stephen became good friends with one of his classics professors at UCLA. Nenna, the nurse from the UCLA/Amgen study, and her husband Al, became close friends of ours.

Stephen, crushed by abandonments, began to turn inward to avoid more pain from being shunned, and he stopped going to Blue Book Society events. People noticed that he disappeared, and they started leaving messages on his answering machine, which he did not return. No one from this group of people had ostracized him yet, but he was convinced they would, so before they could do it, he beat them to the punch. He didn't want anyone in Blue Book Society to know that he was gay and sick, especially when some of our supposedly more understanding friends already were dropping us.

One Saturday afternoon, my private line rang and I answered, and it was Jessie, the now eighty-three-year-old Blue Book Society grand dame. She was the only person in this group who really knew me, who knew I lived with Stephen, and who had oddly bonded with me many years earlier. Jessie, in her spry, crackly voice, demanded to know what was going on with Stephen. Whether Stephen liked it or not, the time for secret-keeping had ended. I took a breath, and then told her the truth in one sentence: "Stephen is sick with AIDS; I'm not just his roommate, I'm his partner; and he has been avoiding you and everyone else because he is ashamed about being gay and sick." I figured that would be the end of the call and the friendship.

Her immediate response shocked me.

"Well, for God's sake, of course I know that you're his partner, Chris. What is there for Stephen to be ashamed of? Don't you know that [Jessie listed several names of well-known men from Los Angeles Blue Book Society] are all gay? Some of them are married to women, too. I'm coming over to visit, and I won't take no for an answer!"

Red was black, and black was red.

Jessie then came to our house in her chauffeured car and visited Stephen. When she saw him, she gave him a big hug and kiss without any hesitation. Then the three of us talked and laughed for a long time. The next week, she visited him again and took him to a lunch where his Los Angeles Blue Book Society friends welcomed him with open arms. She led the cavalry by telling everyone in advance what was going on with him, and not one of these people ostracized him. It turned out that they all just liked him for who he was, AIDS and all. No social climbing needed. He was enough. These people, in our time of need, did my Los Angeles hometown proud. Los Angeles wasn't Kokomo. A wonderful, surprising turn of events, and Stephen beamed with happiness from being so accepted by the very people who we both were sure would reject us. Jessie visited Stephen regularly for the rest of his life.

But Jessie didn't stop there. She made everyone aware that Stephen had a partner and gave people my private telephone number. Suddenly my phone rang off the hook. All these conservative WASPy wealthy people, whom Stephen at one time had tried so hard to impress, whom I had written off as superficial, now reached out to be my friend, too. I was in Blue Book Society. It was crazy. I even went to lunch one day, filled with conflict and trepidation, at the Los Angeles Country Club, hosted by a couple who told me that when I felt ready someday, they would sponsor me for membership there if I wanted to join. Oh, the irony of this couple's generous offer to sponsor me for membership in a private club that I could never allow myself to join because of its history of discrimination. But their gesture was honest and heartfelt, and I thanked them for it. These Blue Book Society people were among the least homophobic and least afraid of AIDS of anyone. I sure did misjudge this group of people. Red was black, and black was red.

My sister, meanwhile, close to earning the college degree that I had hoped would launch her journalism career back into the big leagues, continued to act out her anger while serving on the UCLA Communications Board. She couldn't choose to help herself. She was also now embroiled in a wrongful termination lawsuit against California State University, Los Angeles, where she had worked part-time, over a first amendment freedom of the press issue. Her anger continued to simmer and grow, and it seemed to consume her, but I was proud to see her finally standing up for herself. Increasingly, Joan drained me of energy when I was around her. The universe was reinforcing to me the lesson that one person cannot fight another person's life challenges. This was a very hard life lesson for me to learn.

And where in the hell was my friend Bryn? He had moved to Minnesota to live with his sister nearly a year ago, but I still hadn't heard a word from him. Was she taking good care of him? I had no way of reaching him because of my stupid mistake of not asking him for his sister's name, phone number, or address. Why was he not calling me? I worried that he had died already.

My ongoing worries about my increasingly angry sister and growing concern over my disappearing friend Bryn only added to my already mounting worries about Stephen's health, his care, and our precarious finances. Fortunately, Stephen's health was relatively stable. The AZT and the Amgen miracle drugs seemed to be slowing the progression of his disease.

In May 1989, shortly after my twenty-seventh birthday, Disney hired me into a full-time position in its Corporate Treasury Department, to start after my imminent graduation from business school. My new boss, Marcia, told me that my job would focus on two areas: first, investment management for Disney's $350-million pension fund portfolio, $800-million corporate cash portfolio, and various executive compensation investment accounts; and second, the company's investor relations program. At that moment in time, I didn't even know what a corporate treasury department did, but I soon learned that it is the most interesting finance group in any company, the place where the most important financial decisions are made.

At home, Stephen and I celebrated my Disney full-time job assignment. He presented me with a small white wooden rabbit, mounted on a platform with wheels, with a little carrot by his front paws. I added him to my growing rabbit collection. Then, we frantically planned a shoestring-budget trip to Greece and Italy funded by the unspent portion of my student loans and scholarships, the last bit of money that I possessed in the world at that moment in my life. Stephen felt healthy enough to travel to Europe, and I figured that this could be our last chance to attempt a trip together of this distance and magnitude. So, carpe diem. We scheduled our departure for immediately after my June 16 graduation, and our return just before my mid-July start date at Disney. Three entire weeks.

Joan and I celebrated our two newly earned university degrees, MBA and history, with a joint graduation dinner attended by my parents, Stephen, Jane, and my first boss Margaret, whom I now also called my second mom. Stephen and I departed for our trip to Italy and Greece the next day, twelve days after the world watched the unidentified "tank man" stare down four approaching Chinese military tanks in Beijing's Tiananmen Square on live television. The day before our departure, he received a complete medical checkup with his doctor, a blood transfusion, a preventative treatment for pneumocystis carinii pneumonia, and a clean bill of health to travel abroad. I hoped that we would be crisis-free for the three-week trip. In tow with us, we brought an Igloo ice chest filled with his Amgen medicines and Blue Ice packets to keep it cold, a three-week supply of needles and syringes, a sharps container to safely store the used needles, and all of his other AIDS medicines. We also traveled with doctors' notes to explain the medicines and needles to the various authorities, and prescriptions for emergency treatments, should they be necessary. Stephen and I looked a bit like traveling paramedics.

En route to Greece, we arranged a long layover in Rome so that Stephen could show me the city's highlights. In about ten frantic but fun-filled hours in the Eternal City, we saw Saint Peter's Basilica and the Vatican, the Trevi Fountain, the Pantheon, and the Spanish Steps, all while eating our weight in pizza and gelato. Rome, my first ever European city, with Stephen was glorious. Then on to Athens, Greece.

We arrived in the middle of a Greek election. First, we toured the Acropolis, the Parthenon, Areopagus Hill, and the Theatre of Dionysus.

Then, we received a special back-of-the-house tour of the museum at the Stoa of Attalos right next to the Agora of Athens, arranged by Stephen's UCLA classics professor friend. A phenomenal experience. The Greek professor who escorted us opened drawers throughout the museum and allowed us to hold ancient artifacts. At one point, she opened a drawer filled with broken shards of pottery.

"These are ostracons," she said.

She explained that ostracons functioned in the way that ballots do today. In ancient Greece, citizens used them to write the names of people they wanted banished from society. We were allowed to hold several of these ostracons, and we could see the names scratched on them. What really resonated with us was that "ostracon" was the basis for the English word "ostracize," a word that had become so painfully central to our lives.

I turned to Stephen and quietly whispered: "Hey, I think I see our names on this ostracon. It says that we should be banished from society because we are gay."

The Greek professor overheard me and said, "That's a horrible thing to say."

"You're right," I answered. "It is a horrible thing, but we live it every day." Stephen gave me the irritated eye.

After Athens, we started our Peloponnesus tour in our rental car, and for the next ten days we drove hundreds of miles. We ate Kalamata olives in the village of Kalamata. In Olympia, we each ran a lap in 100+ degree heat on the stadium track for the ancient Olympics games. At the Temple at Delphi, Stephen took a photo of me, the new Disney Treasury team member, standing in front of the ancient Athenian Treasury. We also listened for the Delphic Oracle, trying to hear a glimmer of our future. Our Peloponnesus trip was epic.

In the month of July, Greece's weather is brutally hot. Everywhere we went, we lugged Stephen's ice chest full of Amgen medicines in one hand and a container of an ever-increasing number of used needles in the other. This did not seem like a burden because Stephen beamed with happiness. It was carpe diem. I worried constantly about his health, but thankfully his energy held up marvelously.

Finding a steady supply of ice or refrigeration for our Blue Ice, however, presented its challenges. We had one close call, in Sparta, where our barebones hotel had no ice and no refrigerator, but the hotel owner sent out a call for help and several nearby villagers contributed trays of ice from their homes to keep Stephen's medicine cold. Twice. Once at our check-in, and then again the next morning. Unbelievable. These absolute strangers in a foreign country showed us such kindness. These people were not casting ostracon ballots.

Throughout Greece, I also carried investment books to prepare me for my new job, including my favorite, *Investments: Analysis and Management* by Jack Clark Francis. I set aside time to read these books every day. I read everywhere we went, at beaches, in restaurants, and even at archaeological sites. At one point, I took things a bit too far and dropped my favorite investment book into the Mediterranean Sea. I still have that book, with its waterlogged pages and dented pink cover.

We stopped to swim at beaches, and compared them to Hawai'i and California beaches. We dumped bottles of water over our heads to stay cool, and we doused ourselves in the fountains in village squares. We ate delicious Greek food. Beer in Greece cost the equivalent of twenty-five US cents. We drove and toured each day until we were tired, and then searched for an inexpensive hotel, where I would give him his evening and then morning shots of Epogen and Neupogen, which anchored our otherwise carefree days by reminding us of the inevitable sword of Damocles hanging over him. We visited nearly every church that we came across, and Greece has a lot of them. We became experts on the differences between Doric, Ionic, and Corinthian columns. We met several welcoming Greek people along the way, too. In one village, we encountered two brothers who barely spoke English, and they invited us to dinner at their house. We met their wives, parents, and sisters, and we drank their homemade wine, and then we all got up and danced the Hasapiko just as I had done with my sister in Chicago in the summer of 1978.

Everywhere we went, Stephen translated for me. He could read ancient Greek, and translated the inscriptions on the columns, walls, floors, and grave markers. In addition, many excavations of Greek ruins had been completed by the French, and so many museum displays were presented only in modern Greek and French with no English, so he translated the modern Greek and French for me, too. Groups of people surreptitiously followed the two of us through the archaeological sites and museums once they figured out that Stephen could translate everything. He became a de facto tour guide. It was hilarious, and I was so proud of him. Once, someone even tipped him five dollars. That was huge! In Greece in 1989, five dollars could buy you twenty beers!

Stephen and I grew closer, and we lived like there was no tomorrow because we were well aware that one day there would be no tomorrow for him. So throughout the trip, we lived for today.

At one point, I asked Stephen why he was so distant from his parents. I knew that ever since Stephen's near-death experience with pneumocystis carinii pneumonia the previous summer, his mother had started volunteering at local AIDS organizations in Yorktown, Virginia, which I thought was interesting. But strangely, his parents hadn't visited us in Los Angeles, which I thought odd given his terminal illness. How could they not visit their only child, their prodigal son who was dying from AIDS, in more than a year? Did they not want to see what was actually happening to him? Did they not want to spend time with him? This parental behavior didn't compute, and I knew that it hurt Stephen a great deal, so I tried not to poke at it. His mother still telephoned him, though. But he still kept her at a distance. He continued to have her leave messages on his answering machine without picking up the phone. He still didn't call her back very often, either.

Stephen shrugged at me and said, "She's always trying to follow me into everything."

"What do you mean?" I asked.

"Well, she went to college for her Bachelor's Degree after I got mine. Then when she found out that I was gay, she made some gay friends. Then when I got diagnosed with AIDS, she started volunteering at AIDS organizations."

"Steve, that's a good thing," I responded, trying to encourage him to open up more to his parents. "Your mother is trying to reach out to you, and to connect with you. Except for her extremely poor judgment when she sent you her Valium and Xanax, it sounds to me like she just wants to be a part of your life in some way even though she hasn't visited you."

"Chris, she even followed me into the Episcopal Church," Stephen said, deadpan.

What? This was new territory. Stephen never mentioned before that he had once been a member of another religion.

"What do you mean she followed you into the Episcopal Church? What religion were you before you were an Episcopalian?"

After a pause, Stephen replied, "Well, I was Jewish."

Stephen and I had been together five-and-a-half years and he never once mentioned that he had been born and raised Jewish. This blew my mind, and I got angry, not because Stephen had been born Jewish, but because in five-and-a-half years and thousands of conversations, he didn't tell me, his partner, this important and intriguing fact about himself.

"Why did you not tell me this before, Steve?" I demanded to know. "It had better not be because you are ashamed of your Jewish roots. You know that many of my closest friends are Jewish, and I love them. You already know that my last name, Zyda, which should really be Zeida, means 'grandfather' in Yiddish, so at some point my ancestors were Jewish, too. I don't understand why you wouldn't share this part of yourself with me. If this is due to shame because of Blue Book Society, I'm going to smack you. You already know that they all know that you have AIDS and a gay partner and they still love you."

Then Stephen told me about how he had felt lost when he attended Yale University and Yale Law School. This led him to spirituality, and during law school he converted to the Episcopal faith, and that made him feel much more content. That experience sparked his lifelong quest for all things spiritual. Stephen's hospital bed conversion in Scripps Memorial Hospital to the Roman Catholic faith with Basil the monk now made a lot more sense. I already knew that a quest for life's spiritual meaning was deep in Stephen's DNA. He apparently was just ashamed to share the whole history of it with me until now. He had so much shame about so many things. Then I said, "Well, it's ridiculous that you waited so long to tell me this about yourself. You should be proud of your heritage. When we get back to Los Angeles, we are going to eat potato latkes once a week for the next six months and I won't take no for an answer."

Stephen very much wanted to take a three-day detour to visit Greece's Mount Athos, as our friend Basil the monk had done. But this would be far too dangerous. Mount Athos is completely isolated from society. No hospitals or doctors if something went wrong. No ice or electricity for refrigeration for his medicines. Accessible mostly by foot, with long hikes up the sides of mountains in blistering heat. We had to skip it.

We finished our Greece trip on the island of Crete. We stayed at the Creta Beach Hotel in Agios Nikolaos, which had a white grand piano in its large dining room that was in terrible condition. For fun, I played a few notes after breakfast one morning and the hotel's owner ran over to me and excitedly said, "Wow, you can play the piano?"

"Yes, but this piano is very out of tune, and the pedals are broken, and the piano bench is downright dangerous to sit on," I replied.

The hotel owner asked me, "Can you fix it?"

Well, I'm not a piano technician, but I have seen many technicians in action over the years, and piano tuning is not rocket science. I looked inside the rickety piano bench and the tuning wrench hammer was there. I thought to myself, "Well, it's only eighty-eight keys, what can possibly go wrong?"

So, I told the hotel owner, "Let me see what I can do."

Then I tuned the piano. Without a tuning fork to guide me, I used the middle C piano key as my benchmark and tuned the entire piano around it. By the time I was done, the piano sounded playable. Fortunately none of the strings broke. Then, I turned my attention to the broken pedals, which turned out to be pretty easy to repair. The hotel owner was ecstatic.

Then he exclaimed, "You must give a concert tonight at dinner!"

Before I could even answer him, Stephen interjected, "Of course he will."

Stephen had thrown me under the bus so quickly that I didn't even see the bus coming!

So, on one special night in July 1989, on the Island of Crete, in the middle of the Mediterranean Sea, with Stephen watching, I gave a piano concert to a dining room of hotel guests. Guests who, when they walked in, had seen the sign the hotel owner had made in marking pen—"Tonight: Piano Concert by Christopher Zyda from America." My European concert debut.

I didn't have any piano sheet music with me, so I just played songs from my memory. I was able to remember enough to play for around two hours. Stephen beamed with happiness and enjoyed a delicious dinner while I worked. He snapped photos of me playing the piano and of the hotel owner shaking my hand in appreciation. I cherished every moment of this experience, one of the happiest memories of my life. The hotel owner was so overjoyed that he comped Stephen's and my entire stay, including our food and drinks.

That one wonderful trip to Greece and Italy with Stephen, done on a shoestring budget, still stands out as one of the great trips of my life. We may have been living our lives in the "valley of the shadow of death," but we triumphed with carpe diem. Today was all that mattered. Not one health problem in three weeks, a huge stroke of luck that made for a European trip with Stephen for me to remember for a lifetime without him. It was the best thing that I ever could have done with every last bit of money that I possessed in July 1989. I would do this trip with Stephen all over again in the same threadbare hotels on next-to-no money, just as Cher sang about in her 1989 Heart of Stone album hit, "If I Could Turn Back Time."

In mid-July 1989, I started my new job at Disney. My first office as a full-time cast member was located on the second floor of the original Streamline Moderne Art Deco Animation Building on the studio lot, where Walt Disney himself once had his office. Original framed animation cels from Disney's historic films decorated the long, quiet, carpeted hallways: *Snow White and the Seven Dwarfs, Dumbo, Bambi, Cinderella, Alice in Wonderland*, and on and on, drawn by famous animators who had once worked in this building. I felt a sense of awe and pride as I walked into my office there, knowing that I was now a part of this one-of-a-kind company that had created many of my favorite films from my youth. At the age of twenty-seven, I was working in the most interesting finance group in any company, in the world's greatest entertainment company. Truly a Disney dream come true.

Rolf, the Cash Manager with whom I initially worked closely, was one of the few remaining Disney old-timers, having actually known and worked with Walt Disney himself. Rolf had joined Disney in 1950 and, among many other roles, had worked as the production accountant for *20,000 Leagues Under the Sea*. He was one year away from his well-deserved retirement after forty years of service. His slightly prickly personality was just his curmudgeonly mask for his heart of gold. Rolf taught me a great deal about cash management during my first year at Disney.

More importantly, he told the most amazing Walt stories. My favorite: when Walt died on December 15, 1966, Disney's stock soared 15.26 percent the next trading day because the titans of Wall Street believed that the company would then abandon his "ridiculously stupid" plan to build a giant new theme park in the middle of an alligator-infested swamp in Orlando, Florida. After telling this, Rolf laughed, and laughed, and laughed. This was a time-capsule scorecard that contrasted the creative dreams of a visionary company founder with the shortsightedness of Wall Street analysts. An exceptional finance lesson, too, that I never forgot.

I quickly realized that I had stepped into a very big job and it would soon take over my life. My new job required me to travel a great deal to meet with investment management firms located all across the country. I took frequent trips to New York City, Chicago, Boston, Houston, Philadelphia, and of course Walt Disney World in Orlando. During my first week of work, my executive assistant signed me up for every frequent flyer program and frequent hotel guest program in existence. I used them all, and racked up status points quickly. The downsides: I continued to be a very nervous flyer who gripped my armrests with white knuckles while tightly closing my eyes during every takeoff and landing, and I worried about leaving Stephen at home alone every time I had a business trip.

MGM Grand Air was one of the approved airlines by Disney for travel from Los Angeles to New York City. It flew only one route: LA to New York's John F. Kennedy Airport, out of a private air terminal located on the south side of Los Angeles International Airport, far away from the passenger crowds at other airlines. Each airplane, a Boeing 727, had been designed as all first class with only thirty-three seats. The center of the plane featured a full open kitchen, with a chef who could prepare nearly anything that you wanted during the flight. The plane also featured billowing gold drapes throughout, a gold-plated lounge bar area, bathrooms with gold-plated faucets, gold-plated sinks, and gold-plated toilet flusher handles. So much gold. The MGM Grand Air experience embodied the spirit of the late 1980s post-Tax Reform Act of 1986 decadence. It was unbelievable, especially for a fresh graduate like me. It underscored for me the contrast between the two completely different worlds in which I now lived—at work and at home.

My Disney job was both intense and exciting. Everyone with whom I worked was an A-player, even the executive assistants. The work hours were long, over sixty hours per week, which, in hindsight, turned out to be the shortest work-week hours of my entire career. I quickly learned how to multitask, and how to pump out a high volume of work in a compressed time period, all while managing to juggle caring for Stephen at home, who was starting to get weaker. I soaked up everything I could about the investment management industry. My brilliant boss Marcia, as well as the best and brightest minds of Wall Street with whom I now worked, willingly taught me everything they knew about the equity and fixed-income markets. On one trip to New York, Marcia took me to the trading floor of the New York Stock Exchange and introduced me to the specialist who traded hundreds of millions of dollars of Disney stock every single day. He showed me his order book and explained how he controlled the price of Disney stock in the market, and this blew my mind. As I looked across the frantic trading floor and up at the balcony where dignitaries rang the stock market's opening and closing bell, I thought about how incredible it would be for me to ring that bell someday. I sat on trading desks in downtown Los Angeles, Newport Beach, New York City, and Boston, and learned how to value and trade equities and fixed-income instruments. The most remarkable aspect of all this was that I was actually getting paid to learn all of these fascinating investment strategies. To fill in the gaps, I voraciously studied investment books at home on weekends and after work each day, even while malathion-spraying helicopters buzzed our house at night to combat the Mediterranean Fruit Fly invasion that threatened California's multi-billion dollar citrus industry. Imagine Stephen reading his Greek and Latin textbooks, and me reading my investment books, sitting side by side on the couch in our sunroom. One big academic geekfest. Reading alone together became one of our favorite pastimes.

In addition to investing the company's money, I also worked on investor relations, which managed the company's financial communications with stock analysts and major investors. Earnings press releases. Stockholders' meetings. Wall Street analyst conferences. Executive speeches. Gently guiding analysts so they could prepare accurate company earnings models, while not disclosing any insider information.

My new job was fantastic. I cut my investor relations teeth on handling Wall Street analyst queries surrounding the November 6, 1989, initial public offering (IPO) of Euro Disneyland SCA stock on the Paris Bourse, France's stock exchange. An honor for me to be able to work on one of the most successful IPOs of 1989. At age twenty-seven, I answered questions about Euro Disneyland's growth prospects from heavyweight entertainment analysts, such as David Londoner from Wertheim Schroder & Co., and my boss Marcia trusted me to do it. That was one of the many great things about working at Disney. The company allowed young people to handle some fairly significant job responsibilities. But you had to learn how to swim quickly. If you sank, Disney would easily cut you from the team. The pressure to perform at Disney was high, but I loved it, since, with my ongoing studying at home, I made sure to learn how to swim.

I took note that just four days before Euro Disneyland's blockbuster 1989 IPO, the *Los Angeles Herald-Examiner*, where I had worked during my summers in college and where my sister had worked with me, published its last edition and went out of business. An eighty-six-year-old LA institution and an important part of my personal history, now a ghost. Then just three days after the IPO, the Berlin Wall fell and Soviet communism started to crumble. The world was changing so much, and so quickly for me. An incredible new finance career, the demise of a major newspaper, an end to the dreaded Cold War.

Working at Disney came with some wonderful fringe benefits, too, that I was able to share with Stephen. Free screenings of Disney films in an impeccable screening room on the studio lot, shown with zero coming attractions beforehand. Heaven. That's how we saw *The Little Mermaid* in late 1989. Disney management also received a Silver Pass, which allowed free admission to Disneyland for four people. Many weekend evenings after we were done reading and studying, Stephen and I would hop in the car and drive to Disneyland at 9:00 p.m. if he felt well enough just to go on a few rides before the park closed at midnight. Also heaven. As a management team member, I was allowed to park about fifty yards away from the Disneyland entrance. Again, heaven, the ultimate in Doris Day parking for this native Angeleno.

As I settled more into my demanding new job and learned to manage my stress from working while caring for Stephen, the AIDS pandemic around us continued to rage and Alvin Ailey, the talented African-American choreographer who popularized modern dance and founded the Alvin Ailey American Dance Theater in New York City, died from AIDS on December 1, 1989. Yet another bright light in the arts was extinguished, calling for more action. By the end of 1989, according to amfAR, AIDS cases reported to date in the US were 117,508 with 89,343 deaths, a mortality rate of 76 percent, and the CDC estimated that approximately 683,000 Americans were living with HIV.[11,27]

Stephen and I took a third and final trip to Hawai'i, our special, wonderful romantic place, in late February 1990, after the Office of Thrift Supervision seized Imperial Savings and Loan and assigned the failed company to the government's Resolution Trust Company, and also shortly after the incredibly talented artist Keith Haring, whose art I love, died from AIDS on February 16. Stephen struggled with his energy levels for much of this trip, and took frequent naps huddled underneath blankets because he felt cold even in the eighty-three-degree tropical weather. We kept our itinerary for this trip simple, staying mostly in and around our low-budget condominium on the north shore of Kaua'i. I started to worry that the AZT and the Amgen drugs were losing their potency.

Stephen turned forty on March 26, 1990, the same day that the American fashion designer Halston died from AIDS. I threw a small birthday party for him at my mom and dad's house. Joan and Jane attended. I splurged on a fancy birthday cake, the top decorated at Stephen's request in a country western theme with a cowboy riding a bucking bronco. He loved it. It cost me a small fortune, but I wanted it to be a special birthday cake because it likely was his last one. I sensed some tension in the room at the party. Not surprising tension from my parents. But I also noticed some tension between Joan and Jane, something that I had not seen before.

Shortly after his birthday, Stephen came down with cryptosporidiosis. Also known as crypto, this illness is caused by the microscopic one-celled Cryptosporidium parasite that lives in soil, food, and water. When Cryptosporidia parasites enter the human body, they travel to the small intestine and burrow into its walls. This causes a watery diarrhea, along with dehydration, weight loss, stomach cramps, fever, nausea, and sometimes vomiting. A person with a healthy immune system recovers from crypto in a week or so. But in 1990, people with AIDS couldn't battle this parasite, and so they would have crypto for the rest of their lives, as Stephen did. It's a horrible parasitic condition. AZT and the Amgen drugs didn't combat it. The worst side effect for Stephen was that his weight started to drop due to his constant loss of fluids.

Also around this time, Stephen started to have problems with cytomegalovirus, also known as CMV, a common virus that infects people of all ages. CMV is related to the viruses that cause chickenpox and infectious mononucleosis. Once CMV enters a person's body, it stays there for life, but people with healthy immune systems show no signs or symptoms. However, it can cause serious health problems for people with AIDS, specifically through cytomegalovirus retinitis, also known as CMV retinitis, which causes an inflammation of the retina of the eye that can lead to blindness, as it eventually did for Stephen. AZT and the Amgen drugs didn't combat this either.

That's the confounding thing about all of the AIDS-related illnesses that attacked Stephen and slowly withered him away in front of my eyes. Pneumocystis carinii pneumonia, KS, thrush, cryptosporidiosis, cytomegalovirus—they exist all around us, but people with healthy immune systems fight them off, often without them even knowing it. This is why it's important to realize what those two middle initials in AIDS stand for: immune deficiency. The immune system can't do its job, like a castle whose walls are crumbling. With no defenses against these illnesses, in 1990 people with AIDS experienced a disease domino effect on their way to the grave. AZT and the Amgen drugs could only do so much.

On April 8, 1990, Ryan White died from AIDS at the age of eighteen. Ryan was the brave young man who brought AIDS into focus for the whole world in December 1984, and he had lived just over five years and three months from the time of his diagnosis. Elton John sang at his funeral. Michael Jackson later recorded a beautiful cover of "Gone Too Soon," one of my favorite songs, in honor of him. Around the world, people mourned Ryan White's passing. His death shook me to my core because I followed him as my benchmark of someone who probably received the best AIDS care available in the United States. Now he was gone. I stared at his obituary in the *Los Angeles Times*—it was like a cannon shot to open the last battle of a war. Using an approximate January 1986 start date for Stephen's illness, my mental math projected that the same five years and three month time span would peg his potential death somewhere around April, 1991—one year away. Time was running out for Stephen. Time was running out for us. I was so aware of the preciousness of time. I felt increasingly powerless about this horrible disease of AIDS.

From April through August 1990, Stephen's health declined at an accelerating pace. The month of May saw the release of the film *Longtime Companion*, about the surviving partner of a man who dies from AIDS. My career continued to blossom at Disney, but I knew that soon I would be a longtime companion, too. In June, we spent a weekend near Santa Barbara on Sandyland Road at Carpinteria Beach with Joan and Jane. Stephen swam and bodysurfed in the Carpinteria waves for hours, beaming with happiness, as though he would never do it again. In June, I worked on my first financing deal at Disney, helping my corporate finance colleagues raise almost two billion dollars for the company. Stephen's crypto got worse. The United States entered a recession in July, with the Savings and Loan Crisis in full swing, and Los Angeles real estate values started to decline. I received my first big raise. Stephen started to wear a diaper to avoid crypto accidents. Disney started to assign more projects to me. Stephen started to lose too much weight. I dreaded that the AZT and the Amgen medicines weren't working anymore. That damn crypto just wouldn't go away. Stephen's life really was ending. The stark dichotomy between my rising corporate finance career at Disney and Stephen's significantly declining health at home, which I kept secret from my work colleagues, created much conflict, worry, and guilt for me. I was juggling my stress close to the limit of my ability.

More than two years now also had passed since Stephen's near-death in La Jolla, and his parents still hadn't visited him. They were running out of time, damn it. Stephen was very hurt by their abandonment. This family dynamic, with his death now looming, was painful for me to witness, but by this time I had seen so much of the dark side of life that nothing really shocked me anymore. I thought to myself, "These horrible choices made by his parents are going to eat them up after he is dead." I took some level of comfort that at least my own parents were still in our lives and supporting us.

Believing that it would help matters, the micromanager in me strong-armed Stephen and his parents into one final trip together before his health passed the point of no return. In August 1990, just after Iraq invaded Kuwait, we all went to Southwest Harbor, Maine, one last time. This time, as part of my strong-arming to make it happen, I split the cost of the rental house with Stephen's parents, who initially were reluctant to go. David, Stephen's best friend, couldn't join us because by this time he was close to death at his apartment in New York City, being cared for by his Yale classmates Carl and Janie. David's boyfriend in Los Angeles, Jeff, dealing with his own health issues, visited him as much as he could. Stephen and I flew to Bar Harbor after connecting through Bangor Airport in a tiny puddle-jumper aircraft that terrified me.

I remember feeling so tired on this trip. The stress from Stephen's accelerating health decline and the high pressure of my job were catching up to me. In Los Angeles, I had been going nonstop, which generated a sort of self-fueling energy, but now that I stepped away from my routine I felt drained. I tried to sneak off during the first two days to take naps, and Stephen's mother oddly hassled me about this. His energy was quite low by this point, so he slept a lot. It was difficult to make conversation with his parents on this trip because of the elephant in the room. On day three, Stephen said to me, "I've got to get out of this house," so we drove to Bar Harbor and rented a speedboat for the afternoon. We drove it all around the bay, with Stephen doing most of the driving, and he beamed with exhilaration in the wind and the splashing sea around us. I have a photo of him with his broad smile, his blue eyes squinting in the bright sun, but looking so thin. The odd thing about living with someone experiencing AIDS wasting syndrome is that you don't notice it happening. It creeps up bit by bit. But it's right there in that photo on the boat, and hits me right in the face when I see it today. So thin. This was the last good photo I ever took of him.

After our day in Bar Harbor, Stephen wanted to get out and away from his parents again, and he proposed a three-day driving trip through New Brunswick, Canada. We climbed into our rental car and drove to Saint Stephen, and spent the night there. Then we visited Saint George and Saint John. On the third day, we navigated by car and ferry to Campobello Island in the Bay of Fundy, where President Franklin D. Roosevelt's family had maintained a summer home. In fact, it was at Campobello Island, in 1921, that he was stricken with the polio virus that left him paralyzed from the waist down. Then we drove back to Southwest Harbor. When we crossed the bridge that links Campobello Island to the US, we were greeted at the border by two US customs officers who, upon realizing that we were a gay couple, condescendingly detained us, searched our car from top to bottom as we waited in the street, and almost confiscated Stephen's medicines from the UCLA/Amgen study even after Stephen showed them his doctors' notes.

While well-intentioned, my strong-arm peacemaking skills failed in this final Southwest Harbor trip with his parents. I didn't see the reconciliation or healing between Stephen and his parents that I had hoped for. He was still running away from them. It was the first time that we both had seen Stephen's father since he learned two years earlier that his son was gay, had AIDS, and I was his partner. In fact, it was the first time that we had seen Stephen's father in person at all since Thanksgiving 1986, nearly four years earlier. His father seemed more distant than ever. Both his parents seemed to not really know or understand the Stephen that I knew and loved. Why didn't they ever visit him when he was healthy, or ever? Airline tickets aren't that expensive when love is involved. My grand total of time spent with Stephen's parents in my nearly seven-year relationship with Stephen, other than during his near-death in the summer of 1988, amounted to only ten days. They still didn't really know me, and I didn't know them. I had hoped for so much more on this trip, but I returned to Los Angeles disappointed.

Despite the disappointment to this last trip, the carpe diem strategy that Stephen and I adopted in the summer of 1988 had really worked. Living for today works. In the span of two years, on shoestring budgets we managed to travel to Hawai'i three times, Greece and Italy, Maine, and now even New Brunswick. Plus, Stephen had pursued a classics doctoral program at UCLA. The two of us certainly packed in a lot of life together once we knew that Stephen's days were numbered, and I'm proud of that.

After we returned to Los Angeles from Maine, Stephen developed neuropathy, which causes tingling, numbness, aching, or pain starting in a person's toes and spreading up the leg. As neuropathy advances, a person can have difficulty walking, as Stephen eventually did.

Everything in Stephen's body by September 1990 seemed to be slowing down, falling apart. He knew it. He enrolled at UCLA in the fall Quarter of 1990 but he dropped out midway and did not finish the term. He was so close to earning his Master's degree in classics, but it was not meant to be. It was painful to see how little sand was left to pass through his hourglass. None of the AIDS drugs were working.

In the fall of 1990, Stephen went through a phase of increasing frustration and anger. One night, as I drove us home heading east on Beverly Boulevard in the poorly lit stretch of road that cuts through the Wilshire Country Club, he lost his temper about a topic that I can't even remember today. Suddenly, his rising emotions overpowered him and he rolled down his car window and threw his wallet out into the street. I quickly pulled over to the side of the road and screeched to a stop.

"I'm going to die, Chris," Stephen sobbed and shook. "I'm going to die!"

What do you say to a person whom you love who has a terminal disease and who finally reaches this emotional crux between anger and acceptance? How do you comfort him? How could I possibly help Stephen in this moment when he was dying from AIDS, and I was perfectly healthy, with a bright future ahead of me? Stephen had been my biggest cheerleader about my MBA, my new finance career, and my future at Disney and beyond, even when he knew that he wouldn't be there for it. I felt terrible, guilty, and inadequate all at the same time. This is the moment that I learned that sometimes in life, words fail. Sometimes words aren't needed either. There was literally nothing that I could say to Stephen, so I leaned over to the passenger seat, and I embraced him and held him tight, and we both cried together for a good long time. No words at all, just love. Then, eventually I composed myself as Stephen still cried, and said, "I love you more than anything, you know that? I wish that I could change the world for you, but I can't. I will walk this road with you for as long as you are still here, until I know that you are safe in whatever happens after this life is over. I promise."

Life absolutely crushed my heart when this happened.

In that dangerous stretch of poorly lighted roadway, cars are not supposed to stop. We had partially blocked the flow of traffic. Cars whizzed by us, and some honked their horns as they passed, and Stephen's wallet still lay in the middle of the street behind us. Eventually, I climbed out of the car and retrieved it, and then, silently, we drove home.

◆◆◆

I THINK THAT IT was sometime in October 1990. It was definitely after August, when Stephen and I had returned from our trip to Southwest Harbor, Maine, and it was definitely before Thanksgiving because I remember that Stephen and I spent Thanksgiving in 1990 alone. I don't, however, remember what had led up to the heated argument with my mom on the telephone. I just remember that she grew more angry with me as we spoke. I think that part of our conversation was about Stephen's declining health, but it was mostly about my parents, and how Stephen's illness was affecting them, and how the two of us were embarrassing them in front of their friends. The conversation turned ugly.

I think that my brain has somehow protected me from the intense pain of this conversation with my mom by locking much of its memory tightly deep inside me, never to be completely recalled, or more importantly, felt again. It's a very dark, walled-in chamber of my brain.

There is one thing from this phone call that is seared into my mind forever. Eventually, my mom shouted at me, "I should have had that abortion when I was pregnant with you, and then none of this would be happening to us."

A hot dagger right to my heart. No child ever wants to hear, or ever should hear, such a horrible statement of rejection from their parents. In that painful instant, my mother confirmed for me what I had always suspected since my childhood. My birth was not a Roman Catholic "surprise." My birth was not even an "accident." My birth was, in fact, "unwanted." My mother had only begrudgingly completed her pregnancy. The storm finally had stretched my mother and father beyond their limits, beyond their capabilities as parents, as human beings. Their twisted American experience of *Fiddler on the Roof* had morphed into their worst nightmare, and they couldn't deal with the world around them any longer. My parents, the two valedictorians, were failing at their relationship with me. In my mother's anger, she had slipped and blurted out the truth, the ultimate secret.

My mother didn't, in the heat of that moment, shout in the abstract and say, "I wish that I had an abortion." Even an abstract angry comment such as this would have been devastating in its own right. No, my mother hadn't said that at all. Instead she had said, "I should have had *that* abortion." She had admitted indeed that an abortion had been considered and weighed when she was pregnant with me. Perhaps my parents had made a list of pros and cons about me. Perhaps they decided to go ahead with the abortion, but had a change of heart. Perhaps they consulted a priest who, of course, would have railed about it being a mortal sin. Perhaps a doctor was involved in deciding if there should be a me. Abortions in 1961 weren't legal in California, but you could get one, especially if you were a medical professional who had connections, as my mother certainly did. Regardless, I now knew the devastating truth: there was a period of time, in the fall of 1961, when the few tiny cells that ultimately would grow into me hung in the balance of my parents' deliberations about my fate. Worse, my mother was now telling me that she wished she had done the deed.

In light of this devastating revelation, it suddenly made sense to me why my mother had an emergency hysterectomy immediately after I was born. In 1962, the only allowable form of Roman Catholic birth control was for a doctor to order a hysterectomy for medical reasons. Any doctor could make up a "medical reason" to justify a hysterectomy to satisfy the Church's doctrine. After my parents' unwanted pregnancy with me, they ensured that there would be definitely, absolutely, positively, no more children for them.

This revelation was too much for me to take. I felt crushed. Angry. Furious. Rejected. Instantly orphaned. My parents and I were all floundering, lashed to our core by the storm. We were all living through Samuel Coleridge's *Rime of the Ancient Mariner*, adrift on a ship in a churning ocean while life went haywire all around us. AIDS phobia, homophobia, religion, family history, grief, shame, and guilt all combined to create a vortex of hurricane winds and a powerful, cresting wave of fury between us. The AIDS Vortex of Insanity. This was the first time that I was sucked into the Vortex, but it wouldn't be the last.

I was beaten down and exhausted from taking care of Stephen, from seeing him wither away, from my demanding finance career, and from years of fighting so many swirling forces in the world around me to protect him. I didn't have any energy left for my toxic parents. My subconscious psyche sprang into protection mode. I lashed out at my mother with all that I had left to defend myself, "That's it. I am done with you. You are no longer my mom and dad. Don't contact me ever again. I mean it."

Then I hung up on my mother.

I immediately collapsed into a ball on the carpeted floor of my home office, and lay there and sobbed for a long time. I tried to remember all of the good and loving things that my parents had done as they raised me to adulthood. They drove me to my piano and trumpet lessons. In fact, they bought a piano for me when I was seven years old so that I could practice. They attended all my music recitals, and watched me play the trumpet in my high school marching band and orchestra. They came to the Hollywood Bowl to watch me play trumpet in a concert with the Los Angeles Philharmonic Orchestra, a special honor that I earned during high school. They encouraged me to learn how to ski, which certainly requires special effort in the Los Angeles winter. They bought me a chemistry set for Christmas one year, and were more impressed than upset at me when I learned how to create an explosive compound that detonated, making a huge mess inside our garage. They paid for my college education. They fed and clothed me. They took me on vacations. There was so much good in my parents, and I knew they loved me deeply. But they could also be meddling, bossy, judgmental, self-centered, and so falsely guided by their rigid religion. I couldn't reconcile how these same two people who had shown me so much love for so much of my life were now rejecting me because I was gay and the man I loved was dying from AIDS. That's the mind-blowing experience of the AIDS Vortex of Insanity. It truly is insane. I realized that my parents didn't know the meaning of unconditional love. I realized that their understanding of the Roman Catholic religion hinged on rigid, illogical rules instituted by humans, and not the Church's more important spiritual messages of love, compassion, forgiveness, and grace. I realized that they didn't possess the strength to be there for Stephen and me in our most dire time of need. I realized that they were fallible, imperfect human beings. They crumbled like pillars of salt as the storm rained down on them.

It was all horrible.

Then, eventually, I picked myself up off the floor, because I had to keep going, for Stephen. For his sake, I was not going to let this miserable fucking storm in my life beat me, even with hurricane force winds now lashing me from every angle as my parents rejected me and I rejected them.

My sister bizarrely sided with my parents in this argument, and so I cut off all my contact with her, too. The time for accommodating destructive and negative people in my life had ended. I was tired from Joan's ongoing and escalating drama that resulted from her anger at the world. Her anger now had finally even driven her wonderful partner Jane away from her, too. She was still hiding in the closet from our parents at age thirty-eight. I didn't have any energy left anymore for negative people in my life. Not with Stephen dying.

After this telephone call, my parents almost immediately sold their house in Porter Ranch and moved to Las Vegas, where virtually no one knew them. At least they abided by my final request: they did not give me their new address or telephone number. They were gone from my life. My family was Stephen.

CHAPTER 7
STORM SURGE

THE DAY THAT I HAD feared for nearly five years finally arrived on December 23, 1990: Stephen checked into the hospital for the last time. I returned home the day before from a business trip to Walt Disney World in Orlando. He assured me, during my check-in phone calls with him from the road, that he was doing all right. But when I saw him, I could tell that his health had deteriorated significantly. He could no longer walk well from his neuropathy, and he was quite weak. He was having difficulty changing the diaper that he wore for his crypto. David, his best friend, had died just over one month earlier, on November 10. Stephen took that news quite hard. In his current condition, there was no way he could travel to attend David's January 20 memorial service at the Witkin Gallery in New York City.

I now worried about leaving Stephen home alone during the day because he had to navigate the stairway from our bedroom to the kitchen. I tried to objectively analyze the situation. I could no longer care for him while also working at my demanding job at Disney. I had to face the reality that we were really beyond this, and Stephen needed to be in the hospital so his condition could be stabilized. Looking back, I realize that thinking he could be stabilized and his health would improve again was pure denial on my part. I guess denial is where we go once we have exhausted all rational coping mechanisms.

Stephen accepted my decision to go to the hospital. That evening, I carried him, which was disturbingly easy to do, from our bedroom down the stairs, and out to my car, loaded his personal effects including his Amgen medicines, and drove him to Sherman Oaks Hospital. After the hospital staff assessed him, they told me that his condition would continue to deteriorate, and that he would likely die within a few weeks. In 1990, this was all part of the predictable progression of AIDS. My calculations based on Ryan White's lifespan were proving to be accurate.

I called Stephen's mother in Virginia and told her that he had been admitted to the hospital, and that I was being told that his illness was in the home stretch. At my request, she agreed she would fly to Los Angeles, but she made no mention of his father coming. I didn't ask.

After I settled Stephen into his hospital room, I talked with him, we held hands, and I sang him Christmas carols, and then, after he fell asleep, I cried. Even though I had known for years that this day would arrive, the reality hit and crushed me: this was it; Stephen was going to die from this horrible disease; he would no longer be part of my life. We would not make it through the storm together. I stayed with him until midnight when the nursing staff made me go home. A heartbreaking day I knew would come one day, and will never forget.

After I left the hospital, however, I did not go home. Instead, I went to a gay dive bar near our house called the Gauntlet II and got drunk on shots of tequila mixed with 151-proof rum that the bartender lit on fire before he served me. I told the bartender what was going on in my life, and he said, "These are on me, you need this," and the shots kept coming while an upside-down motorized decorated Christmas tree, mounted to the bar's ceiling, spun around in the air above me. The searing pain of life for me at that moment in time was simply too much to bear. I felt all alone with the storm surge up to my neck. In an empty bar, I cried and spilled my private life to a bartender I didn't even know, numbed by alcohol.

Very early the next morning, Christmas Eve, I received a frantic phone call from Stephen. With the sound of terror in his voice, he told me that one of the UCLA doctors in charge of the UCLA/Amgen study had driven to Sherman Oaks Hospital, seized all of Stephen's Amgen experimental medicines, and announced to Stephen before leaving, "Everyone else in the study is dead, so the study is over." Stephen cried tears of despair to me over the phone.

The Sherman Oaks Hospital staff was shocked and in an uproar over the doctor's reprehensible behavior. The nurse on duty got on the telephone and said to me, "Get over here right away, and bring some more medicines so that we can give Stephen his morning shots!"

I could not believe this doctor's behavior, and on fucking Christmas Eve! My blood instantly boiled over at the audacity of this AIDS doctor stealing a dying man's medicine from his hospital room. I vowed an all-out war.

Luckily, we had an additional supply of the Amgen medicines in our refrigerator, but it would only last us about two weeks. I rushed over to the hospital with Stephen's morning doses, leaving the rest safely stored at home. For the next week, I made two trips daily between our home and the hospital with these meds so that the nightmare doctor couldn't steal any more of them.

Stephen's mother arrived in Los Angeles on Christmas Day and spent most of the following days at the hospital with him. At night, she slept at our home in our downstairs guest bedroom. Once again, Stephen's father stayed home in Virginia. I didn't understand. Didn't he understand that his son's life was nearly over?

But I couldn't fixate on this because it was time to go to war, with all guns blazing, against the UCLA doctor, the UCLA School of Medicine, and the Amgen Company.

I faxed a strongly worded letter to the School of Medicine and the CEO of Amgen, demanding a meeting. My letter threatened all sorts of legal and public relations mayhem if they didn't give Stephen the experimental drugs. The UCLA general counsel attempted to erect a roadblock with the oldest anti-gay discrimination trick in the book. On the telephone, she said to me, "The only person who can discuss this with us is Stephen. He is not married to you, so you have no rights to discuss this situation with us."

I was appalled that my own alma mater, UCLA, would engage in this homophobic discrimination, the ultimate Gay Catch-22 before we were able to legally marry. But the general counsel was only doing her job, invoking the letter of the law in California and the United States. In fact, thanks to our bruising battles over Stephen's health insurance claims, he and I had already planned for this sort of discrimination.

I yelled back at her, "What about the power of attorney form that I have from Stephen to handle his affairs because he is too sick to handle them himself?"

The general counsel immediately backed down. Soon afterward, the dean of the School of Medicine invited me to a meeting. I asked Stephen's mother to join me at the meeting so that she could witness our latest battle with the world in taking care of him.

As I drove from my Disney office in Burbank to UCLA in Westwood, I thought about what to say. By this point, I was exhausted, worn out, furious, grieving, and barely keeping it together at work. The theft of Stephen's drugs had brought me to my breaking point. I thought to myself, what is the worst thing that could happen in this meeting? The meds were already gone. With no further downside for me, I thought that maybe this actually gave me some power. I abandoned my fantasy of grabbing this ghastly doctor by the throat and choking him to within inches of his life. Instead, I would stay cool, speak calmly, and simply be resolute. There is nothing more ominous than a justifiably angry person who remains contained.

When we arrived at UCLA Medical Center, an assistant ushered us into a conference room adjacent to the dean's office. Inside, there were three men: the doctor who stole Stephen's medicines, that doctor's boss who we learned had directed him to do the stealing (who was also a doctor), and the dean. The two doctors looked distressed and worried. I didn't shake anyone's hands, but simply sat down and stared at them. Stephen's mother stared at them, too. She was as angry as I was. The two doctors could barely look us in the eyes.

The dean began the meeting, saying, "Thank you for meeting with us. What do you want?"

What I *wanted to say* is the following fantasy monologue that I considered at the time, and have replayed in my mind dozens of times in the decades since that meeting:

"I apologize in advance if I lose my temper, but as you can imagine, I am angry. Stephen would be here with us today, too, but unfortunately, he is in Sherman Oaks Hospital—dying. That's right, he's dying.

"Once upon a time, I briefly considered becoming a medical doctor myself because I admired how doctors helped people. I like helping people, too. I admire the 2,500-year-old Hippocratic Oath: 'First do no harm.'

"Imagine the irony for me today. I'm here at a conference table in this world-renowned medical center whose mission is to cure and heal people. And today, I'm looking at two doctors that are trying to kill my partner."

This is the part where the dean would try to interrupt me for bringing up murder, but I would calmly speak right over him and continue:

"Please, please don't interrupt me. Let me say my piece. Yes, these two doctors are trying to kill my partner. I do not understand what warped logic justifies you barging into Stephen's hospital room on Christmas Eve to steal his medicine. What a Merry fucking Christmas present. You made a dying man cry. You should be proud of yourselves.

"You two doctors are in the wrong profession if you want to steal medicine from dying patients. You should be working in the health insurance industry instead. That's the industry that prevents people from getting their medicines so that they die instead. Your profession, the medical profession, is supposed to help people. What has happened to integrity in the world today?

"But I am tired. I'm exhausted from taking care of Stephen for the past nearly five years. We have fought with health insurance companies. We have lost our friends, either to death or because they have ostracized us. We have been shunned by our own family members, too. We have spent a fortune on AIDS treatments that haven't worked, trying to find some glimmer of hope for his life. The entire world has turned against us. Now, you doctors, too.

"But luckily, for me, I am young and I am not HIV positive, so I can fight for Stephen. You had better believe that I'm going to fight for him.

"I am about to become your worst living nightmare. I will file a lawsuit, and both of you doctors will be personally named in it, as well as UCLA, and also the Amgen Company. One of the causes of action in my lawsuit will be the attempted murder of Stephen."

In my fantasy, when I say this, the two doctors look up from the conference table and stare at me with their eyes wide open, scared. Good. Then I continue:

"I will do it. I make a lot of money at The Walt Disney Company to pay for lawyers. A lawsuit against you for trying to kill a person with AIDS isn't going to help you two build your AIDS medical practices.

"I also will fund a public relations campaign. This lawsuit will be covered in every newspaper and media outlet in the country. I will do it. I have friends in the news media and they will love to publish this story.

"I will sue you forever. Long after Stephen dies, I will keep suing you. It will be a long and nasty fight.

"I will ruin your careers. The American Medical Association will know what you did. The California State Medical Licensing Board will know what you did. I will do everything in my power to have your medical licenses revoked. I will do it.

"People will picket outside the UCLA Hospital. People will picket outside your doctors' offices. People will protest every time that the two of you present an AIDS research paper or speak at an AIDS conference. I will do it.

"I don't care how much money it takes, or how long it takes. I am losing the man that I love, and you are trying to hasten his death. So I'm going to hasten the death of your careers.

"I can make all of you miserable for a long, long time. I will do it.

"Do not underestimate me simply because I am only twenty-eight years old. I will do it. This may sound like a threat. It isn't. It's a promise. I give you my word that I will do it. All of it."

Then, usually in my fantasy monologue, I take a deep breath and end it with a more upbeat and innocent tone of voice, and say, "Now, does anyone have any questions?"

But sometimes, I end my fantasy monologue by jumping across the conference table and choking that horrible doctor within inches of his life.

Regardless of the ending, my fantasy monologue is always an Oscar-worthy performance.

But the fact was that I had already written much of my fantasy monologue into the letter I had sent to UCLA and the Amgen Company, so it didn't need to be rehashed in person, but I did calmly make clear at the outset that I would file a lawsuit against all of them. Then I pivoted into a solution because I wasn't dealing with fantasy, I was dealing with reality, and the reality was that I needed a quick solution. Stephen needed those drugs. So, instead of delivering my fantasy rant, I responded to the dean's question by saying, "I want Stephen to have access to the two Amgen medicines for as long as he needs them. Those Amgen medicines work and you know it. I have only one week of medicines left, so you have one week to figure out a way to get them to him.

"If you provide him with the medicines, and if you two doctors stay away from him, then I *might* decide to not sue all of you.

"Otherwise, you had better get ready for a long, public fight. Because I am young and I am healthy, and I make a lot of money to pay for lawyers, and I can make you miserable for a long time. You are doctors. You are supposed to help patients, not steal their medicines." So, yes, I did sneak in some of my fantasy monologue at the end.

UCLA is a teaching hospital, but never in my wildest dreams did I think that one day I would be teaching there. Stephen's mother sat through this meeting almost completely silent, but looked at me with some measure of admiration, I like to think.

"We are truly sorry for what happened," responded the dean. "We are going to fix this."

I could already tell that the dean was going to do the right thing.

"Thank you," I responded. "We have one week. If Stephen runs out of his medicines, I will file the lawsuit."

I would have filed that lawsuit, funded a public relations campaign, and pursued everything from my fantasy monologue. Even though Stephen and I were financially stressed and in debt up to our eyeballs at the time. I was so furious that I would have figured out a way.

Two days after this meeting, Gordon Binder, the chairman and CEO of the Amgen Company, called me in the early morning at home.

He said, "On behalf of the Amgen Company and UCLA, I apologize for what happened. I personally will make sure that Stephen gets the medicines that he needs for as long as he needs them, free of charge, compliments of Amgen."

I couldn't believe it.

"Thank you," I replied. "You are a hero in this horrible saga. Thank you for the medicines."

The Amgen Company and UCLA both quickly showed integrity, and for that they should both be commended.

I hung up the phone. I trembled with relief, an emotion that I didn't even know still existed in me. Then my trembling gave way to an ocean of tears of relief, amplified by exhaustion. I sobbed, all alone, for a long time. I had won my war against the two doctors, the UCLA School of Medicine, and the Amgen Company.

The two doctors stayed away from Stephen, and we switched him to the best AIDS doctor in all of Los Angeles, Michael S. Gottlieb. We found out from our friend Nenna, who worked in the UCLA/Amgen study, that the two doctors got into a fair amount of trouble for what they had done. That was enough for me, and I let the battle go. Luckily for those two doctors, who both still practice medicine at two major westside hospitals in Los Angeles today, online review websites didn't exist in 1990. My reviews would have

The simple life: me swinging in my parents' backyard, 1965.

*Me at my confirmation ceremony at Our Lady of Lourdes Roman
Catholic Church in Northridge, May 1974.*

My junior year UCLA Delta Sigma Phi fraternity composite photo, January 1983.

Stephen in his law office wearing his Metropolitan Club of Washington, DC jacket, 1983.

A *very* SPECIAL NIGHT WITH
JOAN RIVERS
BENEFIT FOR A.I.D.S.
SUNDAY, MARCH 11, 1984 STUDIO ONE, 652 N. LA PEER

DO NOT WRITE BELOW THIS LINE

	SEATING $25	STANDING $15	RECEPTION $20	NAME Christopher Zyda
8 PM	75⁰⁰			ADDRESS 888. N. West Knoll #339
11 PM				CITY LA.
				ZIP 90069
	$75¹² $	$	$	TOTAL 75⁰⁰

A.I.D.S. PROJECT/L.A.   TAX EXEMPTION I.D. #95-3842506

A historic night to remember: my receipt for the Joan Rivers' AIDS benefit at the Studio One disco in West Hollywood, March 1984.

Happy days: Joan at her desk at the Chicago Tribune, *1976.*

David (left) and Stephen in front of Yale University's Sterling Library, August 1985.

Stephen with one of his parents' cats at their house in Southwest Harbor, Maine, August 1985.

Stephen and my mom dancing at my dad's sixtieth birthday party
at Joan and Jane's house, September 1985.

Stephen and me at the Del Mar train station shortly after he almost died from pneumocystis carinii
pneumonia at Scripps Memorial Hospital in La Jolla, July 1988.

My mom, dad, and me in front of UCLA's Royce Hall at my business school graduation, June 1989.

Margaret, my second mom, and me at my UCLA business school graduation.

Stephen poses at a beautiful waterfall on the road to Hana, Maui, September 1988.

Stephen cooling himself from 100+ degree heat in a village fountain in Greece, June 1989.

Stephen and me standing in the Mediterranean Sea on the island of Crete, Greece, July 1989.

A memory for a lifetime: my impromptu evening piano concert in Crete, Greece, July 1989.

(Left to right) Joan, my dad, Jane, Stephen, and my mom at Stephen's fortieth birthday party at my parents' house in Porter Ranch, March 1990.

Me with the Disney Corporate Finance team and Disney Chief Executive Officer Michael Eisner celebrating at Walt Disney World after raising $2 billion, June 1990.

Stephen beaming with happiness while boating in Bar Harbor, Maine, August 1990.

How I will always remember Joan: enjoying her prized 1963 Mercury Comet convertible, 1988.

STANDARD INSURANCE COMPANY

home office: Portland, Oregon 97207
P. O. Box 711
(503) 248-2700

FACSIMILE (503) 321-6407
Writer's Direct Number
(503) 248-2934

February 25, 1992

██████████████████

Attorney at Law

████████████████████████

    Re: Stephen ████████ Deceased
          Imperial Savings Association
          Group Policy No.
          Claim No. ███████

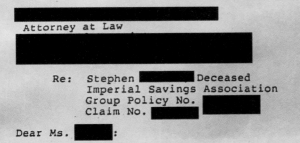

Dear Ms. ██████:

    During a telephone conversation we had yesterday, you asked me to provide you with a copy of the above-referenced group policy. A copy is enclosed with this letter.

    This letter will also serve to confirm an earlier telephone conversation we had on Friday, February 12, 1992. During our conversation you confirmed that you represent ██████████ ██████, but only with respect to one matter.

    During that conversation I informed you that ████████████, deceased, had been receiving long term disability benefits under a group policy. Under the terms of the policy, benefits would terminate upon his death. Standard Insurance Company was not notified of Mr. ████████'s death until January of this year. The long term disability checks, which were issued and cashed after the date of his death, bear his forged signature and the purported signature of ██████████.

    Standard Insurance Company is seeking recovery of the long term disability benefits that were paid after the date of Stephen ████████'s death. The amount of the overpayment is ████████.

    I understand that you will be discussing this matter in more detail with ████████████. You will then let me know what her position is in regards to this matter.

DEDICATED TO EXCELLENCE

Stephen's parents' over-the-top felony disability insurance fraud perpetrated in their son's name after he died, February 1992.

Me in the chute moments before the gate opened, competing in bareback bronco riding at the Denver gay rodeo, July 1993.

My rodeo posse: (left to right) Doug, Tom, Doug, me, Juan, and Tim at the Tim McGraw concert at the In Cahoots country western dance club in Glendale, 1993.

(Left to right) Kelley, me, Dana, and my second mom, Margaret, celebrating my company's IPO and ringing the bell at the New York Stock Exchange, January 2004.

My first day at Amazon.com in Seattle, all settled in at my "door desk," July 1998.

An afternoon reunion trip from Marina del Rey to Malibu on my boat with my friends from the Beckford Avenue Elementary School class of 1974, August 2015.

(Left to right) Kristoffer, me, Shalene, Guiliano, and Laszlo at the finish line of the Camp Pendleton Mud Run near Oceanside, June 2013.

(Left to right) Carol, me, and my husband, Michael, at my fiftieth birthday party in the dinosaur gallery of the Los Angeles Natural History Museum, May 2012.

Me at UCLA's Pauley Pavilion delivering my commencement speech to the English graduating class, June 2013.

Michael and me at the Elton John AIDS Foundation's Academy Awards party in West Hollywood, March 2014.

Michael and me in front of the historic Stonewall Inn in New York City celebrating the fiftieth anniversary of the Stonewall Riots, June 2019.

skewered them. I sincerely hope that both of them have since learned to be more compassionate, make better choices in life, and, more importantly, not steal from their patients.

Even though I won the war over the Amgen medicines, the larger battle for Stephen's life was being lost. I believe that those Amgen drugs gave him an extra relatively healthy two years of quality life. But in those early days of AIDS, it was impossible to know what did what. Maybe the Amgen drugs worked, and the AZT didn't work? Maybe the Amgen drugs allowed him to swim upstream for a while by helping him make red and white blood cells so that he could better withstand the AZT dosages? But ultimately the pace of growth of the AIDS virus in his body overwhelmed whatever benefits the Amgen drugs provided, and this pushed his health downstream. I will never know for sure. At least we now had whatever benefit the Amgen drugs could provide for the rest of Stephen's life.

This fight with UCLA and Amgen constituted only the latest round of the storm's smashing of my beliefs...beliefs that I learned during my childhood, and upon which I had depended in my early adulthood. The rigid and illogical Roman Catholic Church had already wreaked havoc on my life and crumbled into a heap of flawed doctrine. The health insurance industry that I thought existed in order to help sick people instead seemed focused on denying their claims. People whom Stephen and I had considered friends deleted us from their lives. My parents, who I thought would always be there for me, succumbed to the AIDS Vortex of Insanity and abandoned us in our time of need. Anti-gay discrimination, enshrined by my own elected government, to which I now paid a huge amount of income taxes, created more obstacles in my efforts to protect Stephen and our relationship. And now, licensed medical doctors were sneaking into hospitals not to administer life-sustaining medicine but to steal it! Human integrity seemed to vanish all around me at an astonishing pace—the dawn of the Age of Truthlessness in my life, a world in which few people seemed to do the right thing anymore. A great shift started to happen inside of me at this time because of these smashed beliefs. I wondered: is this all just a part of me growing up? Or is this part of a new Truthless Era that is emerging? Sadly, it turned out to be the latter.

Despite being in Sherman Oaks Hospital, Stephen's health continued to decline and he lost most of his appetite. His crypto was unrelenting, and the chronic diarrhea from it accelerated his AIDS wasting syndrome. By the 1991 New Year, he weighed under 100 pounds, less than half of what he weighed when I first met him. Skin and bones. The hospital installed a permanent line called a Hickman catheter in his chest so that he could be fed and medicated intravenously. Every day, he received a large bag of total parenteral nutrition, also called TPN, which looked like a big vanilla milkshake, through the catheter. This liquid nutrition kept him from starving to death. In preparation for his release from the hospital for the final phase of his life in home hospice, the hospital staff trained me on how to keep his Hickman catheter sterile, how to flush the line so that it wouldn't get clogged by blood clots, and how to administer the TPN.

Stephen was running out of time. Who was I kidding? He already was out of time. Deep down, my hopes had faded, and I knew that no lifesaving treatments would suddenly appear to save his life now. This really was the end. There would be no miraculous moment when his immune system would recover enough for him to survive so that he and I could ride off on a horse together like the characters played by John Travolta and Glynnis O'Connor at the end of *The Boy in the Plastic Bubble*.

In late January 1991, just after President Bush launched Operation Desert Storm in the first Gulf War, after four weeks of hospitalization and a staggering hospital bill, Stephen's condition stabilized enough for him to be released from the hospital. He would live the rest of his life at our home in a hospital bed with twenty-four-hour-a-day home nursing care, at a cost of about $3,500 per week. Underscoring both the milestone size of the AIDS pandemic by 1991 and the world's attempts to downplay it because of the disease's stigma, on January 25, 1991, the *New York Times* published an Associated Press article with the headline, "US Reports AIDS Deaths Now Exceed 100,000." It was buried on page A-18, below a much lengthier article decrying the ugliness of, and excessive wording on, the US Postal Service's newest stamp. One might think that 100,000 American deaths from a deadly virus would warrant a front-page news story, or at least more prominent coverage than postage stamps, but sadly that was not the case with AIDS because gay men comprised most of those deaths.

We turned our master bedroom into a hospital room, and at night I slept in my home office in the next room. His mother slept downstairs in our guest bedroom. The nurses woke me up at night when Stephen needed me. He went on a constant morphine drip to alleviate his pain, the crucial final medication for a person dying from a terminal disease. In addition, he received periodic shots of Ativan for his anxiety. Stephen and I watched the battles of Operation Desert Storm play out live on the television news each night after I came home from work, and on weekends. A time when all Americans still received the same news. In between the news coverage, almost every night, we watched Touchstone Pictures's film *Pretty Woman* over and over on VHS videotape at Stephen's request. He loved that film. Shockingly, his new AIDS doctor made house calls. But the good doctor's focus now was solely on keeping him comfortable.

With three shifts of nurses at home to help me care for Stephen, I was able to worry a little bit less about him during the day and give more attention to my demanding work at Disney. Then there was our houseguest: Stephen's mother. She decided to stay in Los Angeles for the remaining duration of her son's life. I welcomed her staying with us, since I thought that this would provide the two of them with some quality time together to experience some healing of their long-strained relationship, and to say some proper goodbyes, just as the characters played by Shirley MacLaine and Debra Winger had done in the film *Terms of Endearment*. I thought it could be good for her to glimpse a bit of Stephen's Los Angeles life, and to meet our remaining LA friends since she had never once visited us during our entire seven-year relationship. In addition, I thought that it would help to have her keeping watch over the nurses and Stephen while I was at work. On a personal level, I hoped she and I might get to know each other better. Finally, I thought that she and I would be able to comfort each other in our grief. After all, we were both losing a central person in our lives.

The state of Stephen's and my finances by January 1991 truly terrified me. At this point, I was making significantly more money than he ever did as an attorney, but he and I were sinking further into debt with each passing month. The copayments for his twenty-four-hour nursing care were going to crush us when his company finally processed the health insurance claims. The only saving grace was that ever since the Office of Thrift Supervision had seized Imperial Savings and Loan Association in February 1990, it took about nine months to process health insurance claims. So, this financial assault wouldn't happen until around September 1991. The ominous countdown clock for Stephen's twenty-nine months of COBRA health insurance would run out at approximately the same time—August 1991. We had only eight months left before we faced financial ruin. After that, I had no idea what we would do for Stephen's healthcare costs. Disney did not offer domestic partner benefits at that time, so I couldn't add him to my excellent company health plan: another downside of gay people not being able to legally marry.

I projected that the only thing to save us from falling off a financial cliff was to sell the house in order to unlock our now sizeable home equity. But then where would Stephen and I live? How would I even move him in his health condition and with all of his hospital equipment? September 1991 was still eight months away, so I focused on each day right in front of me. This is when I learned the meaning of the Alcoholics Anonymous Twelve Step Program's philosophy of "One Day at a Time." In fact, it's another version of carpe diem, but in a different context. It works. But not enough to eliminate my worries and high stress level.

My single Visa credit card was maxed out to its credit limit. I prioritized bill paying. To create more financial breathing room, I stopped paying on my student loans even though I knew that it would ruin my credit rating (with every intention of paying the loans back once this was all over). I reviewed the rules for cashing in my Disney 401(k) plan account. I started to eat less to save money. I was so sleep-deprived and depressed by this point that I didn't have much of an appetite anyway. I didn't bother Stephen with any of these financial worries. This left me with no outlet, and I was a grieving, financially stressed out, exhausted, wrecked shell of a human being. I continued working at my job and taking care of Stephen at home, but the rising storm surge all around made me feel like I was slowly drowning.

I also realized in January 1991 that the music had stopped in my life. Somewhere between Stephen's crypto and neuropathy, I had stopped playing the piano. Since the age of seven, playing the piano had always enabled me to release stress and improve my mood. I had also stopped listening to music on the radio and my compact disc player. Since early 1990, the music playlist of my life had been completely empty. For me, the musician, my realization that music had disappeared from my life constituted an ominous sign that depression was getting the best of me. Exhaustion, hopelessness, anger, frustration all swirled inside me, and I could see the stepping stones of a pathway to a life of permanent bitterness. I desperately needed a life raft. So, I created one.

I turned to psychotherapy. I found a gay psychotherapist in Silver Lake named Guy who allowed late-night appointments, so I could see him after work and after Stephen was asleep. Thankfully, Disney's great health insurance plan covered this.

Guy became one of the saviors of my life. I am not entirely sure if I would be still here on planet Earth without him and his wise counseling. Guy, about sixteen years older than me, has an insightful perspective on life. My favorite part about him is that he never, ever minces words of honesty—whether or not you are ready to hear them. His painfully direct approach to psychotherapy was exactly what I needed. I saw Guy weekly from the beginning of 1991 through the middle of 1993. I navigated through many of the known and unknown maps of my life—my childhood, my family, my being gay, my Roman Catholic upbringing, my negative tapes, my career, my personal obstacles to happiness, and, most importantly, grieving for Stephen—all with Guy's help.

Guy's psychotherapy practice centered on gay men, and by 1991 he had seen the movie that I was living hundreds of times before. After I explained my situation to Guy, he steered me to accept, and focus on, five important realizations, starting with, "Chris, you are taking care of everyone around you except for yourself."

Yes, this was true. It was exhausting me.

Realization number two: "Stephen is going to die, it's not your fault, and there is nothing that you can do to stop it."

Yes, I knew this, and I hated it, but I was slowly coming to accept it.

Number three: "When this is all over, you will still be here to live your life and you need to prepare for that."

I wasn't ready to accept this quite yet, but I knew that Guy was right, though it felt like something of a betrayal to me as long as Stephen was alive.

Number four: "Don't quit your job at Disney; you have a great career there."

As I felt I was drowning in the storm, I felt that a possible life raft was to quit my Disney job so I could stay home and take care of Stephen. While this had its appeal, I had to accept that Guy was right since it made no logical financial sense. We desperately needed the money from my job to pay for Stephen's care. This, of course, continued to create terrible guilt for me because of the stark contrast between my world at work with my big league finance job, and my world at home with Stephen, 100 pounds, lying at home in his hospital bed, dying from AIDS.

And number five: "Chris, stop keeping your light under a bushel at work, you are too smart for that."

By "keeping my light under a bushel," Guy was referring to my career strategy of keeping my head down at work and not letting anyone at Disney know what was happening in my personal life. This was all because of Joan's terrible experience being fired by the *Chicago Tribune* eleven years earlier. I didn't want to be fired from Disney for being gay, or for having a partner dying from AIDS. I was not "out" at Disney. The company had lots of gays and lesbians working in its Studio division, but I was in Corporate Finance, a completely different professional world and culture, much more conservative like Wall Street. So, I worked hard, I said yes to every project the company threw at me, kept to myself, and kept my home life a complete secret from my colleagues.

To me, this strategy made sense in light of my sister's disastrous experience. I was not being paranoid. The *Tribune* and Disney were both huge media companies. They both were located in major metropolitan cities, too. In California in 1991, gays and lesbians still didn't have any legal protections from employment discrimination. In early 1991, the California Legislature had only just started to debate AB 101, a bill to prohibit employment discrimination against gays and lesbians, which would not pass until the fall of 1991, only then to be vetoed by Republican Governor Pete Wilson. 1991, even in a more progressive state such as California, was still quite a scary time for gays and lesbians in the workplace. I was terrified that if I came out at work, my career would instantly be over.

To me, the obvious solution was to be so diligent in my job that Disney wouldn't fire me for being gay because it would then lose one of its high-performing employees.

I tried so hard to keep my work life and my personal life completely separate, but with the overwhelming stress from Stephen's looming death, my personal life and my work life now were on a collision course. My strategy was unsustainable. Something had to give.

Guy nudged me forward and helped me realize that the time had come for a repeat of January 1984, when I stood in front of my eighty-plus fraternity brothers and announced I was gay. Now, almost exactly seven years to the day after that emotional experience, I prepared to do it again at Disney. Except this time, I would be telling everyone not only that I was gay, but that I also had a partner, and that he was dying from AIDS. I had no idea how Disney would react, and it terrified me. Would I even have a job after this? Would Disney be sucked into the AIDS Vortex of Insanity? Would red be black? Or, this time, would red be red? There was only one way to find out.

CHAPTER 8
EYE WALL

A s I prepared to come out to dozens of colleagues at Disney, I reflected on how, from the night I told my UCLA fraternity brothers I was gay in 1984 until now, early 1991, I had come out to hundreds of people. Each one of these "coming out" discussions required some level of risk assessment on my part. Can this person handle my disclosure? Should I talk to our mutual friends first to determine if this person can handle it? Will I be all right if this person rejects me? What is the potential collateral damage for me if this person shares my revelation with other people I know but whom I haven't yet told? Most terrifying, might this person hurt my career as what happened to my sister? Or discriminate against me? Or otherwise hurt me?

Ah, the Coming Out Dance. LGBTQ+ readers will understand because many of us have danced this dance our entire lives. No one teaches us the steps, and they vary with each dance partner we approach. Like any dance, at first you stumble around a bit while you figure out the steps and rhythm that work best for you. Then you improve. This is a dance you must master because it's one you must perform with each new person who comes into your life. Otherwise, your sexual orientation will form a barrier to reaching a true friendship. Some people, however, choose to not dance at all—they are just "out" because they either can't hide their sexual orientation, or they don't try to hide it as I did for so many years. These are the bravest people of all. During the course of my life, I have become a world-class coming out dancer. I have perfected the steps, some bold, some more nuanced. The steps I choose depend on my latest dance partner and how much I care about the person.

In January 1991, at the age of twenty-eight I was still not a polished coming out dancer, and the Disney dance I was about to perform particularly terrified me. But it was time to take to the dance floor.

I came out to all my closest work colleagues on the same day. Not in one fell swoop as I did with my fraternity, but through multiple individual meetings held behind closed doors, beginning in the morning and continuing through the day. I wanted to see the whites of each person's eyes as I told them that I was gay and that my partner was dying from AIDS. I had found from my years of dancing the dance that I could tell more from a person's eyes than from their words.

I knew that my news would spread like wildfire through the rest of the company's corporate staff, into the top echelons of the Theme Parks and Resorts management team, and a bit into the Studio division, as well as into Consumer Products. Disney had multiple gossip grapevines for news such as mine. Even though I was not a senior executive, I regularly worked with top executives throughout the company and I knew my news would quickly make its way to them. That's why this dance required my most adept performance. The potential repercussions were great. Stephen and I had been ostracized by people we had considered friends, several of them gay. I could hardly be confident of how this would play out.

I started with Richard Nanula, the treasurer, and the boss with whom I worked most closely, in his office on the fifth floor of the brand new Team Disney Building—the Michael Graves designed Greek Revival corporate headquarters building that featured the Seven Dwarfs from *Snow White* holding up the roof as caryatids. We had all just moved into our new offices there. My office was on the third floor, right below and behind Bashful.

I don't remember exactly what I said to Richard because my heart pounded so strongly throughout the entire meeting, but I know that I told him that Stephen would be dying soon. As I spoke, I saw what I thought were the tiniest tears well up in his eyes. I do remember what he said to me after I finished delivering my news, "I wish that you had shared this with me earlier. It pains me to think that you have been dealing with this all alone while you are working here. I want you to take off as much time as you need to take care of things: doctors' appointments, arrangements, whatever you need. If you need an advance on your salary to cover anything, just say the word and I'll approve it."

My entire body released a huge sigh of relief. Not only was I not getting fired, I was being embraced. A senior executive, who was not constrained by anti-gay-discrimination laws, was acting like a caring friend. My pounding heart pulsed emotions of relief, shock, and happiness throughout my veins. But this was just one down. Would Richard be the exception? I moved on to Judson Green, the chief financial officer, to deliver my news. Judson was another boss with whom I worked closely. After I finished speaking, he said to me, "Chris, whatever you need from us, we will be here for you. I am so sorry to hear that you are going through this."

So it went throughout that momentous day. One after the other, I told colleagues about my situation. I was met with a collective resounding, overwhelming, and unqualified response of support and sympathy. Some actually cried. It was a day of shining a bright light on the elephant in the room and, as I left the building that night, I felt like the weight of an elephant had been lifted off my shoulders. Without doubt, the best dance of my life.

Over the course of the next few days, I told the same news to everyone on Wall Street with whom I had a close working relationship. The largest investment management firms, research firms, and brokerage firms in New York City, Boston, Los Angeles, and Newport Beach with whom I worked closely now knew my situation, too. Once again, I was met with support and sympathy.

Red was black, and black was red, again.

Then the Disney grapevine did its job and my news bounced around the company until seemingly everyone knew. That week added well over 100 additional people to my lifetime coming-out scorecard.

No one cared one bit that I was gay. No one. Nothing changed for me at work. No one treated me any differently. In fact, I now felt closer to my Disney and Wall Street colleagues. All that anyone cared about was how they could help and support me as Stephen died. Even though I never took a salary advance, just knowing that this was an option relieved a huge amount of stress for me. Disney's support saved me as I teetered at the brink during this critical time in my life.

In the aftermath of the second, and last, mass coming-out experience of my life, the time for secret-keeping had once and for all ended. Done, completely done. Never again in my life would I hide my sexual orientation from anyone.

As Stephen and I made our way through the eye wall of the storm in January and February 1991, he was fully alert as he spent time in and out of his hospital bed, even doing some unsteady walking with my help. Now that I was out at Disney, he called me every day at my office around lunchtime to check in. Jeanne, my executive assistant, became friends with him, and remembers him as having a calm and soothing voice.

We adjusted to our loss of privacy with the round-the-clock nurses in our master bedroom and his mother as our long-term houseguest. But "houseguest" is a misleading term. She made herself the "bedroom guest," because of her loudly proclaimed determination to conduct a nonstop bedside vigil until the moment that he died. Stephen and I set up a system for us to get private time together every night after I got home from work. This also gave his mother a break, though I'm not sure she wanted one.

She quietly started to fight a bit with the nurses while I was at work. They weren't fast enough, attentive enough, or they talked back to her. By contrast, from everything I saw, the nurses were quasi-saints who treated Stephen wonderfully. His mother kept clashing with them, and eventually she fired one—a very good nurse, and I was not happy that she did this without discussing it with me first. After the firing, the owner of the nursing company called me at work and asked if I would speak to Stephen's mother about being more polite to the nurses. She told me the nurses had voiced concerns in their reports about how his mother was handling such issues as "control," "death and dying," and her "non-acceptance" that he was gay. Non-acceptance about him being gay? What? Well, I did ask her to be nicer to the nurses, but it had the opposite effect. Soon, another nurse quit because of rough treatment by her. By the end of February, I could feel the tension in our master bedroom between the nurses and his mother. I tried to be extra nice to the nurses to compensate for his mother's behavior because they were amazing godsends.

I tried to be empathetic about his mother's behavior, understanding that it emanated from the incredible stress she was under due to the impending death of her only child, her prodigal son. But the nurses did not deserve to be abused.

Then she started making our friends feel unwelcome. She ignored them when they visited, barely even saying hello. This made no sense to me. These were important people in Stephen's life, and she had an opportunity to get to know them and make connections that would last beyond his death and comfort her. If not that, then at the very least she could be pleasant to our friends simply out of politeness as a guest in our home. But she had zero interest in getting to know anyone. I knew she had gay friends back in Virginia and that she volunteered with AIDS charities, so this odd behavior was puzzling to say the least. Perhaps she was realizing how much of Stephen's life that she had missed by never once visiting him when he was healthy, and she resented our friends' shared history with him, and she wanted them to disappear.

Regardless, our friends ignored the cold shoulder and still visited. Jessie came, too. Stephen's mother definitely did not like Jessie. She was blatantly rude to her one day. As Jessie left our home that day, she turned and said to me, "I know bullshit, Chris, and that hussy is full of bullshit." It was kind of awesome to hear this tiny, spry, Blue Book Society grand dame say "bullshit" and "hussy" in the same sentence. Jessie, it turned out, had incredible foresight. She recognized Stephen's mother's descent into the AIDS Vortex of Insanity long before I did.

Another odd behavior was that Stephen's mother stopped calling him by his name. Instead, she now only called him "my son." From December 1991 through the end of Stephen's life, she never once referred to him by his identity, his name. Instead, she referred to him only in reference to herself, almost as if he were her possession. Even when she spoke directly to him, she said "my son," with an odd articulation. Creepy.

The conversations between Stephen and his mother in my presence focused on superficial banalities, nothing deep or worthy of *Terms of Endearment, Steel Magnolias, On Golden Pond, Driving Miss Daisy*, or any other story that involves losing someone you love. Every conversation was about the news, or the weather, or things that happened twenty years ago when he was at Yale. To be fair, I wasn't home during the weekdays, so maybe they had deep conversations when I was at work. But I didn't see any evidence of emotional healing between them, much as I had hoped for it to happen. These superficial conversations highlighted for me that they didn't have much to talk about with each other, because they hadn't spent regular time together for so many years, and this was a damn shame.

Then, at the same time Stephen's mother was shunning our friends, she developed a close relationship with two complete strangers in Los Angeles who had been introduced to her over the telephone by friends in Virginia.

Again, odd. She welcomed these two individuals into her life with open arms while ignoring our actual friends. It seemed like she was trying to create a parallel universe inside our home for herself—one in which no one from Stephen's California life existed at all, except for me—and I was starting to suspect she wished that I didn't exist either. At the time, however, I was thankful that she had found some companionship to help with her grief, even if it wasn't from our circle. I worried because her own husband, still back home in Virginia, didn't appear to be much of a companion to help her with her grief during this stressful, difficult time. He certainly could have come to Los Angeles to spend time with his son, and also to support her. But he chose to stay home. Was watching television back home in Virginia more interesting than supporting his wife and dying son? What. The. Fuck.

I didn't understand the reason for her increasingly bizarre behavior at the time, but I understand it now: she was angry and devastated about Stephen's impending death from AIDS, and she blamed everything and everyone in his California life for it. In her mind, we were all responsible for "her son's" death. So, she needed to shun our friends, who in her mind were complicit in his death. As for these two strangers, who I believe genuinely tried to help Stephen's mother with her grief, they unwittingly helped her descend further into the AIDS Vortex of Insanity by allowing her to create a parallel universe, one in which she controlled their entire narrative of Stephen's life.

Then, came "diplomagate." I arrived home from work one day in February and Stephen was very upset because his mother had removed his two Yale diplomas from the wall of our master bedroom, right as he watched from his hospital bed.

I asked him, "Did you tell her to leave them where they were?"

Stephen responded, "Yes, but she didn't listen."

It seemed this woman was really going crazy. I found the diplomas leaning against the wall of our guest bedroom where she slept and I confronted her about them.

"I paid for those diplomas," she shrieked at me.

I answered, "Of course you did, but he's not dead yet. By taking them down, you're basically telling him that he should just get it over with and die already. Is that really the message you want to send your son?"

After a tortured discussion, I convinced her to rehang his diplomas. As she did so, Stephen smiled at me, and the nurse on duty looked at me and rolled her eyes. From this point on, we were all officially in Stephen's Mother's Hell.

During that tortured discussion, she also confessed to me that she had gone to the Department of Motor Vehicles and signed the title of Stephen's car over to herself. Totally nuts, and I was aghast by this. His car was a well-worn, eleven-year old, red Volkswagen Rabbit Cabriolet convertible with over 100,000 miles on it, maybe worth at most $1,000. This behavior directly contradicted the bedside vigil she professed she would conduct for him until he died because she loved him so much. Instead, she was scheming and plotting.

As Stephen lay dying in his hospital bed, the days were emotionally hard on him because of his mother's increasingly odd and upsetting behavior. He did not have the strength to stand up to her by this point. Frankly, even when he was healthy he could hardly summon the courage to disagree with her. It explained why he moved 3,000 miles away from home, and all the years of unanswered and slow-returned phone calls. Now, here he was, in his hospital bed, helpless to stop her from transforming into Norma Desmond from *Sunset Boulevard*, trapped inside her own self-made house of mirrors. Everything was about her. Her opinions. Her reaction. Her reflection. Her judgment, which was searing on everyone around her. When your son whom you allegedly love is dying, what type of mother chooses to spend his remaining days of life going through his home claiming mementos and signing over nearly worthless assets to herself instead of spending quality time with him before he is gone from the world forever? She couldn't let him die in peace. She and I regularly argued, out of Stephen's earshot, as I tried to manage my household, and keep him calm, and keep her from doing too much harm.

All of this went on in our house as Stephen's death approached. I tried to make the most of my remaining time with him, but in addition to caring for him, I now also had to worry about his mother's deteriorating mental state as she self-medicated with Valium. I tried to connect with her, I wanted to like her, but she made everything so difficult, and she just wouldn't listen to others. This added another level of stress to a situation that already had plenty.

One weekend, Stephen's priest, Father Alexei, visited us, and Stephen turned the conversation to a discussion of his funeral wishes. His mother freaked out, said that it was inappropriate for him to discuss this, and she desperately tried to change the subject. But since the subject wasn't going to get any easier to talk about, and because he was worried about her declining mental state and concerned that his parents would not follow his wishes, he disregarded her objections and told all three of us what he wanted: embalming and burial in a Roman Catholic cemetery, not cremation. She bristled at this because she intended to cremate him, and he knew this. He continued. A Roman Catholic funeral service. A plaque at the Memorial Hall at the Basilica of the National Shrine of the Immaculate Conception at Catholic University in Washington, DC. And, finally, definitely no AIDS quilt panels in his memory. He had previously discussed funeral arrangements with me, and he had even recorded these wishes on an audio tape, but banning us all from making AIDS quilt panels in his honor surprised me. Even though I didn't agree with him, I could live with this because it was what he wanted. I realized this was one more reflection of the shame that Stephen felt about having AIDS. He had evolved so much in his journey of self-acceptance, but an AIDS quilt panel was a bridge too far, and even in death, he didn't want to be associated with this disease that carried so much social stigma in 1991. Of course, I felt he was completely missing the point of AIDS quilt panels, which was to comfort those who are left behind just as much as it is to honor those who had died. But the time for me to debate this with him had long since passed.

The great thing about this discussion was that Stephen had now expressed his funeral wishes to his mother, in front of witnesses. This would prove to be very important, and damning, because I didn't trust his mother one bit.

In the ensuing nights, after Stephen and I finished our private alone time, his mother would join us in our master bedroom and the three of us would watch the evening news together, and then *Pretty Woman*. Over and over. It was ironic because *Pretty Woman* was a Disney movie, and she had professed three years earlier how much she disliked everything about The Walt Disney Company and its films. But she didn't realize that *Pretty Woman* was produced by Disney's subsidiary, Touchstone Pictures. I never told her. We had enough stress in our household.

By March 1991, Stephen stayed in his hospital bed most of the time but he still was conscious and mentally alert. Early that month, he and I watched the permanent cease fire for Operation Desert Storm on the television news on the same night that we watched the horrific videotape of the Rodney

King beating by members of the Los Angeles Police Department. A few days after the King beating, we watched news coverage of fifteen-year-old African American Latasha Harlins's murder by Korean grocer Soon Ja Du over a $1.79 bottle of orange juice, which inflamed Los Angeles racial tensions even further. On March 14, The Walt Disney Studios legend Howard Ashman, who had written the lyrics for Disney's animated films *The Little Mermaid* and the soon-to-be-released *Beauty and the Beast*, which he also produced, died from AIDS. His death dealt a huge blow to everyone at Disney, and was another sign that AIDS continued to mushroom everywhere around us and decimate the world's arts and entertainment communities. By the end of 1991, according to amfAR, AIDS cases reported to date in the US would be 206,563 with 156,143 deaths, a mortality rate of over 75 percent, and the CDC would estimate that approximately 748,000 Americans were living with HIV.[11,27] One of those 1991 deaths would be Stephen.

Throughout March, Stephen's mother continued descending into the AIDS Vortex of Insanity. She wasn't interested in speaking to me, or knowing anything about Stephen's and my life together. She periodically hassled me about my working during the day, which of course exacerbated my guilt about my high-pressure job, and made no seeming connection to the fact that my salary paid for the house in which she house-guested. She regularly demeaned the entertainment industry and, by extension, my career. If I had been a research scientist, she would have demeaned research scientists, too. She needed to disapprove of my work to fit her narrative. If she had believed that Stephen's partner was a successful finance executive at a Fortune 100 company who paid for almost all of Stephen's bills, for a significant portion of Stephen's medical care, and for the house in which she was living, it would have conflicted with her parallel universe with its narrative about the evil of Stephen's California life, Stephen's friends, and me.

I tried hard to put myself into Stephen's mother's shoes and understand her situation. Her only child was dying, which is arguably the ultimate tragedy. In his novel, *An Orphan's Tale*, the author Jay Neugeboren wrote, "A wife who loses a husband is called a widow. A husband who loses a wife is called a widower. A child who loses his parents is called an orphan. But…there is no word for a parent who loses a child, that's how awful the loss is!"[29] Perhaps this explained why she removed his diplomas from our master bedroom while he

---

29   Jay Neugeboren, *An Orphan's Tale*, Holt Rinehart, & Winston, copyright 1976, page 154.

was still alive. Maybe they reminded her of all the hopes and dreams that she had once had for Stephen that were dying along with him. Maybe staring at those diplomas all day long while she performed her bedside vigil was simply too much for her to bear.

This strange behavior, however, was the unfortunate harvest of a lifetime of dysfunctional relationship dynamics between Stephen and his parents. His parents had placed all of their hopes and dreams in him, but in an unhealthy way. After law school, Stephen moved across the country, 3,000 miles away from them, to try to build his own life without them bearing down on him. His AIDS diagnosis and looming death must have been truly unbearable for these people. It shattered their whole worldview and dreams. He would never get married to a woman and have children, their grandchildren. He wouldn't have the successful legal career they wanted him to have. He wouldn't become a member of the Los Angeles Country Club. He wouldn't be around to take care of them in their old age. All that money they spent on expensive Yale and MIT tuition was now completely wasted in their eyes. That's why his mother took down those diplomas. I get it—in addition to the searing pain of losing her only son, looking at those diplomas all day long must have felt like looking at the fancy home or vacations she could have bought instead. The death of her own dreams. That's also why his father never visited either: Stephen was already dead to him. His father never visiting him spoke volumes about their fractured family dynamics. Where was unconditional love in any of this? It was horrible, hurtful, and inexcusable for him to not visit his son. Horrible, despicable rejection.

On top of it all, Stephen's more than seven-year relationship with me, twelve years his junior, a guy who loves the beach, from, of all places, Los Angeles, the world's "vapid" entertainment capital, who didn't attend an Ivy League college, who really wanted to be a writer, and who now worked at Disney, was just too much for his judgmental parents to bear. They couldn't simply be happy that their son had found love. In their eyes, I was not good enough for him, and I would never be good enough for him, and there was nothing I could ever do for them to accept me. Given the intense grief I grappled with at the time, I didn't understand this perspective when I lived through it, but I can see it all now. At the time, all I really knew was that his mother seemed increasingly crazy, his father was outright cruel, I was fairly sure that neither of them liked me, and I didn't think that we would stay in touch after Stephen died, a damn shame because we all could help each other through our respective grief.

When Stephen and I were alone together in March, we talked a lot about death, God, spirituality, and the afterlife. One night as we talked about what comes after this life, Stephen and I joked about him sending me signs from the hereafter to let me know when he was all right. We came up with three different methods: the first was for him to appear to me in a dream. But we both agreed that dreams can be unreliable, so we devised two backup methods. So, the second was for Stephen to send me a rabbit, in honor of his pet nickname for me. The third method, just in case God didn't allow the dead to send their loved ones pre-agreed-upon signs from the hereafter, was for Stephen to send me some other sign that only he and I would know, but he would have to send it to me multiple times so that I could accept that it actually was a sign, especially since I didn't believe in signs in the first place. We laughed about our strategy of trying to outsmart God. We were laughing in the face of death, which was really a beautiful thing.

Stephen celebrated his forty-first and final birthday on March 26, 1991. What do you give someone when you know that it's their last birthday? A heavy assignment to carry out, for sure. I devised a gift for him that spanned each of his five senses, as best as he could enjoy them by that point. For sight, we watched *Pretty Woman* yet again. For hearing, I arranged a bedside concert by a harpist from the Los Angeles Philharmonic Orchestra. For touch, I gave him a gentle foot massage that did not upset his neuropathy. For smell, a bottle of Stephen's favorite men's cologne, Ralph Lauren's Polo. And for taste, at his request, a selection of sushi from our favorite sushi restaurant at the Beverly Center. Even though Stephen had virtually no appetite by this point, he managed to eat all of the sushi and keep it down that day, which in itself was something to celebrate on his birthday. The beaming smiles from Stephen as I unfurled the five stages of his birthday celebration made it all worthwhile for me, even as my heart was breaking inside.

During this sad/happy birthday party, I thought about how, in 1984, my first birthday present for Stephen was a ticket to the Joan Rivers benefit for AIDS Project Los Angeles, and now on his final birthday AIDS was killing him. Bittersweet bookends for our relationship.

In mid-April, during our time alone together Stephen suddenly blurted out, "I'm sorry, Chris."

"Sorry for what?" I replied.

"Everything. I don't know what's going to happen, or how fast it will happen when it's my time, so I want to say all of this to you now.

"I'm sorry about the drugs and alcohol, and for making such a mess of my life. I'm sorry that I couldn't give you the life that I wanted to give you. I'm sorry that you gave up your writing career, and then you had to deal with all of this. I don't know what I would have done without you in my life to help me fight this disease. I'm sorry that I'm dying and leaving you alone in the world. I'm sorry for my anxiety, my fears, my insecurities…everything. I am so, so sorry, Chris."

I took a deep breath. This was *Dark Victory* time; the sky was blackening above him.

"Well, Steve, I'm sorry too, for a lot of things," I responded. "I'm sorry that I can't make you healthy again. I'm going to miss you so much when you're gone. I'm sorry that I have to work while you're home here sick. I'm sorry for all those times when I lost my temper because I was frustrated with you. I'm sorry that I will never see the beautiful salt-and-pepper hair that I'm sure you would have someday. I'm sorry that you won't be here to enjoy the fruits of my finance career."

Then, we forgave each other for everything that we had ever done to each other. We talked about the things we hated about each other, what we loved about each other, the things that made us grateful about life and our time together, and all of the things that we appreciated. We called each other names (both good and bad), we made faces at each other, we laughed, and we cried, and we said everything that we needed to say. Eventually, he said, "You saved me, you know that, Chris, right?"

"How, Steve? You're dying. If I had saved you, you wouldn't be in this hospital bed. Maybe rescue is a better word, and by the way, it was mutual. I climbed the tower and rescued you, my Prince Charming, and then you rescued me right back. We rescued each other. Just like in *Pretty Woman*."

"Chris, promise me that you will go on and live a great life. Don't forget me, don't forget what we did together, and don't forget carpe diem. I will be pulling for you from the other side. I'm so proud of your finance career, but please write something someday. I love you so much."

"Of course I will never forget you, Steve. You are a part of me, forever. I love you more than anything."

Then I kissed him, and with tears streaming down our faces, we held hands and let the love flow between us in a wonderful silence. Partners, and best friends, saying goodbye.

That's the moment when I learned what true love really means. When Stephen first started getting sick, I remember feeling angry and cheated by life because we got only two short years before his illness appeared. For a while during his illness, I did feel cheated by life on some levels. But was I really cheated? Or did I actually get a better, more real version of what love actually is, and can be, and should be, in the face of the tough challenges that we all ultimately face in life? As I look back on my life, some of my happiest memories from my relationship with Stephen occurred after his near-death in La Jolla: when the whole world turned against us, when our time together was short, when we fought together as a team, when we carpe diemed the hell out of everything, when we had little money, when we crammed in so much life together even with death bearing down upon him, when he freed himself from the external pressures that had left him so unfulfilled in his life, when he focused on his true passions with his remaining time on this planet, when he found inner peace and happiness, when my Prince Charming turned into a frog and I loved him even more and then he turned back into a prince again, when I learned that deep love can exist in the midst of the searing pain of what most people would say is a horrible situation and therefore not even bother to look for it. Not to mention all the life lessons that Stephen and I learned together, and that I was so lucky to learn at such a young age. He stopped caring about impressing Blue Book Society, and then he learned that these people loved him for who he was all along. Together we learned that we could take darn good care of ourselves in the face of huge adversity. We had been through so much of life together. He became a changed man, and I became a changed man, and our love had grown very deep. We both rose, in our respective ways, to meet the incredible and heartbreaking challenge at the center of our lives, and we both grew from it immensely. A couple of my well-intentioned friends have made comments to me over the years along the lines of, "You only got two good years with Stephen," or, "You stuck with him for better or worse, but it was mostly for worse." I don't see my relationship with him this way at all. I lived through all of it, and I can see the good, the growth, and the redemption in the entirety of my relationship with Stephen. We got life. We got love. Real, gritty, angry, unfair, frustrating, painfully heartbreaking, wonderful, deep, resilient, triumphant, beautiful, raw life and love. In other words, the truth.

That was the last deep conversation that I remember having with him.

By the end of April 1991, Stephen was completely bedridden. Much less consciousness. He pushed the button on his morphine drip machine frequently. The machine allowed him to push it every ten minutes, and so he did. He started to hallucinate. His mental faculties declined notably. He stopped calling me at work. The hardest part for me in losing Stephen was my pain in seeing his incredible brain, that intellect that once drew me to him like a magnet, slowly recede from me and the world.

Stephen's father still remained in Virginia, and I wondered when, or if, he would ever come to say goodbye to his son. Stephen's mother's emotional state continued to deteriorate, too. Father Alexei came to visit Stephen one day while I was at work, and after meeting with him he also had a private meeting with her at my request. After his visit, he telephoned me to say, "Be careful, Chris." He never returned to visit Stephen again.

In May 1991, I turned twenty-nine. I certainly didn't feel like celebrating. A lost birthday for me. Stephen now was conscious much less often and had more hallucinations. He saw people sitting in the room who weren't there, and he heard voices. Our finances were a total disaster by this time. On May 6, two days after my birthday, The Walt Disney Company was added to the Dow Jones Industrial Index, a huge milestone, and I didn't celebrate that either. When my Wall Street friends called my office to congratulate me on Disney being added to the Dow, it only seared more guilt into me over my ascending finance career while Stephen was at home dying.

Around this time, one of our next-door neighbors, named Hope, stopped me in my driveway as I left for work, and she said to me, "My husband and I have figured out what is going on in your house. We just want you to know that if you ever need a place to come, to get away, to talk, or just sit and do nothing, our home is open to you." It was the most wonderful thing for me to hear at this point. It's common in Los Angeles to never get to know your neighbors, elevating the Robert Frostian view that "good fences make good neighbors"[30] into an art form. Hope and her husband Steve had lived next door to us for almost seven years and we had only waved polite Angeleno

---

30   Robert Frost, *"Mending Wall," Selected Poems of Robert Frost,* Holt, Rinehart & Winston, copyright 1963, pages 23–24.

waves to each other as we pulled in and out of our respective driveways. And now, Hope was purposefully and bravely breaking through the secure walls of anonymity. Red was black, and black was red, again. I lived next door to hope.

Toward the end of May, Stephen stopped asking to watch *Pretty Woman*. He stopped wanting to watch any television. One day, he removed his eyeglasses and never wore them again. Then, he took off his wristwatch. He had gone blind. But he could still hold, and grip, my hand. He could still talk, but only during the moments when he drifted back into consciousness, a place where he lived less and less.

By June 1991, Stephen's eyes mostly just stared blankly at the ceiling above him, with a glassy appearance. His eyes didn't even look blue anymore, and were turning gray. When I held Stephen's hand, his grip back to me was weaker. I instructed the nurses to wake me up at night whenever Stephen was even slightly alert so that I could talk to him for a few minutes before he lapsed back into unconsciousness again. I wanted to grab every last remaining second of time that I could have with him. Of course, this added to my exhaustion, but I figured that soon enough I would have plenty of time to sleep while I drowned in my grief. Time seemed to move slower as Stephen and I moved through the eye wall of the storm. Thankfully, as they had promised, my Disney colleagues were being incredibly accommodating and not asking me to do any work-related travel. So, Stephen and I had no unnecessary time apart.

Nearly six months into her self-imposed bedside vigil, Stephen's mother finally admitted that she was cracking under the stress and needed to get out of the house for a bit. The nurses were overjoyed to hear this, too. So, one weekend afternoon I took her to see the newly released film *Thelma and Louise* at the Hollywood Pacific Theater. She liked it very much. But, as I look back, it's as if the AIDS Vortex of Insanity caused her to adopt *Thelma and Louise* as her future life plan.

Stephen's father—finally—traveled to Los Angeles at the end of June. I thought to myself, "Why come now? You have missed your chance. Stephen's life is essentially over." But at least he finally came. I doubt that Stephen ever knew that his father was there because he was mostly unconscious or delirious from the morphine by this time. His father didn't show any emotions whatsoever, and seemed to be more interested in inspecting the furniture in our house and going through the papers in the file cabinets in Stephen's home office than in spending time with him. It seemed that this was the main reason for his visit.

In early July 1991, Stephen's mother once again told me that she wanted to cremate Stephen because she never wanted to be separated from him again. Of course, this was in direct contradiction of Stephen's explicit wishes, so I reminded her of his conversation with her in front of his priest, Father Alexei. She exploded in anger. She yelled at me: "He is my son, I know what's best for him! Don't you dare tell me what to do!"

I became angry because of the utter hypocrisy of the situation. Here was this woman, conducting her bedside vigil, and grieving, and saying how much she loved "her son," and talking about how she volunteered with AIDS charities in Virginia, and how religious she was, and how she had all these gay friends, and meanwhile she was fixated on pursuing her own self-centered agenda of ignoring Stephen's wishes. She was taking the AIDS Vortex of Insanity to new extremes. Of course, with Stephen on the verge of death, he couldn't stand up and fight for himself. So, I told her, "Frankly, I don't really care one way or the other if a person wants to be embalmed and buried, or cremated. For myself, I choose cremation. But since Stephen specified to you that he wanted to be buried and not cremated, I think that you should listen to him. But since I am not legally married to him, this is your decision and it's on your conscience, not mine. I know that I could not live with the guilt if I chose to ignore a dying person's wishes."

She most definitely did not appreciate my commentary.

But I didn't care. I was pissed that Stephen's parents would do this to him. Their "son." Utter bullshit. Jessie was right.

Regardless, Stephen's life was almost over. In a strange way, I felt already as though he had died weeks earlier. His body was still alive, and he still breathed, but the Stephen that I knew and had loved for seven-and-a-half years had already moved on to another plane of existence. He and I were almost through the eye wall and to the center of the storm that I would be left to weather alone.

CHAPTER 9
THE EYE

My 2,724 days with Stephen ended in the mid-morning of Saturday, July 13, 1991. It rained that morning, something that hardly ever happens in Los Angeles during the summer. But it was all too fitting as the storm claimed him during what should have been the summer of his life. After his five-and-a-half year fight with AIDS, Stephen transitioned into the great beyond and I moved into the eye of the storm. I became a twenty-nine-year-old widower.

Earlier that morning, I could tell that it was the end. Stephen showed no signs of life other than shallow breathing. His hand was unresponsive when I held it. His now-gray eyes were glassy, and seemed full of a pool of tears.

Stephen's mother wailed and pounded her chest and ran upstairs to his bedside when the nurse told us that he was gone. I suppose it made sense for her to finally let out her emotions after her six-month-long bedside vigil, which ironically ended with her not being next to his bed at the moment that he died. His father showed no emotions. Our cat Edith spontaneously jumped on the hospital bed and laid down between Stephen's legs and purred. Edith knew.

I was quiet. Stephen finally was at peace. His nightmare with AIDS was over. I didn't even cry. I had already cried so much during the past five-and-a-half years that now that he finally died I only felt a combination of relief and numbness. My journey with Stephen was done. I knew that my crying would come later.

After his mother's emotions subsided and his father took her out of the bedroom clutching the two Yale diplomas in her hands, I leaned over the hospital bed and kissed Stephen on his forehead and quietly said to him, "Goodnight, sweet prince." Our tragic Shakespearean ending: Stephen my Hamlet, I his Horatio.

Within a few minutes of his death, my telephone rang and it was our friend Basil the monk. "I'm sensing that something happened to Stephen," he said when I answered. If that's not clairvoyance, I don't know what is.

Stephen's death certificate listed his official cause of death as "respiratory failure, due to pneumocystis carinii pneumonia, due to AIDS." What this means in plain English is that the sacs inside his lungs responsible for exchanging oxygen and carbon dioxide slowly built up fluid and stopped working, which then restricted the oxygen needed for his organs to function, and this caused his brain and heart to stop.

The nurse on duty methodically sprang into the prescribed post-care procedures, turned off all of the machines and the morphine drip, cleaned up various medical supplies, and left our house.

The mortuary promptly came to pick up Stephen's body. The attendants gently placed it into a brown body bag. They zipped it up and respectfully carried the remains of my partner out our front door and into their van. And then, just like that, Stephen's body was off to be cremated against his wishes. Our house was empty of him forever.

The hospital equipment company soon came to pick up the hospital bed, IV equipment, morphine drip machine, and the other medical devices and supplies. The underground pharmacy picked up his unused medicines to deliver them to people who didn't have any health insurance. Within the span of a few hours, our master bedroom almost looked like a normal bedroom again. Life already was moving on.

Stephen's presence in our home started to fade, too. I could feel it. To try to hold on to what I was losing, I went into our clothes closet and smelled some of his clothes that he hadn't worn for months. I clung on to Stephen through the faint drift of him that remained in his clothing.

Our house became eerily quiet. So empty. So different. I already knew that I didn't want to stay there long-term without Stephen.

I called our friends to let everyone know. Suddenly, I had all the time in the world now to talk on the telephone. No more rushing around to take care of him.

Stephen's parents started planning his memorial service. They may have cremated him against his wishes, but at least they planned a Roman Catholic service for him, to be held at Georgetown University in Washington, DC. To help organize the service, his parents reached out to the same gay Roman Catholic priest in Washington, DC, who had severed his friendship with Stephen two years earlier and whose partner was a doctor. This priest was connected to Georgetown University, and could book a chapel there. I didn't have the heart to tell his parents how this hypocritical priest had hurt Stephen, and let them think he was still Stephen's friend.

Stephen's mother started to obsess about her son's ashes. She wanted to get them back from the mortuary as soon as possible so that "her son would never leave her side again," a phrase I would hear again and again. She wondered whether anyone else's ashes would be accidentally mixed in with Stephen's. I didn't want to have this conversation with her. It sounded too much like Lady Macbeth's obsession over hand-washing.

Then, I went about the things in life that still needed to be done regardless of my devastation. I bought my airline ticket to Washington, DC. I made arrangements to stay there with Stephen's and my friend Marc. I called Richard Nanula, my boss, to give him the news. He told me to not come back to work for at least three weeks. I cooked some food for Stephen's parents and me to eat. I scheduled a short meeting at my office with my work colleagues for the next day so that while I was gone they could keep working on Disney's upcoming Wall Street Analyst Conference in September 1991 at Walt Disney World, a major company project.

I paid some bills that I knew would come due while I was on the East Coast. As I paid them, I realized that I wouldn't fall over the financial cliff that I had thought was approaching in September. Stephen's health insurance copayment bills wouldn't arrive for weeks or months, and I would be able to cover the ones that I had guaranteed. Also, we never reached the expiration of his COBRA health insurance coverage, which would have happened just six weeks after he died. These were both huge financial reliefs for me. I thought about how I had achieved my goal, set two years earlier, to be making a good salary by August 1991 to pay for his medical expenses. We had come so close to the edge of the financial cliff.

I took out the trash. I straightened up the house. I did a bit of laundry. I fed our cats. I gave one of our cats to one of Stephen's nurses, and I asked his parents to take our other two cats back to their home in Virginia because of my allergies, and they agreed. I was relieved to know that all three of our cats would be in good homes, and that soon I would be able to breathe again without constantly taking allergy medicine. But our adorable cat Edith would never get to play trampoline again. His parents didn't know how to set it up, and now was not the time to teach them.

Then, a couple of Stephen's and my friends came by to take me out and provide some comfort. I figured that his parents might want some private time alone to grieve together, too. They didn't even say hello to our friends when they picked me up.

I was going through the motions, and the motions helped me keep going.

On Monday morning, piles of flowers and cards arrived at my home, sent by my Disney colleagues.

On Monday afternoon, I discovered a large white rabbit hopping around on my front lawn. In the middle of Hancock Park! A rabbit was one of the signs that Stephen and I had discussed him sending me months earlier to let me know that he was okay, but we were just joking. Or so I thought. I couldn't believe it. Stephen's mother saw the white rabbit too, but she didn't know what it meant. None of my neighbors had a pet rabbit, and Hancock Park is an urban neighborhood. The rabbit hopped around the lawn for several minutes. Then it went around a corner to disappear into the bushes and never be seen again. Seriously, this happened. Was this rabbit actually a sign? Or was it simply a really strange coincidence? I didn't believe in signs, but wow.

On Tuesday, Stephen's ashes came back from the mortuary. They were delivered in a plain cardboard box, sealed with scotch tape.

"I will never let my son out of my sight," Stephen's mother announced, yet again. "I'm going to hold him in my lap tonight for the entire flight home to Virginia. Even when I go to the bathroom on the flight, I'm taking him with me into the lavatory." Creepy.

I flew to Washington, DC, on Friday for the memorial service the next day. When I boarded my flight, I noticed that I didn't have my usual fear of flying. I didn't care anymore if the airplane crashed. Somehow, Stephen's death cured my longtime fear of flying, except for flying in helicopters, which still terrify me.

Stephen's memorial service at Dahlgren Chapel at Georgetown University was surreal. If you didn't know him at all, you would have thought that it was a beautiful memorial service. Indeed, Dahlgren Chapel is one of the most beautiful small churches I have ever seen: an intimate space with gorgeous stained-glass windows, intricate mosaic tiles, stations of the cross sculpted in metal, an impeccable and detailed wood ceiling, and a soul-inspiring church organ. The small group of guests mostly included Stephen's parents' friends, Stephen's and my friend Marc, and a few of Stephen's friends from Yale University. I encouraged our California friends not to attend because it was so far away and this was his mother's show, and she had been so unfriendly to them.

Stephen's ashes, now in an urn, occupied the front of the center aisle of the chapel. The gay Roman Catholic priest who had severed his friendship with Stephen helped assist with the service. At least this priest had the good sense to not actually preside. Our friend Basil the Monk presided, a good call by Stephen's parents. Michael, a close friend of Stephen's mother who didn't know Stephen well—they had only met a few times—gave the eulogy. Because of this, his eulogy did not focus much on Stephen but instead on Stephen's parents. He looked right at them as he spoke, and at points it sounded like he was pleading with them. In hindsight, I think Michael knew that the AIDS Vortex of Insanity had already largely swallowed both of them. Although this was not a service for the Stephen I knew, it was a very nice service.

Stephen's parents insisted that I sit between them. I wondered whether they were putting on a show of a united grieving family for their friends, or perhaps they simply were following *The Godfather*'s Corleone family motto of "keep your enemies closer."

In reality, I was barely present. I looked at the ashes and my anger grew, thinking, "What kind of parent cremates her son against his wishes?" Then, "Why did Stephen's father avoid visiting him until he was almost dead?" And finally, "How hypocritical for a gay Roman Catholic priest who lives with his gay doctor lover to ostracize his former good friend, never call him while he suffered, and then swoop in to help with his former friend's memorial service?"

Hypocrisy surrounded me, and then my anger moved on to organized religion, and specifically the Roman Catholic Church. I fumed about what I call "the Missing Commandment" in the Bible, the one that somehow fell through the cracks when Moses had his chat with God on Mt. Sinai. In my opinion, the Missing Commandment is "thou shall not force your own damn religious beliefs on other people." Or perhaps a more friendly version of the Missing Commandment is "your spiritual journey is yours alone." I have always believed this, and even suggested the Missing Commandment in my catechism class at Our Lady of Lourdes Church, which got me sent to the chair outside Monsignor Stroup's office. But just imagine the murders, wars, and genocides in the names of the world's organized religions that might not have occurred with this one simple, extra commandment. A biblical typo, if ever there was one.

As I sat there in that church, I steamed about how the Missing Commandment was responsible for the world's homophobia and so much pain in my life. Homophobia that prevented me from marrying Stephen so that I could have ensured that his parents didn't ignore his funeral wishes. Homophobia that drove this gay priest to live in secret with his doctor lover because their lives contradicted the Roman Catholic Church's doctrine. Homophobia that has resulted in the overt persecution of millions and the self-persecution of millions more who are afraid to be who they are.

All of this homophobia rooted in a handful of Bible verses that come from the same sections of the Bible that contain laws people ignore to not eat pork, to have multiple wives, to rape and pillage one's enemies, to have sex slaves, and to kill people for a whole host of reasons in direct contradiction of the Commandment "thou shall not kill." People use the Bible to justify almost anything in the name of organized religion, all while missing the entire point of God and spirituality just like the Pharisees did. The few Bible verses that address same-sex relationships pale in comparison to more than 100 Bible verses that promote slavery. Yet slavery in America today is illegal, but fundamental religious conservatives still constantly rail against homosexuality. All of it, utter hypocrisy.

The Missing Commandment would have solved all this by commanding us to let others be. But alas, Moses stopped at ten.

I grew more and more angry in Dahlgren Chapel during the memorial service while these thoughts streamed through my head. The Missing Commandment. Bible verses that made no sense and contradicted themselves yet wreaked havoc on my life. Homophobia. Why unconditional love was so difficult for people to grasp. Hypocrisy. The Age of Truthlessness. Stephen's memorial service pushed me further out the door of the Roman Catholic Church.

After the service, Stephen's parents hosted a reception at 1789 Restaurant at the corner of Thirty-Sixth Street and Prospect Street, a short walk away from the chapel. Again, beautiful but surreal. 1789 Restaurant is located directly across the street, only sixty-nine feet away, from the top of the Exorcist Steps, where the Roman Catholic priest character Father Damien Karras in the film *The Exorcist* threw himself to his death after he exorcized the young girl's demon into his own body to save her. Stephen's parents could not have selected a more fitting Roman Catholic backdrop for the reception if they had tried. In my view, it was the Roman Catholic Church that needed to be exorcised.

After the memorial service, I flew to New York City and spent a few days with my friend Robert. I don't even remember what I did there. Then, I returned to Los Angeles to a pile of sympathy cards and letters from our friends, including our friends in Blue Book Society. The heartfelt wishes from these people were incredible. Kindness that was that much more comforting because it was unexpected.

I opened every window in my house for an entire day to air it out of all the medical smells, the cat smells, and to get some fresh air into the house after such a long time. I didn't care that it was 100 degrees outside, I needed air in my home. The smells of Stephen aired out of my home too, but it was time to release them.

Then, finally, I cried an ocean of tears, all by myself, the twenty-nine-year old widower. Stephen really was gone. Life still needed to be lived, I knew that. But what do I do now? I, the consummate planner, felt crushed and directionless. For over five years, I had planned for everything except for living again.

It was time for me to take the first steps into my new, uncharted life. The eye of the storm had passed.

But do you know what comes after the eye of a storm? More storm.

CHAPTER 10
FLOODING

THE SIX MONTHS AFTER Stephen's death constitute the lowest point of my life. It felt like living inside of a foggy world filled with molasses. Everything difficult. Everything slow. Everything exhausting. Everything devoid of color and texture. Everything music-less. Everything other than the most basics of life seemingly impossible to attempt, and so I mostly didn't attempt to do anything outside of working. Immobilized in molasses. This is what devastation feels like.

I didn't sleep well. I dragged myself out of bed and aimlessly through my days. I didn't even want to do a basic thing such as go to the grocery store. Friends invited me out, but I stayed home. I just existed, directionless. In shock, shaken to my core.

At the age of twenty-nine, I needed to put my life back together. At the same time, I had to focus on my demanding finance career and not screw that up. I also needed to take care of myself, something that I had not done properly for many years.

I didn't even know where to start. I was in a bad emotional state, spiraling downward. A journey back upward into life seemed insurmountable, like pushing a giant flywheel that had stopped turning, with all the forces of inertia working against me as I strained to move the wheel again. During these months, I lived at a dangerous crossroads where I easily could have turned into a bitter person, devoid of hope.

My psychotherapist, Guy, helped me a great deal, but my therapy sessions occurred only once per week. His sessions gave me an idea, though, as I sat at home at night after work, paralyzed, grieving. I now had the time to embark on an exploration of myself as an adult man, a journey of self-discovery. What better time to engage in self-discovery than when you are a broken man on the ground? With great struggle, I chose to do something each day that forced me to get out of my house and mix with living people in the world around me. Therapy and self-discovery became my new project. The best idea that I could think of at the time. Something was better than nothing.

AIDS Project Los Angeles held a weekly support group for surviving partners of people who had died from AIDS, so I attended every week. On another night, the Los Angeles Shanti Foundation held a similar weekly support group for surviving partners, so I attended that every week, too. I discovered a woman named Dr. Jackie, a grief counselor who specialized in hypnotherapy. I saw her weekly, too. Then, on another night each week I saw Christine, a shiatsu masseuse recommended to me by Dr. Jackie. On weekends, when I wasn't working I sometimes saw friends, but more often I visited the Bodhi Tree Bookstore on Melrose Avenue. Thankfully, I remembered the Bodhi Tree from Marty, my first boyfriend during the summer of 1983, who had introduced me to it. I would linger there, reading spiritual and self-exploration books, and sipping their herbal tea. On Sundays, I went to church. Yes, this man who is against organized religion, with nearly both feet out the door of the Roman Catholic Church already, actually went to church. But I went to Saint Andrew Church, the same church Stephen loved, because it was a connection for me to Stephen.

An important start. All good comebacks must begin somewhere.

I returned to work just over three weeks after Stephen died. Soon after, his parents returned to Los Angeles from Virginia, allegedly to help me sort through my home and then list it for sale. But they started acting strangely antagonistic toward me. Both of them had now mostly descended into the AIDS Vortex of Insanity. The hurlyburlies from *Macbeth* had finally arrived in the center of my life.

This antagonistic behavior did not surprise me. In 1991, it was common for the parents of people who had died from AIDS to descend into the Vortex and treat surviving partners quite badly. I had already witnessed this terrible phenomenon before when our friends had died from AIDS. Another example of the problems created for gays and lesbians because they could not get married and therefore could not benefit from the legal protections taken for granted by heterosexual married couples. Typically, this homophobic discrimination revolved around money and ignoring or challenging wills. With no legal protections, it was difficult for surviving partners to fight back.

But the good news for me, I thought, was that there was really nothing to fight over with respect to Stephen. He died with no assets, only a mountain of debts. Our house wasn't in his name—it was owned 92 percent by his parents and 8 percent by me, so nothing to argue about there. Clean and simple. The furnishings in our house were old and worn, and I certainly did not want most of them. Other than my piano and bench, my books, my clothing, my photographs, my personal papers, the furniture in my home office, and a few sentimental items, I planned to take nothing. Once we sold the house, I intended to rent a condominium in Burbank near my office so that I could start paying down the sizeable debt I had accumulated caring for Stephen. Finally, Stephen had a $100,000 life insurance policy from Imperial Savings and Loan. Three years before he died, he had named his parents as the beneficiaries of 55 percent of this policy to repay them for a loan they had made to him before he and I met. He left 34 percent of this policy to me, and the remaining 11 percent to some religious organizations. Simple, clean, nothing to argue about. Or so I thought.

Well, tensions continued to escalate, and one night his mother finally admitted what I had suspected all along—that she didn't like me one bit, and that she believed I killed Stephen. She was very angry at me, even if her logic was lacking. After all, how could I have killed Stephen with AIDS if I was HIV negative? Then, she accused me of being a freeloader off his money. More faulty logic, since I made significantly more money than he ever did, and I had been paying the lion's share of our expenses for the past two years. Next, his father accused me of exerting undue influence over Stephen to coerce him to specify $34,000 for me and $11,000 for religious organizations from his life insurance. He told me that he was certain that his son never intended to leave money to anyone but them, and only designated me and religious organizations as beneficiaries because he was sick with AIDS and not of sound mind. His father told me they intended to claim undue influence and challenge Stephen's life insurance policy. Finally, his father told me they were certain that all the furniture and furnishings in the house belonged to Stephen, and therefore it all now belonged to them.

I was incensed. I told his parents that Stephen made his life insurance designations years earlier when he was mentally healthy. I explained to them that he left them the majority of his life insurance, and that he designated his insurance beneficiaries without even discussing them with me. Furthermore, why on earth would I coerce him to give money to religious organizations when I distrusted organized religion? It was the madness of the Vortex. I told them that I planned to only take a few things from my house that belonged to me and that there really was nothing to fight about. I would be gone soon, and then they could hate me forever. During this heated discussion, I was somewhat bemused by that fact that his father sat on the cushion of our sunroom couch right where Stephen once had a nasty diarrhea accident, the stain of which I had miraculously scrubbed out. And now, I, the scrubber of diarrhea stains, was being accused of taking advantage of Stephen!

I tried to calm his parents down, but to no avail. Yes, they were arguing with me about money at that moment, but their anger went far beyond dollars and cents. These two people wanted to obliterate Stephen's relationship with me. They needed to do this for their parallel universe narrative. Seeing the dark place this was going, I stood up for myself, and for Stephen, and said, "Be careful. You have already dishonored your son by cremating him against his wishes. Not everything in this house belonged to him. Remember, I own part of this house, too. If you sue me for undue influence, I will fight back. You have no idea what he wanted. Neither of you were here the entire time while Stephen was dying until the very end."

It certainly seemed to me that we were headed for a fight over virtually nothing. This made no logical sense, but that's how the Vortex works.

Later that night, Stephen's parents completed their descent into the Vortex, adopted *Thelma and Louise* as their life plan, and chose to drive themselves over a cliff. Unbeknownst to me, as I slept in my bed, they plotted.

I left for work the next morning, August 13, 1991, hoping Stephen's parents would be more reasonable by the time I returned home. That day around 2:00 p.m., his father called me at my office to tell me that they had changed the locks on my home, and to never come there again. Then he hung up on me. The torrential flooding from the storm had begun.

I was stunned and outraged. How dare they change the locks on my own home? How dare they continue to dishonor Stephen by treating me like this? Stephen's parents were trying to eradicate his California life. I decided that if they were so intent on driving off a *Thelma and Louise* cliff, then I would help them step on the gas pedal. I vowed to fight for my relationship with Stephen, and to make a stand for all gays and lesbians who had ever experienced this sort of reprehensible homophobic discrimination. His parents messed with the wrong gay man. My laid-back California personality retreated, and my take-no-prisoners New Jerseyan attitude took front and center stage.

By the end of that day, I had hired my neighbor Paul as my attorney and he began work on an emergency restraining order to prevent Stephen's parents from removing anything from my house. Then, I hired a moving company to show up at my house the next morning so that I could remove my personal belongings. I also had arranged to have about twelve of my friends serve as witnesses for me by being present while I moved out. Finally, I had found a place to spend the night. My friend Sandy, who wrote her business school applications with me, now worked as a finance executive at Largo Entertainment, a film studio run by Larry Gordon, a powerhouse Hollywood producer known for his action movies, and she told me that I could stay at her West Hollywood condominium. My next morning was shaping up to be quite the action movie itself.

The next morning, my friends showed up at my house promptly at 7:45, including Margaret, my first boss, and Stephen's priest, Father Alexei, who had been chased away by Stephen's mother months earlier. The moving truck arrived as planned. Everyone armed themselves with moving boxes on my front lawn. I instructed everyone to remain calm, be polite, not provoke anything, and not respond to anything that Stephen's parents said or did. My attorney Paul knocked on the front door. Stephen's parents refused to open it, and yelled expletives at me through one of the front windows. They certainly possessed quite a colorful gutter vocabulary. I walked around the back of my house and I pulled on the door handle to the sunroom. That door never shut properly. If you pulled hard on it, the door always popped right open. Sure enough, it did. I calmly walked through my house and saw his parents screaming in my living room. I smiled and said a chipper "good morning" as I walked right past them and opened my front door. Paul and my friends streamed inside my house.

Then, utter bedlam ensued. Stephen's mother ran screaming into the kitchen to call the police. Good. Stephen's father ran to the guest bedroom. I directed my friends upstairs to my home office that contained several of my personal belongings. Suddenly, his father reappeared in the living room with a large green crowbar and attacked Paul with it, screaming, "Get out, I'm going to kill you." Stephen and I never owned any crowbars. His father had made a special trip to a hardware store to purchase it, and I'm fairly certain for the sole purpose of using it on me. Paul ducked and grabbed the crowbar in defense, and thankfully convinced Stephen's father to let it go.

Stephen's mother now entered the living room, still screaming. Oh, the slew of terrible anti-gay obscenities hurled at my friends and me by the two of them! She repeatedly shrieked that I was a "whore" and that I had "killed Stephen." As my friends tried to carry my belongings to the moving van, his parents wrestled boxes from them on my front lawn and took the boxes back inside my house. My Hancock Park neighbors stood on their porches and witnessed this insane spectacle unfolding in my front yard, and the neighborhood buzzed about it for weeks afterward. The movers stood outside my home, dumbstruck and in shock.

The police arrived quickly, thankfully. Four LAPD officers, with their guns drawn, took control of the situation. Stephen's parents screamed that everything in my house belonged to them. The officers tried to calm them down, and in their police report later described them as "abusive, uncooperative, and often irrational" while noting that my friends and I were "friendly, quiet, and cooperative." Paul threatened to press charges for assault and battery against Stephen's father for the crowbar attack. The police seized the crowbar as evidence. One of the shocked movers tried to call his supervisor from the kitchen phone to ask for guidance. When he picked up the phone to dial, Stephen's mother ripped the cord out of the wall, screamed that it was "her phone," and no one could use it. The four officers did an excellent job of diffusing the situation and helped Paul negotiate an agreement with Stephen's parents and their attorney via the telephone: no one could remove anything else from my house pending a court order, and in the meantime they agreed to be responsible for safeguarding my house and all of its contents.

One of the officers, a young African American woman, stayed by my side the entire time, and she said, "You're going to be all right, these people are crazy."

I didn't feel all right, though. I felt terrible and humiliated.

After the police finished with the attorneys, my friends and I left my house and I went to work. The officers instructed me to not return to my house, and to let the attorneys sort everything out. I left hoping that Stephen's parents and I would be able to resolve our disagreements quickly since, after all, there really was nothing to fight about.

Well, it turns out that agreements, even if negotiated between attorneys in the presence of police officers, only work if people actually follow them. Stephen's parents had no intention of following any agreement, or the law. The AIDS Vortex of Insanity had transformed them into Thelma and Louise, laws and agreements be damned. They already were far over the cliff.

For the next month, they offered to "sell" me my personal belongings back at a "fair market value," set by them. I refused to pay their ransom.

Then, they packed everything in my house into a moving van and left town. I returned to my house, and confirmed that everything in it was gone, stolen. Mission accomplished: Stephen's parents had obliterated his California life.

I was shocked. What kind of human beings do such a thing?

The kind who wear large religious crosses, apparently.

Also, by this point, Stephen's father had spent significantly more time in Los Angeles poring through Stephen's and my belongings than he ever did visiting his son while he was dying from AIDS. Priorities.

Fortunately, my friends and I had been able to retrieve a few things from my house before the police arrived that fateful day. The most important things, things that could never be replaced: a few photographs of Stephen and me, a few important papers, the audio tape that he had recorded of his funeral wishes, a few of my books, Stephen's Batman pin, one of his favorite shirts and his favorite tie, and the small ceramic rabbit and small wooden rabbit on wheels that he had given me as gifts. And randomly, his passport. But everything else that I owned now was on its way to Virginia. My clothing. My diplomas (apparently Stephen's two Yale diplomas weren't enough for them?). My piano and bench. My sheet music. My metronome. Most of my books. My file cabinet. My file box of creative writing ideas. My home office desk that I had built out of a door. My mail. My bills. My income tax returns. My telephone. My answering machine. My computer and dot-matrix printer. My stereo system and my compact disc collection. All of my belongings, stolen, gone to Virginia.

I was furious that Stephen's parents would violate an agreement between our attorneys, negotiated in front of police officers. They had completely dishonored their son, first by cremating him against his will and now by treating me—his partner—like I was nobody in his life. I gave up any hope of reasoning with them. I was going to do battle with the AIDS Vortex of Insanity, and I vowed that somehow I would remain sane.

I filed a police report for the theft, and then I sued Stephen's parents over my stolen belongings and several other actions designed to rattle them. I hired a process server to serve the lawsuit at their home in Yorktown, Virginia.

In response, they countersued me for twelve causes of action:

1. Partition (to force me to sell my 8 percent of my house)
2. Interference With Prospective Economic Advantage ("undue influence" because Stephen designated me and some religious organizations as life insurance beneficiaries)
3. Assault (Stephen's mother alleged that I assaulted her in February 1991 in front of Stephen and the nurses during "diplomagate")
4. Battery (related to her alleged assault claim)
5. False Imprisonment (related to her alleged assault claim)
6. Assault (Stephen's parents alleged that my friends and I assaulted them as a group when I tried to retrieve my personal belongings from my house)
7. Battery (related to the alleged group assault)
8. False Imprisonment (related to the alleged group assault)
9. Conspiracy to Intentionally Inflict Emotional Distress (related to the alleged group assault)
10. Intentional Infliction of Emotional Distress (related to the alleged group assault)
11. Intentional Infliction of Emotional Distress (against me for allegedly verbally abusing Stephen in front of his mother and the nurses)
12. Declaratory Relief

Their twenty-one-page cross-complaint overflowed with hyperbole. I was "willful, wanton, malicious, oppressive." Also "reckless." I "exercised undue influence" with "ill will." I "threatened," and was "harmful and offensive." I caused them "great mental, physical, and nervous pain and suffering," "extreme and severe mental anguish," "permanent disability," "humiliation," and "emotional and physical distress." They didn't sue me for killing Stephen, though, which surprised me given how many times his mother accused me of this. The cross-complaint stated that they were required to "employ physicians for medical examination, treatment, and care of these injuries, and did incur medical and incidental expenses," and they would "continue to incur medical and related expenses" for their "permanent disability." By reading this lawsuit, you would think that I was Baby Jane Hudson incarnate!

I fought back and I fought to win. I stopped paying the mortgage on the house. I stopped paying the utilities, too. I shut off the electricity, gas, and water. Why not? Everything was in my name. I fired the swimming pool service and the gardener, and the pool promptly turned green and the landscaping turned brown. I canceled the house insurance, knowing that the bank would replace it with an expensive insurance policy and then add the cost to the mortgage. Stephen's parents had forgotten that I had been paying the house's expenses, and there was no way that they could afford to pay them on their retirement income. They didn't think their *Thelma and Louise* strategy through very well. As the mortgage fell into delinquency, Home Savings started to pile on late charges, fines, interest upon interest, special servicing fees, and legal fees. The hundreds of thousands of dollars in equity in our home that existed when Stephen died started to disappear. This lit a financial fuse for all of us, but mostly for his parents since they owned 92 percent of the house. For every one dollar that I lost, they lost $11.50. They were apoplectic about this. But they refused to recognize the simple solution: just give me back my belongings.

Throughout the fall of 1991, while eastern European countries declared their freedom and independence from the Soviet Union like falling dominos, Stephen's parents desperately tried to force me to sell the house. I refused. As an 8 percent owner, this was my right, and they couldn't sell the house without my signature. They were stuck. I always responded with, "Return my belongings, and I'll agree to sell the house." They wouldn't return them, so I refused to agree to sell. Their hatred and greed blinded them to this rational and obvious resolution. Meanwhile, the house fell into disrepair and became a neighborhood eyesore. His parents then hired a real estate agent to list the house for sale, but I wouldn't sign the listing agreement. He still tried to sell the house without a valid listing agreement, which of course is unethical. By the winter of 1992, he had presented five separate purchase offers, including one from a fellow Disney executive in the Studio division, each one for a successively lower price because the Los Angeles real estate market was collapsing due to a trifecta of the Savings and Loan Crisis, a terrible US economy, and massive defense industry layoffs in the wake of the fall of Soviet Communism. With each new purchase offer, I asked Stephen's parents if they were ready to return my belongings. Each time they said no, so then I said no to the offer. I was living through a real-life version of *The Little Foxes*, Lillian

Helman's classic play about human greed that was made into a film starring Bette Davis. His parents were so fixated on the money. But mostly, I think what really sent them over the edge was that a gay man whom they hated was preventing them from getting what they wanted.

Meanwhile, Home Savings continued imposing hefty late fees and other penalties, and the home equity continued to evaporate into thin air.

By playing such hardball with Stephen's parents, I was hurting myself as well, since this was ruining all three of our credit scores. I didn't care—I was *that* angry. My FICO credit score fell to an un-bankable level, a complete credit disaster. But so did theirs.

This was the first lawsuit of my life. I was blown away by how much Stephen's parents lied in the documents they filed with the court. I was stunned to see people blatantly lie under penalty of perjury in court filings, but unfortunately it would not be the last time I would witness such behavior. My attorney Paul told me, "This is what people do in lawsuits when they know they are on the losing side. They lie, make up facts, and assassinate their opponent's character. I've seen this dozens of times. Eventually it will all blow up on them. Be patient." He was right. But trust me on this: telling the truth in the face of boldfaced lies is much harder than it sounds.

In early January 1992, I switched attorneys, from my neighbor Paul to Lloyd, one of my best friends from college and a member of my fraternity, even though Gloria Allred, the high-profile civil rights attorney, had expressed an interest in taking my case. I had also consulted with Sheila Kuehl, another well-known attorney and former actress in the television series *The Many Loves of Dobie Gillis*, and an openly lesbian woman who later served in the California State Senate and State Assembly and who today is one of the five Los Angeles County Supervisors. She emphatically told me, "Make sure that you sue the hell out of those homophobes." Lloyd was a litigation expert. My marching orders to him: do everything legally possible to fight Stephen's parents until they returned my belongings, I didn't care how much it cost me. For me, this war wasn't about money, it was about principles.

Home Savings eventually recorded a notice of default on the house, and Stephen's parents filed an "ex parte" motion to appoint a court receiver to sell it before it went to foreclosure. At that time, I didn't know anything about ex parte motions, but they cut right to the front of the line with the judge for immediate consideration. There's a very short notice and response period, which requires attorneys to rush around and work overtime to deal with the motion. The best part: ex parte motions are *really expensive*. When I saw the bill from Lloyd's law firm for the ex parte motion, I thought to myself, "Wow, if I'm paying these sky-high legal fees then his parents must be paying them, too." I wanted to make our lawsuit as expensive as possible for them so that they would give up and finally return my belongings. So I called Lloyd and said, "We need to have a lot more ex parte motions. Let's do ex parte motions as much as possible from now on."

Lloyd agreed. From January onward, my lawsuit with Stephen's parents consisted mostly of ex parte motions. I made peace with turning over most of my paychecks to Lloyd's law firm to fund my war of principles.

Lloyd and I fought the good fight on the motion, and we delayed the judge's ruling for a while. The real estate agent, who was gay himself (!), and who I concluded had agreed to share his sales commission with Stephen's parents because of their repeated insistence that he receive a commission even if another real estate agent sold the house, pleaded with the court to force the house sale because "every day that goes by the value of this property continues to decrease." Eventually I lost the motion, and the judge appointed a court receiver to oversee the sale. The court receiver made it clear to me and Lloyd that he was not a friend to gays and lesbians, or to those who represented them.

But the good news is that Los Angeles real estate values continued to plummet. Mother Nature helped, too. Before they fled to Virginia, Stephen's parents broke several windows in the house and then the roof started to leak. Then, the 1991–1992 Los Angeles winter unleashed a downpour of more than twenty-one inches of El Niño rain, forty-one percent more than average, and flooding from the broken windows and the leaking roof damaged the inside of the house. Incredibly, by April 1992, when the court receiver finally sold the house, given the bank's penalties, the crashing Los Angeles real estate market, and the court receiver's fees to sell the house, the hundreds of thousands of dollars of equity that existed at the time of Stephen's death had dwindled in eight months to $7,071.84. The court receiver placed the sale proceeds into a court escrow account pending the outcome of our upcoming trial.

Stephen's parents were furious over the lost money.

This is a good place to backtrack a bit. After Stephen's parents locked me out of my house and during the early days of my lawsuit with them, it occurred to me that my homeowner's insurance might cover me for my stolen belongings, particularly since the insurance was in my name, not Stephen's. Well, it turned out that my insurance covered me for all my stolen belongings, and at replacement cost, too. All I had to do was produce a list of the stolen items, along with photographic proof of them, and a police report for the theft.

This certainly turned out to be an unexpected silver lining. I had already filed a police report for the theft. Two years earlier, I had made a detailed photographic record of everything in our house for insurance purposes in case we ever had a fire. Then, just in case our house burned down, I stored all the photos safely in my desk drawer at Disney. So, one of the unexpected benefits of Stephen's parents' theft was that over the next several years I eventually received an entire new houseful of furnishings, paid for by my insurance.

As my legal battles raged, and with initially no furniture or clothing, I settled into living at my friend Sandy's condominium on Hayworth Avenue in West Hollywood. Because of my grieving and depression, the few items that I was able to take from my house remained in storage at the moving company for several months. At first I slept on the floor of Sandy's spare bedroom, on a yoga mat. Eventually, I bought a mattress for the floor, a dresser, a bookshelf, and some new clothes. But that was about all the acquiring I did. I was too depressed. I didn't even cook much, and mostly went out to eat to either Greenblatt's Deli or Gaucho Grill, both of which were within a short walking distance. I hired my UCLA mentor, Liz, who by that time had started her own accounting firm, to pay all my bills for me since I was too despondent to pay them myself.

Fortunately, I had the mental strength to maintain my therapy and self-discovery journey, even amidst my lawsuit and my increasingly high-pressure job. I didn't participate much in the AIDS grief support group discussions, but I listened intently to other participants, most of whom lived through much worse experiences of homophobic discrimination than I did. I was not alone. It comforted me to know that I was not the only person dealing with the insanity of the AIDS Vortex.

Being with these people who were so impacted by AIDS made me think of my missing friend Bryn. I was sure that he was dead by now. It had been more than three years since he left Los Angeles to live with his sister in Minneapolis. He had to be dead.

Dr. Jackie's grief hypnotherapy truly rocked. At the end of each weekly session, she hypnotized me with affirming messages for me to absorb into my subconscious mind. These messages counterbalanced the negative tapes lodged deep in my subconscious. I still remember one of the messages said in every single session: "You are good, and you are good enough." I cannot tell you how powerfully affirming that simple message was at this devastating time in my life. It was straight out of Louise Hay. It was the parachute that saved my psyche from splatting on the pavement.

My weekly shiatsu sessions with Christine were phenomenally helpful. She possessed an intuitive ability to improve my emotions, my energy, and my sense of well-being. Her treatments were unusual, though. Sometimes she would just rub my toes in a particular way, and not even all of my toes. Sometimes she would just rub my stomach and intestines, or my liver. She also taught me about Chinese medicine, and recommended Chinese herbs and acupuncture. I tried them all.

My therapy with Guy also continued, and with him I sorted out my road maps and emotional cobwebs, and worked on my grief, depression, and anger from a more classical psychotherapy perspective.

Between my two AIDS grief support groups, hypnotherapy with Dr. Jackie, shiatsu with Christine, therapy with Guy, and my weekend dates with the Bodhi Tree Bookstore, I was well on my way to transforming myself into the woo-woo new age Californian that everyone likes to joke about. As difficult as all of this was for me to do, it actually worked, laying an important foundation for me to eventually rebuild my life. Having survived the storm this far, I was determined to stay afloat as the flood waters swirled around me.

My friend Basil the monk visited me a few times during this period on his travels between his work on Lantau Island in Hong Kong and his home monastery in Spencer, Massachusetts. He also comforted me and helped me deal with my grief with his spiritual wisdom. Basil "got" and understood what really should be the core of the Roman Catholic Church. One of the good ones.

One night, as I reviewed my telephone bill before I mailed it to my accountant Liz so she could pay it, my newly issued telephone number caught my eye: 650-8629. It looked familiar to me. I wrote it down on a yellow Post-it note, and above it I wrote my old telephone number from my West Hollywood apartment where I lived when I first met Stephen: 652-9608.

I then made the connection between the two telephone numbers, both numbers assigned randomly by the phone company. The same seven digits, just in a different order. I calculated the mathematical probability of this happening: significantly lower than the odds of being struck by lightning. I still didn't believe in signs, but wow, what a strange coincidence. I still have that Post-it note.

Locking me out of my own home and stealing all of my belongings while I reeled from the searing pain of losing Stephen, just after I returned to work and I struggled to focus on my demanding corporate finance career, was one of the most despicable things that Stephen's parents could have done to me. It rocked me to my core, and the timing could not have been worse. At that moment in time, the stakes in my career were high because Disney had scheduled a three-day Wall Street Analyst Conference at the end of September at Walt Disney World in Florida, and I had a major role in planning and managing it. Over two hundred buy side and sell side analysts plus dozens of members of the press planned to attend the conference, which would feature daily events from early morning to late at night, including "behind-the-scenes" tours of each theme park, speeches by every senior executive, and entertainment. My future career depended on me executing this huge project well. While I grappled with my grief and my mushrooming lawsuit, at work I helped plan the three-day meeting agenda, drafted the content of executive presentations, and cleared the financial disclosures that Disney would make at the conference with the legal department. Multiple agenda revisions. Multiple speech rewrites. Meetings at all hours of the day and night to accommodate busy executive schedules for speech practices. A huge logistical undertaking, and incredible work experience and senior executive exposure for me at the age of twenty-nine, just one month after Stephen had died, my deep grief still raw. I threw myself into this work because I had no alternative but to get it done, and it's a miracle that I executed the project well given how badly I felt.

One of the businesses that we planned to highlight at this Conference was Disney's fledgling Hollywood Records unit. While I worked on a draft of the Hollywood Records speech with one of the group's members, she said, "It's too bad that we wasted ten million dollars on the Queen music catalog when Freddie Mercury is about to die from AIDS. That's going to wreck the value." She argued that I should cut any mention of the Queen music catalog from the Hollywood Records speech because of this. I steamed silently.

Hollywood Records had purchased the Queen catalog in February 1990 for $10 million—its first big acquisition. At the time, there were rumors that Freddie Mercury was battling AIDS, but he hadn't publicly acknowledged it. But what did it matter? The Queen music catalog was fantastic, even if it might not have another new addition. Not only was my colleague's comment insensitive, it demonstrated a misunderstanding of finance, annuity streams, supply and demand, and inflation. I left the Queen references in the speech.

Freddie Mercury died on November 24, 1991, two months after the Analyst Conference. He disclosed that he had AIDS the day before he passed. But his death didn't tank the value of the Queen music catalog; it actually increased it. I would not be surprised to learn that Disney has since made at least twenty times its investment in that music catalog, if not far more than that.

In addition to Freddie Mercury, the AIDS pandemic continued to claim lives throughout the world's entertainment and arts communities throughout 1991. Brad Davis, the actor famous for his role in the film *Midnight Express*, died from AIDS on September 8.

Then, on November 7, the legendary Los Angeles Lakers basketball player Magic Johnson stunned the world by announcing that he was HIV positive and retiring from basketball. His news rocked the media. Just as Ryan White did almost seven years earlier, Magic Johnson helped transform the stigma that AIDS was only a gay disease. Now everyone knew that HIV could even strike a beloved heterosexual basketball star. An incredible act of bravery.

By the holidays in 1991, I was adrift, fully immersed in my grief. I was alone for Thanksgiving. I had invitations to join friends, but I chose to be alone.

I was alone for Christmas 1991. Again, I had invitations to join friends, but I wanted to be alone with my grief. I saw the animated film *Beauty and the Beast* by myself on Christmas Day at Disney's newly renovated El Capitan Theater on Hollywood Boulevard. My work colleague Dan, who worked in Corporate Communications, told me to stay to the end of the credits because it contained a surprise that I would like. The film was fantastic, and at the end of the credits appeared the following dedication:

To our friend, Howard,
Who gave a mermaid her voice
And a beast his soul,
We will be forever grateful.

Howard Ashman
1950–1991

This was the film's dedication to Howard Ashman, the genius who wrote the lyrics for *The Little Mermaid* and *Beauty and the Beast*, who had died from AIDS only a few months earlier. It moved me so much, and made me so proud to be working at a company that would honor Ashman in such a beautiful and emotional way at a time when AIDS still carried such stigma. I told Dan that I loved the film's dedication, and then he told me that he wrote it. That blew me away. To this day, Dan says it's the thing he's most proud of from his eighteen years working at Disney.

I was alone for New Year's Eve 1991 and New Year's Day 1992. Again, my choice to be alone.

Being alone for these major holidays after Stephen's death was fine with me. I was so deep in my grief that I didn't feel like celebrating anything, and my friends understood. That season of holidays didn't matter to me. This underscored, however, that even with all my intensive self-discovery work, it was extremely difficult for me to live again, to turn my flywheel its first few important inches. Los Angeles, for me, was turning into Lost Angeles.

In January 1992, as Stephen's parents and I fought over their ex parte motion to appoint a court receiver, one night I checked on my house in Hancock Park. I hadn't visited it for months. It was still empty, and I could see that it had suffered water damage, but now some lights inside it were on, the landscaping was manicured again, and the swimming pool wasn't green anymore. Someone was taking care of the house. Mail overflowed from the mailbox at the front door. I had long since forwarded all my mail to my office, so none of this could be mine. Inside the mailbox was a letter addressed to Stephen from the Standard Insurance Company, his long-term disability insurance company. I opened it. It was his monthly disability check. Stunned, I thought, "Why on earth would Standard Insurance still mail Stephen his monthly disability check when he has been dead for six months?" Then my mind quickly went to a darker place and I thought, "Oh, no, does this mean that Stephen's parents are still cashing his disability checks?"

Well, this discovery turned out to be an amazing stroke of good luck for me.

I called Standard Insurance Company the next morning. Of course, the customer service representative wouldn't discuss Stephen's policy with me because I wasn't married to him. So, I had to get creative. I said to her, "If someone was committing insurance fraud against you, wouldn't you want to know about it?"

"Well, yes," she replied.

So then she and I did a dance. I said, "Okay, You can't discuss Stephen's disability insurance, but I can tell you things, right?"

"Yes."

"Look in your computer system, and see if his monthly disability checks stopped being cashed after July thirteenth, 1991, the day that he died."

The representative responded, "Well, I can see what has happened in his account, but I can't discuss it with you. But do you have proof that he died?"

Aha, I thought, this means that Standard Insurance didn't know that he had died.

"I have Stephen's death certificate," I replied.

"Please fax the death certificate to me," she said.

I faxed the certificate, and almost immediately Paul, an executive from Standard Insurance Company, called me back. He said, "Someone has been cashing Stephen's disability checks each month since he died. Someone is forging his name on the back of the checks."

But Paul couldn't tell me any additional information because I wasn't married to Stephen. So, I continued the dance and said, "I have a hunch as to who is signing the checks. It's probably his parents."

I told Paul that I would have Lloyd subpoena the forged disability checks so they could serve as evidence in my lawsuit of Stephen's parents' poor moral characters. If one of his parents' handwriting was on the back of those checks, it would blow a huge hole in their case and virtually ensure me victory. Then I would get my stolen belongings back.

Needless to say, Lloyd was excited to hear my news. But, before I could subpoena these documents from Standard Insurance Company, I had to win a court order from the judge because I didn't have legal standing to request them since I wasn't married to Stephen. I filed an ex parte motion to request the judge to issue a subpoena to Standard Insurance to turn over Stephen's cashed disability insurance checks since his death. His parents fiercely fought this motion, but the judge ruled in my favor.

When the documents arrived, sure enough, on the back of each disability insurance check was Stephen's forged signature, in his mother's handwriting. Her writing was very distinctive, almost like a child in elementary school just learning cursive. Un-fucking-believable! Each of these forged checks was deposited in his parents' bank account at First Virginia Bank in Richmond, Virginia. These people had committed criminal felony insurance fraud, forging their dead son's signature for months with no conscience whatsoever after they had cremated him against his wishes. So incredibly sad. I kept a copy of one of the forged disability checks as a lifetime memento of his parents' abject dishonesty, and mounted it in my scrapbook, along with a copy of the threatening letter sent to them by Standard Insurance Company in February 1992.

Lloyd delighted in informing the judge about Stephen's parents' now confirmed felony insurance fraud. I couldn't believe how insane Stephen's parents had become in the Vortex. Compared to them, Thelma and Louise were rank amateurs. They quickly paid back the stolen money to the insurance company, with interest and attorneys' fees, so they wouldn't be prosecuted for a felony. They became even more furious at me now that they had been caught for their crime and embarrassed in front of the judge, but they still refused to return my stolen belongings.

As I thought more about the insurance fraud, I realized that Stephen's parents could only have done it with the help of another person, or persons. Someone in Los Angeles needed to stop by the house every month, fish Stephen's disability insurance check out of the mailbox, and then mail the check to his parents in Virginia. There were only three potential accomplices to their felony: his mother's two parallel-universe friends she had met while staying at my house, and the gay real estate agent who so desperately tried to sell the house to earn his commission. This one mystery I would never solve.

One February weekend afternoon, I had a telephone call with my Blue Book Society friend Jessie that changed my life. I remember that it was one of those "California Dreamin'" days: a sunny and warm day, just after a torrential rain, when the Los Angeles air is smogless and crystal clear, and from the top of Runyon Canyon you can see all the way from the San Bernardino Mountains to Catalina Island and beyond. A winter day when Angelenos run around in shorts, T-shirts, and flip flops. The type of day that makes East Coasters want to move to California.

On my phone call with Jessie, while still wearing my pajamas, I lamented how even on this beautiful day I didn't feel like going outside because of my grief, and Jessie interjected: "Chris, no one can pick you up off the floor except for you. I remember when I lost my husband, Tommy, fourteen years ago, I felt the same way that you do. And six months after your spouse dies is the lowest point: everyone expects you to be fine, but you're not. This is when you have to act, and only you can do it. The therapy is nice, but you have to choose to live again, to be happy again. Happiness is a choice, Chris. You just have to do it. Just do it."

This phone call with Jessie was the slap in the face that I needed. Her timing with that slap was impeccable, too. I was so comfortable in my intensive cycle of grief therapy that I had become, in a sense, addicted to it, and stuck in it. Jessie had essentially told me to follow Nike's new advertising slogan: Just Do It. It's amazing how a well-timed comment from the right person can change the course of your life in an instant.

She was right. After that call, I showered and dressed and went for a long walk. I walked from Sandy's condominium on Hayworth Avenue near Sunset Boulevard south to Santa Monica Boulevard, then west through the main area of West Hollywood all the way to Doheny Drive at the edge of Beverly Hills, and then back again. I hadn't been to the heart of West Hollywood in years. I walked by so many ghosts from my early twenties, including Barney's Beanery, where I wrote my business school applications when I thought that I had AIDS. I thought about my grief, my life, and my future.

As Jessie said, happiness is a choice. On that day, I chose to not become a ghost, a shell of a person. I chose to not become bitter about life. I chose to not let anger eat me up and swallow me. I chose to live again.

I started working out again. I joined the new Gold's Gym Hollywood on Cole Avenue and hired a personal trainer. It felt so good to exercise, sweat, and feel soreness again. I worked out at the UCLA campus too, in intense workouts that cleared my mind of everything as I struggled to catch my breath. I would run up and down the 1,245 stairs at UCLA's Drake Stadium over and over, and do pushups at the top of each set of stairs, and sit-ups or leg lifts at the bottom of each set. I modeled these workouts off a group of US Navy SEALs that I had once witnessed exercising on the beach in front of San Diego's Hotel del Coronado in the summer of 1983. This workout strategy did wonders for me. I learned that if I pushed myself insanely hard in my workouts until I couldn't do one more pushup, pullup, sit-up, run any farther, or even catch my breath, that my mind cleared, endorphins flowed, my stress released, sometimes I bawled my eyes out, I felt better, and I slept like a baby. I didn't know it at the time, but I was doing CrossFit long before CrossFit was invented.

Then I took a class and learned how to ride a motorcycle. I started researching and shopping for Harley Davidsons. My friends Robert and Erika sent me a motorcycle helmet as a gift, partly out of fear of safety for me. I replaced my stolen upright piano with a brand new Yamaha C3 grand piano as a gift to myself for my upcoming thirtieth birthday in May, partly covered by my homeowners' insurance claim. Stevie Wonder shopped for Bosendorfers right next to me in the store. I started to play the piano every single day. I replaced my stolen stereo system and my stolen music compact disc collection. I surrounded myself with music again. I discovered the music hits that I had missed playing over the airwaves during the last two years of Stephen's life. The return of music to my life fed my soul.

I did spontaneous silly things, too. One Saturday morning I woke up to an El Niño torrential rainstorm and convinced my business school friends Dorcas and Anna to spend the day with me at Disneyland in the pouring rain. I bought us matching yellow rain suits, rain hats, and umbrellas at the California Surplus Mart. With barely any other guests in the park and no lines for rides, the operators let us stay on the rides for multiple trips and not even get off. I have a great photograph of us all wearing our rain suits and our purple 3-D glasses standing outside Disneyland's Captain Eo attraction. To top it off, we ate lunch at Club 33, the private restaurant inside Disneyland that serves alcohol.

I started to live my life again, bit by bit. My flywheel turned. Progress.

But I still needed to finish my lawsuit with Stephen's parents and get my stolen belongings back. In February 1992, they asked the judge for an accelerated trial date because of his father's alleged poor health. They told the judge that he had failed kidneys, was on dialysis, and would die within a year. The judge believed their story and moved up the trial date to May 15, 1992. This was actually great news, since in 1991 the average wait for a trial in Los Angeles Superior Court was around three years. So I knew that this legal nightmare would all be behind me by the end of May.

We still had the "discovery phase" to complete. I drafted 393 interrogatory questions for Stephen's parents. I also requested a long list of documents. They responded with long lists of interrogatories and documents for me to produce, too. My blanket response to nearly everything they asked was along the lines of, "I'm sorry, but I can't answer this question or produce this requested document because everything I owned was stolen—by you."

Next up, my deposition. Their attorney who took my deposition was a young, perfectly coiffed and dressed blonde-haired woman around my age.

As I waited for my deposition to begin on March 9, 1992, I looked out the window of the conference room at her law office in one of the two Alcoa Company Towers in Century City, and I jokingly blamed Elizabeth Taylor for my standing there. You see, if 20th Century Fox hadn't made the film *Cleopatra*, which starred Ms. Taylor, then the studio wouldn't have been forced to sell hundreds of acres of its studio backlot to cover the film's huge production cost overruns, and then maybe Century City never would have been developed, and then I wouldn't be in this conference room. Thanks a lot, Liz.

Let the sparring begin. To kick off my deposition, just after the court reporter swore me in and the attorney prepared to ask me her first question, I whipped out a camera to take her photo. I didn't tell Lloyd in advance that I would do this because I didn't want him to stop me. She completely lost her composure. She held up her hand and turned to the side, laughing and trying to block her face from my camera. I took her picture anyway, like a paparazzi. Lloyd burst into laughter. The court reporter burst into laughter. I burst into laughter. I could tell that she was trying not to laugh too much too as she demanded that I turn over my film, which, of course, I refused to do.

I said, "I just want a memento of you. It's a special day for me, my first deposition." I dueled with her for three entire days. Most people find depositions stressful and unnerving. I loved every minute of this one.

Stephen's parents refused to return to Los Angeles for their depositions, and hoped that this would allow them to get away with not being deposed at all. After Lloyd explained to me that depositions can occur anywhere, I flew him to Yorktown, Virginia, to take their depositions—two days for each of them—in a small, windowless, claustrophobic room in a local motel. Lloyd also explained to me that depositions could be videotaped, so I hired a videographer to film them to pile on more stress. They absolutely hated being videotaped. Plus, they had to pay to fly their attorney to Virginia to represent them at their depositions. So their attempt to avoid their depositions altogether ended up costing them significantly more money than simply coming to Los Angeles. If their legal fees were anything like mine by March 1992, they had spent well over $100,000 on this lawsuit.

Stephen's parents then struck back when I attempted to take the deposition of Stephen's psychotherapist, Michael, who at this time was dying from AIDS but who very much wanted to testify against them. This set off more ex parte motions. First, they tried to stop his deposition altogether by asserting that they held Stephen's "psychotherapist-patient" privilege. However, they had never filed any paperwork with the probate court, so the judge wouldn't let them assert the privilege without a probate and he ordered the deposition to proceed. Immediately, they filed a probate action eight months after Stephen's death just so they could obtain his psychotherapist-doctor privilege and prevent the deposition, and this cost them even more money.

Michael had agreed to a videotaped deposition, but it's just terrible what Stephen's parents did to this dying man, who wasn't even practicing as a psychotherapist anymore due to his failing health. At the time of the deposition, they still hadn't obtained the psychotherapist-patient privilege from the probate court, but nevertheless they berated him and threatened him with lawsuits if he disclosed any information that violated the "psychotherapist-patient" privilege. Michael sat there looking deathly ill and terrified while they abused him. I couldn't even watch the video for more than a few minutes, but he persevered and spoke his truth. Michael died seven months later on October 25. He is honored as a Circle of Life Memoriam donor to AIDS Project Los Angeles.

In April 1992, Lloyd told me that he wanted to leave his law firm to start his own practice. This gave me an idea. I told him that I would be his first client and hire him to be my full-time attorney, and I would match his law firm salary through the duration of my lawsuit. Lloyd agreed, quit his job, and suddenly at the age of twenty-nine I had my own personal full-time attorney. I now had 100 percent of his attention. He fought Stephen's parents over every procedural matter as our May 15 trial date loomed. But they still would not return my stolen belongings.

Throughout the month of April, Lloyd and I prepared for my upcoming trial. On April 6, Isaac Asimov, the well-known American science fiction author, died from AIDS. Then, on April 29, on the eve of my trial, a jury found all of the Los Angeles Police Department officers not guilty in the closely watched Rodney King beating trial. Los Angeles instantly descended into terrible riots. Buildings burned, businesses were looted, and people were hurt and killed. The 7th Army Infantry Division and the 1st Marine Division arrived in Los Angeles on May 2 to patrol the streets and help keep the peace. A painful and surreal time for my hometown of Los Angeles. I remember driving east on Sunset Boulevard one morning on my way to work, next to a military truck filled with what looked like two dozen young, uniformed Marines sitting in the back holding their rifles with bayonets. At a stoplight, I waved at the Marines, and the young Marines smiled and waved back at me. On May 4, I turned thirty years old while the entire city of Los Angeles lived under a military-enforced nighttime curfew due to riots. Surreal, and so heartbreaking.

My trial with Stephen's parents started on May 15, 1992, shortly after Robert Reed, the television actor famous for his role as Mike Brady in *The Brady Bunch*, died from AIDS on May 12. My trial was my 1992 "vacation" from work. I had half-hoped that Lloyd and I would show up to an empty courtroom and win the trial by default. But Stephen's parents showed up. I ignored them in that wood-paneled courtroom. Each day in court, his mother sported a large religious cross on the chain around her neck. I thought to myself, "The bigger the religious cross, the bigger the hypocrite."

Jury selection fascinated me. Our trial judge, Dion Morrow, questioned potential jurors about whether they could be impartial in a case that involved a dispute between the parents of someone who died from AIDS and his surviving partner. One prospective juror went on a rant against homophobic discrimination, and how he had several gay friends whose partners had died from AIDS only to then be treated terribly by the partner's parents. I so wanted this man to be on my jury, but of course he was excused. Nevertheless, everyone who became a juror on my case heard what he had to say.

In my trial, we weren't allowed to mention anything about Stephen's parents' disability insurance fraud or their abusive treatment of Stephen's psychotherapist at his deposition, but Judge Morrow knew all about their character. That was good enough for me.

As the plaintiff, I put on my case first. My friends testified about the strength of my relationship with Stephen and our seven-and-a-half-year relationship together.

The nursing service testified that no assault of Stephen's mother and no abuse of Stephen occurred because nurses were present in my house twenty-four hours per day and were legally required to document and report any physical, mental, or emotional abuse. They said that their case notes only contained references about Stephen's mother's "stress and her problems accepting Stephen's terminal situation," and no negative notes about me.

Father Alexei, Stephen's priest from Saint Andrew Church, testified that on one of his visits to Stephen and his mother while I was at work, Stephen broke down into tears and said to her, "You will throw Christopher out into the street," and then said that he wanted to make a will to specify his burial wishes, but that his mother "would not let him call an attorney to make one." In front of the jury, Stephen's parents' attorneys objected and tried to prevent him from testifying by invoking Stephen's "priest-penitent" privilege, but the priest explained that this privilege only extends to private conversations between two people, not a conversation among three people. So the jury heard the testimony. I could see the jurors' growing dislike for Stephen's parents.

Guy, my psychotherapist, was the star witness. He testified about the twisted homophobic dynamics between parents and the surviving partners of people who died from AIDS. The judge and the jury leaned forward and hung on his every word.

Two Los Angeles Police Department officers testified that there was no group assault on Stephen's parents on the day that I tried to retrieve my belongings, and they placed into evidence the three-foot long green crowbar that Stephen's father used to attack my attorney, Paul. Judge Morrow held and stared at the large crowbar, his mouth agape.

I testified about what Stephen's parents had stolen from me, and how they had cremated Stephen against his wishes. I assigned damage values to each stolen item, and entered photos of each into evidence. I testified about how Stephen's mother had removed his Yale diplomas from our master bedroom, right in front of his eyes, five months before he died. I testified how she also transferred the title of Stephen's eleven-year-old car to herself before he died. I testified about my emotional distress, and how much I contributed financially to Stephen's and my household. When I disclosed my annual income, I looked right at Stephen's mother and she stared back at me, aghast, with a "holy shit I never knew that you made that much money" look written all over her face. So much for her assertion that I was a freeloader.

I testified that in addition to Stephen communicating his funeral wishes to his mother and his priest directly in my presence, he had also made an audiotape recording of them. Lloyd tried to introduce the tape into evidence so that it could be played for the jury. This set off bedlam in the courtroom as Stephen's parents' attorneys objected. Judge Morrow lost his temper, yelled at everyone, and sent the jurors out of the courtroom. But he didn't clear the courtroom of the visitors sitting in the audience, which by this point was packed with spectators as word about my trial spread throughout the downtown Los Angeles Superior Courthouse. I couldn't believe that strangers would sit in the audience just to watch the meshugaas of my court case, but the Courtroom Television Network, founded one year earlier, had apparently spurred quite an interest in live courtroom entertainment.

Judge Morrow called for a recess for the rest of the day so that he could listen to the tape and decide whether to allow it into evidence. As I left the courtroom, one of the audience members approached me and told me that he was a reporter for the *Los Angeles Times* and that he planned to write an article about my case. He wanted to interview me, but I told him that I wasn't ready to be interviewed. I rushed back to my office and immediately sought out Erwin Okun, Disney's Senior Vice President of Corporate Communications. I didn't want my lawsuit to create any public relations problems for Disney if it got into the press. After I explained to Erwin my lawsuit and the reporter's plan to write an article about it, he said to me, "Don't worry about this one bit. It sounds like you are in the right and will win this lawsuit. We have your back on this if you need it."

The next day, Judge Morrow ruled that Stephen's tape of his funeral wishes could not be played because it would be too prejudicial. But the jurors had heard that a tape existed, and saw my attorney try to place it into evidence, and heard the attorneys argue about it. That was good enough, and so we moved on and I finished my testimony.

Then, a juror sent a note to the judge. Judge Morrow sent the other jurors out of the courtroom. The one remaining juror had asked to be excused from the jury because he was too angry at Stephen's parents and he didn't feel that he could be objective in the case anymore. Judge Morrow excused the juror, and replaced him with one of the alternates.

The next witness that Lloyd called was Stephen's father. He was instantly combative with Lloyd from the witness stand. He was riled up and looked to me to be shaking a bit. He admitted, and even boasted, that they had stolen my belongings—selling some, throwing some in the trash, and taking the rest back to Yorktown.

Eventually, he blurted out, "Stephen wasn't gay." Then Judge Morrow stopped Lloyd's questioning, and he turned to Stephen's father and from the bench said to him, ever so kindly, gently, and with the greatest sensitivity, "Yes, Stephen, your son, he was gay. The other witnesses have already established this as a fact."

Then there was a pause, with the entire courtroom completely silent. Stephen's father sat there frozen on the witness stand, with Judge Morrow, the jurors, the attorneys, the court reporter and bailiff, Stephen's mother, the rapt courtroom audience, and me all watching him. A horrible, painful, dramatic courtroom moment. He didn't say anything. Lloyd didn't ask another question. The silence was deafening.

I knew in that instant that it was time for me to end my lawsuit. I had won. I had proved my point in standing up to Stephen's parents for dishonoring his wishes, for dishonoring my relationship with him, and for stealing my personal belongings. Seeing his father on the witness stand, still after all these years denying that Stephen was gay didn't make me angry. Instead, it made me feel incredibly sad. I finally understood why Stephen's parents had treated him, and me, so badly. I finally understood his lifelong strained and distant relationship with them and why they never visited him. I finally understood the dark center of the Vortex that they were sucked into. Neither of them could accept who their son was.

Stephen's parents' attorneys asked the judge for a recess, and then went into a side conference room with his parents. It looked as though the attorneys dragged them into that room against their will.

When they finally emerged from that conference room, the two attorneys asked Lloyd if I would be willing to settle the lawsuit. They said that Stephen's parents were ready to return my stolen belongings.

Next, Lloyd and I went into the side conference room to talk. Lloyd told me that we had Stephen's parents on the ropes, right where he wanted them. They were going to lose the lawsuit, and I would take them to the cleaners. I knew that all of this was true. I had been watching the eyes of the jurors during everyone's testimony and I could tell that they felt only contempt for his parents. But I didn't sue them for money. I didn't need their money, and I didn't want to take them to the cleaners. This lawsuit for me was about principles, and respect for Stephen, and me, and our relationship, and the return of my stolen personal belongings.

I also wanted to forgive his parents so that I could move on with my life. Yes, after everything that they had done to Stephen, and to me, and after this insane lawsuit, I wanted to forgive them. I needed to put vengeance behind me. I had discovered an incredible book at the Bodhi Tree Bookstore called *Forgiveness*, and its message was quite powerful for me: if you forgive someone, it actually frees you to be able to move forward. Forgiving actually helps the forgiver. This is true. Forgiveness also is a central, but unfortunately mostly ignored, tenet of the Roman Catholic Church. As for the forgiven, they must still live with what they have done.

I told Lloyd that it was time for us to settle. All six of us went into the side conference room. I told his parents that I would settle for the return of my personal belongings, including my diplomas, my piano and bench (which they shockingly told Judge Morrow were being held hostage since September 1991 by the gay real estate agent who had sold my house!), my clothing, my books and personal papers, my mail, my piano sheet music, and a few pieces of artwork, plus all of the proceeds from the sale of the house—the $7,071.84 in the court escrow account. And the large green crowbar. I definitely wanted the crowbar to save as a memento. I still have it. In addition, my settlement required Stephen's parents to follow his last wishes and purchase the plaque that he wanted in the Memorial Hall at the Basilica of the National Shrine of the Immaculate Conception at Catholic University in Washington, DC. Finally, my settlement required that they never contact me again. They agreed to all of it. They insisted as part of the settlement that we would all only "say nice things about each other" to the *Los Angeles Times* reporter who was covering our trial. I whispered to Lloyd, "Can I say that I thought it was 'nice' that they cashed Stephen's disability checks for six months after he died?" Lloyd glared at me and said "no."

As we settled the lawsuit on June 1, 1992, I forgave Stephen's parents and it freed me. That's what forgiving does. Forgiving is powerful. After all, these were the people who created Stephen, my wonderful partner, the first love of my life, whom I still missed terribly. Forgiveness was the fertilizer that allowed me to grow again. I said goodbye to them in that courtroom, and I wished them well. As agreed, they never contacted me again.

After Judge Morrow announced that my case had settled and dismissed the jurors, several of them crowded around me and Lloyd in the courtroom and asked us questions. Stephen's parents and their two attorneys instantly disappeared. Judge Morrow said to Lloyd and me, "Congratulations to you," and then invited Lloyd to stop by and discuss the case with him someday. As I suspected, the jurors were all on my side. The jurors raved about Guy, the star witness of my trial. The *Los Angeles Times* reporter left the courtroom disappointed that I had settled the case, and never wrote his article, but it could have consisted of two sentences:

Once upon a time, in case number BC 036940, in the Superior Court of the State of California for the County of Los Angeles, in Department 57 with Judge Dion Morrow presiding, a gay man fought back and kicked the asses of two homophobic parents from Yorktown, Virginia. Then he had the good sense to forgive them and move on with his life.

According to one of my judge friends who knows Judge Morrow, he remembered my case long after it settled and talked about it until he retired. Anyone can visit the basement of the Los Angeles Superior Court archives and peruse the case filings, as I did to refresh my memory while I wrote this memoir. My lawsuit occupies five volumes on microfiche and several hundred pages. The files are all available to the public and nothing is sealed.

After the settlement, I used the proceeds of the court escrow account distributed to me to send Lloyd, his wife, and their two young children on a vacation to Walt Disney World in Florida, with VIP Disney treatment, including cookies and milk delivered each night to their hotel room, one of my favorite indulgences at Disney World.

I celebrated the settlement with a low-key weekend trip for myself to Palm Springs. The searing heat and sun of the bone-dry desert while I relaxed in a swimming pool seemed the perfect place to commemorate that the storm's flooding was now receding from my life.

When Stephen's parents didn't abide by many of the terms of our settlement agreement, I forgave them for that, too. They "lost" two of my diplomas. They "lost" all of my clothing. The gay real estate agent returned my stolen piano that he had been concealing for nearly a year from me, but he "lost" its bench, proving that gay people make the best homophobes because of their negative tapes. They "lost" all my mail, including the wonderful pile of letters and cards sent by Stephen's and my friends after he died. They "lost" many of my personal papers, too. Nearly everything that Stephen's parents returned to me came back damaged in some way, scratched, broken, or incomplete. Their behavior was spiteful and sad, but it no longer hurt. It was the best that they could do.

But then I had to put forgiveness on hold. I learned that Stephen's parents somehow had conspired to steal $17,327 of hidden proceeds from the house sale from me. I also learned that they hadn't purchased the required plaque for Stephen at the Memorial Hall at the Basilica of the National Shrine of the Immaculate Conception at Catholic University in Washington, DC. Stephen's parents' continued dishonest behavior reignited my fury. So, back to court I went.

My subsequent Motion to Enforce Settlement Agreement was like the last scene of a horror movie, the moment when the hero thinks that the monster is dead but it's really not, and it comes back to life, and the hero has to kill it one more time. My motion was our last dramatic courtroom showdown to finally subdue the monster.

It turned out that Stephen's parents and the gay real estate agent had somehow convinced the escrow company to withhold $17,327 from the house sale proceeds for alleged California state income taxes that they knew weren't ever going to be due. This, I believe, was done on purpose to hide money from the court and me, in case I won the lawsuit. Now that our case had settled, Stephen's parents somehow convinced the escrow company to divert these funds directly to them without going as required through the court escrow account. Otherwise, the court would have distributed them to me because, pursuant to our settlement agreement, I was to receive all of the house sale proceeds. This is a fraudulent action that the court receiver should have caught, and prevented, but he didn't and you can probably guess why. Somehow Lloyd figured out that all of this had happened.

Pages of legal briefs from both sides argued about my missing piano bench, and whether pianos are sold with benches or not (they are), and whether my missing piano bench ever existed even though a photo of my piano and its bench had already been admitted into evidence during the trial. In exasperation, Stephen's parents' attorneys offered to pay for a new piano bench with their own money, and sent me a check for $200. The attorneys were waving the proverbial white flag. In more pages of briefs, we debated why his parents hadn't yet ordered, or paid the required $1,000 for Stephen's memorial plaque in the National Shrine of the Immaculate Conception. They accused me of "harassment," and argued "Zyda simply does not want this action to end."

Stephen's parents' attorneys did their best to depict me as the bad guy. For example, they wrote, "[Stephen's parents] also believed [settling] would bring to a close a costly trial which promised to drag on endlessly while Mr. Zyda attempted to litigate 'damages' over items like a garden hose, an ashtray, a can of WD-40, and other 'evidence' he preferred (sic) to this Court, while [Stephen's father], a man in his 70s…was forced to sit through this debacle 3,000 miles from home while being on dialysis more than ten hours a day, looked on."

Ten hours a day for dialysis? Really?

Another example: "Zyda simply won't accept the fact that this litigation is over, and instead is fighting to keep it alive by accusing everyone who was unfortunate enough to be associated with it of a host of misdeeds."

Hmmm, the attorneys now considered themselves unfortunate? Interesting.

And one final example: "To add insult to injury, Zyda has refused to pay the $73.50, which he was obligated to pay for half the cost of insuring the shipment of goods. Despite its demand, payment has not been received."

These were all feeble attempts to distract from the fraud committed by Stephen's parents and their accomplices, and I enjoyed every one of them. Truth and honesty finally were winning. The proverbial karmic chickens had come home to roost on all of them.

Unfortunately, because of work, I wasn't able to attend the final courtroom showdown. But it was epic. According to Lloyd, Judge Morrow blew a gasket at Stephen's parents and pronounced something along the lines of, "You either pay this entire amount to Mr. Zyda right now, or we are going to conduct this entire trial all over again from the beginning, starting tomorrow morning." They immediately paid the $17,327 to me as ordered by the judge. They also had Federal Expressed a cashier's check for $1,000 for Stephen's memorial plaque in the National Shrine of the Immaculate Conception three days before the court hearing—just in the nick of time—so they could claim at the hearing they actually paid it. Otherwise, I'm fairly sure that Judge Morrow would have clobbered them even more for continuing to dishonor Stephen, "their son."

One final Shakespearean hurlyburly of my life now over. Finally, the battle foreshadowed by the witches in *Macbeth* was lost and won.

Then, and only then, did I pay Stephen's parents the $73.50 I owed them for the shipping insurance.

I spent hundreds of thousands of dollars on legal fees over the course of fifteen months defending Stephen's and my relationship. The outcome was worth every penny. At long last, I finally got to know Stephen's parents.

As for the plaque for Stephen in the Memorial Hall at the Basilica of the National Shrine of the Immaculate Conception in Washington, DC, Stephen's parents purchased the smallest possible plaque. But it's there. I visited and saw it with my own eyes because I always feared that they would cancel the order and get a refund. So congratulations to them for finally following their son's last wishes, even if I had to legally beat them into submission to do it. Of course, they never made an AIDS quilt panel for Stephen. I knew that they wouldn't, and that's why I purposely didn't include Stephen's directive to not have one in our settlement agreement. I knew that I didn't need to require them to not do something that they would never do anyway.

Not catching one bit of a break, and while still wrestling with my grief, I went straight from the end of my crazy lawsuit into a plum and highly stressful work assignment drafting a presentation for Frank Wells, Disney's president and chief operating officer, to give at the upcoming high-profile Allen & Company Media Conference in Sun Valley, Idaho, in early July. When I finished drafting it, Frank insisted that I accompany him to the conference in case he needed to make any last-minute changes. I was excited to have this opportunity to witness firsthand how this incredibly brilliant and successful man worked. At the conference, Frank and I practiced his speech over and over while walking around a grassy field outside the Sun Valley Lodge. We grilled each other with potential questions and answers. Then, as we walked into the lodge for his presentation, Frank turned to me and said, "I want you to sit in the front row, Chris. If I get a question that I can't answer, I'm going to call on you to answer it."

During Frank's presentation I sat in the front row, as instructed, in between Warren Buffett, the investment guru and Chairman and Chief Executive of Berkshire Hathaway on one side of me, and Don Keough, the President and Chief Operating Officer of Coca-Cola and recent owner of Columbia Pictures, on the other side of me. I wasn't grieving at that moment; instead I was terrified.

I prayed that no one would ask Frank a question that he couldn't answer, because if Disney's President—who, by the way, was also a Rhodes Scholar—didn't know the answer, I was fairly sure that I wouldn't either.

After his presentation, which went off without a hitch, Frank thanked me for my work and told me to stay in Sun Valley and enjoy the rest of the conference over the weekend.

"Be sure to go ice skating," he said.

Sun Valley Lodge featured a beautiful outdoor ice skating rink, which operated even during the hot summer. It was ninety degrees in the sun, but the ice was perfect and I ice skated as ordered by Frank (just as in the days of Walt, Disney was a first-name company). I loved it. It felt so good to enjoy another weekend of fun relaxation.

When I returned to Los Angeles, I took Monday off, and Frank actually called me at home to thank me and tell me that I had done a great job. Such an amazing, classy man.

The week after Sun Valley, my corporate communications colleague Dan, who had written the Howard Ashman dedication for *Beauty and the Beast*, and I had lunch in the Rotunda, Disney's executive dining room. At one point, we discussed a friend of mine who was dying from AIDS, named Frank, who was an avid fan of Disney animation. Frank had been too sick to see *Beauty and the Beast* during its run in the theaters, and he desperately wanted to see the film but he would likely die before Disney released it on home video a few months later. As I lamented over Frank's dilemma, Dan interjected, "Why don't we ask Jeffrey if you can borrow a copy of the film?"

Dan was surely joking with me. By "Jeffrey," Dan meant Jeffrey Katzenberg, the chairman of the Walt Disney Studios. Katzenberg was many levels above me at Disney. I didn't think that he even knew who I was other than a finance guy who occasionally showed up in meetings to discuss his Wall Street presentations. I felt that Dan's suggestion that Jeffrey Katzenberg would somehow allow me to "borrow" an advance home video copy of *Beauty and the Beast* so that my friend Frank could watch it before he died was absolutely ludicrous. Asking Disney to lend out a home video copy of one of its blockbuster animated films before it was released to the public was akin to a random stranger dropping by Buckingham Palace and asking Queen Elizabeth II to lend out one of her favorite tiaras. These animated films were the company's crown jewels. Disney literally locked them in a guarded vault.

"Ha, ha, ha," I replied, convinced that Dan was joking with me. "That will never happen."

Dan, who has a great sense of humor, joked with me all the time so I didn't believe him. "I'm not joking," he responded, with a serious look on his face. "I'm going to ask Jeffrey."

Well, even if Dan was serious, I was sure that the company would never allow it. "I'll be a good reference for you when you get fired, Dan," I replied.

A couple of days later, Dan appeared in my office with an unmarked VHS videotape, and he delicately set it down in the middle of my desk and smiled at me.

"Here it is," he said. "You need to get this tape back to me in two days."

I screamed, "Are you kidding me?"

I was floored. I could not believe that Jeffrey Katzenberg approved this. Disney lent me one of its crown jewels! I was over the moon. I couldn't wait for the end of the workday so that I could surprise Frank at his apartment that night with the tape.

This was the most wonderful gift that anyone could have given Frank, who by July 1992 was completely bedridden. Frank watched *Beauty and the Beast* twice, and loved it. I didn't let the unmarked tape out of my sight, and I returned it promptly as promised. Dan and I both were emotional that we were able to fulfill my friend's dying wish. Frank died shortly afterward, on August 18.

At the end of July, I came home to a terrible message on my home answering machine. Gigi, a longtime friend of my parents, said that my sister had experienced a brain hemorrhage and was in intensive care at Valley Presbyterian Hospital, that the situation was grave, and that my parents were on their way to the hospital from Las Vegas. Just as I was starting to believe that the storm was no longer flooding my life, it came back in an instant with a giant wave.

I called my brother Michael in Carmel and told him to get to Los Angeles as soon as possible. I didn't give my brother the option to say no. I called Jane, Joan's ex-partner, too. Then, I rushed to the hospital's intensive care unit, saw Joan unconscious in a coma, and received a full medical report from the doctors while I waited for my parents and brother to arrive.

The doctors delivered terrible news to me. Joan's brain was full of blood and completely destroyed, according to two brain specialists. They showed me the CAT scan, and all I could see was the image of a solid pool of blood, no discernable brain matter at all. The specialists told me that they could identify no brain activity. She now was unable to breathe on her own, kept alive only by machines. Both of her kidneys had failed. She had been found at her house by Jeff, an old high school friend, the football quarterback who had once dated her long ago and whose mother was my first piano teacher. She apparently had suffered the hemorrhage anywhere between twenty-four and forty-eight hours before Jeff found her. Once again, I felt the waters engulfing me.

My sister and I hadn't spoken for more than one and a half years, and now here she was in front of me, in a coma, essentially dead. My parents, who had also not spoken to me for more than one and a half years, were on their way. My brother Michael, who had not spoken to my parents or my sister in at least seven years, was on his way, too. We were about to have one horrible estranged family reunion.

When they all finally arrived at the hospital, I rounded up the doctors so that we could hear Joan's grave prognosis together. They told us that she would never recover. I asked almost all of the questions. My parents were in too much shock to ask much. After the doctors' devastating report, my parents, brother, and I had the excruciating family meeting that no family should ever have to endure, and we agreed to remove Joan from life support and donate her organs. We all signed the paperwork.

But before the hospital pulled the plug, I insisted that we all hold hands with her, as a family, one last time. On one side of the hospital bed, I held her right hand. On the other side of the hospital bed stood my parents and brother. My brother held her left hand. My mother stood in between my brother and my father, holding their hands. Our last time together as a family.

From across the bed, I looked across my sister's unconscious body at my parents and brother on the other side. Through my tears, I bemoaned our screwed-up family dynamics. Why couldn't we just love each other for who we are? What is so difficult about this? A lifetime of pain about my family's dysfunction boiled right out of me in that intensive care unit. My parents and brother stared at me and didn't say a word as I lectured away, crying. I was telling the truth and they knew it. Then, I said that I just wanted us to have a few last minutes together as a family, one more time, and for everyone to be quiet. When I was satisfied that we had spent enough time holding hands together silently as a family, I said we could all let go of each other. No one said a thing. Then, the hospital staff wheeled my sister away.

Joan died Friday, July 31, 1992, almost three weeks after her fortieth birthday, in what should have been the summer of her life, just like Stephen.

My parents went to pieces about Joan's death, as expected. I took care of everything for them, but we barely spoke. After all, I was the family expert on death since I had been dealing with death all around me for nearly ten years. I planned Joan's funeral and reception. I played Martha and the Vandellas "Heat Wave" and "Dancing in the Streets"—two of her favorite songs—in the Roman Catholic church at the San Fernando Mission. Joan's ex-partner Jane gave a moving eulogy for her, in which my parents finally learned that their daughter was a lesbian after she had lived her whole life hiding in the closet from them out of fear of their disapproval. The San Fernando Mission's presiding priest was mortified by the music and the eulogy, and yelled at me afterward. I broke so many of the rules for a Roman Catholic funeral and I didn't care. At the reception afterward, someone took a photo of me sitting on an ottoman, my hairline dreadfully receding, looking off into the distance. Still in shock, I was thinking to myself, "Will the clouds finally part and the sun ever break through?" In August 1992, Annie Lennox's song "Why" flooded the airwaves, an appropriate song to mark my sister's passing. Why?

Guess what the *Chicago Tribune* did when Joan died? One of her close *Tribune* colleagues wrote a beautiful obituary at my request and submitted it to the paper's news editor for publishing. This editor, who had joined the *Tribune* as a reporter shortly after Joan did, had also been my sister's friend. In fact, this news editor and his whole family had lived at Joan's apartment with her for weeks when he first moved to Chicago and hadn't yet found a permanent place to live. Well, what did this friend, this editor do? He "spiked" Joan's obituary—journalism-speak for "killing" a story. This editor couldn't be bothered to acknowledge and honor his friend and former colleague, my sister who had housed him and his family, even though the newspaper routinely published obituaries for former employees. One last chance for someone there to choose to do the right thing and they blew it. Fucking *Chicago Tribune*.

This unleashed my anger at the *Tribune*. Not only had this newspaper discriminated against and fired my sister and destroyed her journalism career, sending her life into an ever-descending spiral that finally had resulted in her death, but now it couldn't even be bothered to print an obituary for her. I eventually let this anger go, and trusted that somehow, someday, karma would mete out justice to the *Tribune* and everyone involved in my sister's vicious outing and firing, whether it be a future company bankruptcy, or dead-end journalism careers or unhappy lives for all the perpetrators, or perhaps a future implosion of the entire newspaper industry. I'm afraid my capacity for forgiveness has its limits, especially when my big sister is involved.

I was devastated for not having been in any contact with Joan before she died, but eventually I forgave myself. I focused on my happy memories of her, when she was young and so full of life, before the *Chicago Tribune* fired her for being a lesbian, before life beat her down and made her so angry. My big sister who took me to my first concert, the 5th Dimension, at the Universal Amphitheater, and who owned a beige two-door 1963 Mercury Comet convertible, her pride and joy. One of my favorite photos of Joan is of her sitting in the back seat of that car in front of her house, with the convertible roof down, wearing sunglasses, smiling, and flashing a peace sign. Quintessential Los Angeles, and Joan. That's how I will always remember her.

I moved out of Sandy's condominium and into Joan's house to handle her estate at my parents' request. I divided up her belongings and found good homes for everything. I gave many of them to Jane, even though she had split up with Joan two years earlier. Jane adopted Joan's cat. I treated Jane the way I wished Stephen's parents had treated me. Among Joan's papers, I came across the last words that she wrote before her brain hemorrhage, in her own handwriting, and I kept them as proof that she still had some hope for herself even as she was drowning in her storm. It said:

> *"Think about that tomorrow! Tomorrow is such a long time—alas…looking ahead at my life and trying to think about how I'll spend the rest of it."*

I was now grieving the loss of two loved family members who had died during the past year. There had been so much death in my life over the past nearly ten years, during which time I had fought the world, and I was emotionally exhausted. I needed to take a break, a big break, and reset myself. It was time.

I started planning a vacation to Australia to jumpstart my life. I purposely planned my departure for New Year's Eve 1992 so that I could usher in 1993 in a different country, in a different hemisphere, as far away from Los Angeles as possible, in the middle of summer in the land down under, the opposite of Los Angeles's winter, and begin an entirely different and huge life reset in my new year. My theme songs as I planned my trip were Janet Jackson's "Escapade" and "Roam" by the B-52s. Both songs had been released in 1989, but I was just discovering them.

Anthony Perkins, the famous actor, died from AIDS on September 12. It was around this time that I stopped attending my weekly grief therapy support groups at AIDS Project Los Angeles and the Shanti Foundation. I finished my grief hypnotherapy with Dr. Jackie, too. I also reduced the frequency of my shiatsu treatments with Christine. I stopped going to the Bodhi Tree Bookstore so often. I stopped going to Saint Andrew Church, too. But I still saw my therapist Guy every week. I was starting to feel a bit better, and I looked forward to my New Year's Eve departure.

In the November 1992 election, I switched political parties and voted for Bill Clinton. I didn't so much leave the Republican Party, but rather the Republican Party left me as it continued its death spiral. I didn't want to be a member of a political party that treated gay people as second class citizens. 1992, from my perspective, also seemed to be when the gloves really came off in the culture wars. As one example, on the ballot in November 1992, in Colorado, was Amendment 2, which banned state and local governments from passing laws to prevent discrimination against gays and lesbians. It was called the "Hate Amendment," and Colorado voters passed it by a wide margin of victory.

In early December, I finally went on my first date one-and-a-half years after Stephen's death. A handsome blond-haired man named Max who owned a home security business. At the end of our date, I had already decided that there would be no second one because I just wasn't ready. As I went to hug him and say goodnight, Max said to me, "There are three things that you need to know about me before our next date. I'm HIV positive, I wear a hair piece, and I have a nine-inch dick."

I was dumbfounded. Welcome, Chris, to David Bowie's "Modern Love" and the Los Angeles 1992 gay dating pool in the age of AIDS. Being single and dating again was going to be a challenge for me. The handsome blond man and I never had a second date, but he did become my friend, and he installed the security systems on two of my subsequent houses. I highly recommend his work.

Finally, on New Year's Eve 1992, as it seemed that the storm's flooding was truly behind me, I departed on my trip to Australia. I have a photo of me pointing to my flight on the departure board in the Los Angeles Airport's Tom Bradley International Terminal, wearing an Australian outback hat and a UCLA sweatshirt and sporting my new moustache. I was pointing at my new life, my life past the storm. I flew to Cairns, Australia, through Honolulu, where I had a two-hour layover around midnight. I brought a bottle of Veuve Clicquot champagne on the flight with me (back when you could carry on more than three ounces of liquids!), and I shared it with my row in coach. When I arrived in Honolulu, just like Billy Idol in "Dancing With Myself," I danced to celebrate the New Year in the nearly empty terminal, listening to CeCe Peniston and En Vogue through earphones on my brand new portable compact disc player. Even though it was midnight, I could sense the skies clearing above me—finally. CeCe Peniston's 1992 hit song "Finally" underscored my hopefulness. For the first time in a very long time, I was looking forward to a new year.

CHAPTER 11
CLEARING

I LANDED AT CAIRNS Airport as Australia's 1993 New Year's celebrations continued in the middle of its tropical summer. My taxi driver drove on the left side of the street as we departed the airport, causing me a moment of jetlagged panic until I remembered where I was. I stayed at a gay hotel in Cairns, called BeeBee's, where I made several new friends. Right away, I learned that Australian beer has a much higher alcohol content than American beer. Of course, I learned this lesson the hard way, hangover included.

Restarting my life in Australia with the storm starting to clear was just what I needed. This was my first vacation since August 1990, when Stephen and I went to Southwest Harbor, Maine. My Australia trip theme was "carpe diem, try everything new." I went scuba diving, for the first time, at the Great Barrier Reef. I went river rafting for the first time, on the Tully River, which has some exhilarating class-four rapids, hooking me forever on rafting's adrenaline rushes. I hired a yacht to sail me around the Great Barrier Reef, where the water was so clear that I could see into the water thirty feet down below me. I saw an early screening of the soon-to-be-classic gay Australian film *The Adventures of Priscilla, Queen of the Desert* before it was released in theaters in the United States. After Cairns, I flew to Sydney, where I attended a Mozart concert at the iconic Sydney Opera House. I bodysurfed at Bondi Beach. I explored the city's gay nightlife. By the end of my trip, three Australian men wanted to follow me back to the US and date me—one from Cairns and two from Sydney. Completely impractical, but life-affirming for my still-grieving thirty-year-old ego.

As I explored Australia, I didn't notice that Rudolf Nureyev, the talented ballet dancer who bravely defected from the Soviet Union in 1961 and who served as the dance director for the Paris Opera Ballet, died from AIDS on January 6, 1993, at the same time I was learning how to scuba dive at the Great Barrier Reef. Then, Arthur Ashe, the tennis champion who spent years fighting discrimination against African Americans in his sport, died from AIDS one month after Nureyev, on February 6, 1993. The AIDS pandemic continued to rage around me and, by the end of 1993, according to amfAR, AIDS cases reported to date in the US would be 360,909 with 234,225 deaths, a mortality rate of nearly 65 percent, and the CDC would estimate that approximately 757,000 Americans were living with HIV.[11,27]

After I returned to Los Angeles, I took a big step forward in my healing when my friend Jim, an avid country western fan, took me to a gay country western bar in the San Fernando Valley called the Rawhide and introduced me to a whole new world: country western music and dancing. All with gay men and lesbians. This new gay country western world fascinated me, so different from the West Hollywood world of my twenties. I quickly had a group of gay country western friends: Doug, Tim, Randy, Tom, and Doug #2. I called them my posse, shorthand for my made-up name of the "Rodeo Posse of Farmington, New Mexico," even though none of us had anything to do with New Mexico. We became inseparable.

One weekend night, we went to In Cahoots, a country dance club in Glendale, where Tim McGraw was performing before he became a huge country music star. Being the instigator, I asked one of the waitresses if our group of gay men could join the club's other patrons two-stepping on the dance floor. She replied, "Of course, that would be so cool," so we all went out and danced. We overwhelmingly experienced smiles, thumbs up, and support. During one of his breaks, Tim McGraw came down from the stage to hang out with us. So wonderful.

An even bigger step forward in my healing occurred one night when my posse invited me to a professional rodeo exhibition in Long Beach that featured bull riders and bareback bronc riders. My new friends told me about the International Gay Rodeo Association (IGRA), a group that sponsored amateur gay and lesbian rodeo competitions across the country. As I watched the exhibition and learned about gay and lesbian rodeos, a crazy lightbulb went off in my head. I said something along the lines of, "I could learn how to do this."

"No, you couldn't," they unanimously responded. As soon as I heard my new friends say that I couldn't do rodeo, it made me want to do rodeo more. This is just how I am.

So I quietly investigated at the Burbank equestrian center near my office. Eventually, I heard of a man named Art, a former rodeo competitor, who managed some horse stables on Rigali Avenue in the Atwater Village area just east of the Los Angeles River near Griffith Park. I tracked him down. By that time Art hadn't done anything related to rodeo for years. He thought I was crazy. I thought I was partly crazy, too. But the allure of doing something no one would ever expect me to do, including me, overpowered me as a bold carpe diem statement that I was living my life again and pushing myself to move further through my grief. I convinced him to teach me rodeo, and I promised him that he could teach me how to ride a horse, too.

Art taught me how to "tuck and roll," an important foundation for rodeo where you are regularly thrown unceremoniously to the ground. In my lessons, Art would have me bring my horse to a gallop in the paddock at the stables, then he would yell "jump" and I would have to dive off the horse, tuck myself in the air, somersault before I hit the ground, and roll in the dirt to a safe landing. Over, and over, and over. Terrifying, but so much fun, too. I came home from my rodeo lessons black and blue and caked in dirt, but happy.

Art's daughter Jessica taught me how to actually ride a horse. She let me ride Fling, an American Quarter Horse. Two or three times per week after work, I would ride Fling from the Atwater Village stables into Griffith Park by traversing a dirt path carved into the side of the Los Angeles River's concrete channel down to the river, then trotting alongside the river past the storm drains painted to look like cats, then carefully wading across the river since there was no nearby bridge, and finally into the park through a tunnel underneath the Golden State Freeway. Fling and I would canter and gallop around the various horse trails in the park, behind the old zoo, and all the way up to the peaks of the Hollywood Hills, the outdoor settings for dozens of films and television shows. I loved Fling. One day while I crossed the Los Angeles River, Fling lost his footing in a deep patch of water and fell over. I quickly jumped off headfirst and tucked and rolled into the river, and, to my germophobe horror, briefly swam in my hometown's famous, completely polluted waterway. Fling promptly got himself back up and then waited in the middle of the river, looking at me. I could see the judgment in his eyes as I stood in front of him drenched head to toe. Another carpe diem moment. How many people can say that they actually swam in the Los Angeles River? I took three showers when I got home.

I competed in bareback bronc riding in the gay rodeo circuit a few times. The adrenaline rush lasted for hours, better than any drug. Nothing made me feel more alive, and more scared, than sitting in the chute, on top of the horse, waiting for the gate to open. What happened next was always a blur but it would leave me wired for hours. The horse would charge out of the gate so fast, while bucking, with me trying to balance and not touch the horse with my free hand and with my cowboy hat jammed down on top of my head, and then almost instantly it would be over. Me lying on the ground in some contorted position. Bruised, but happy. I was a living, breathing version of the cowboy on a bucking bronco that was on Stephen's final birthday cake. More importantly, I was living my life. I never did manage to stay on the horse for the full six seconds but this didn't matter. At 5'11" and 195 pounds, I was far too tall and heavy to ever be a serious competitor. If you ever watch rodeo, you'll notice that the best bareback bronc and bull riding competitors are all around 5'7" and about 150 pounds.

I also learned about the interesting gay rodeo subculture. Gays and lesbians, many who lived on ranches and farms in remote locations, traveled from all over the country to compete in and watch these gay rodeos. These events featured the classic rodeo activities of bareback bronc riding, bull riding, barrel racing, and steer wrestling. But they also had fun nontraditional events such as steer decorating and goat dressing. Steer decorating required a team of two, where one teammate lassoed a steer and held him in place while the other teammate tied a red ribbon on the steer's tail. Goat dressing involved teams of two that competed to put a pair of underwear on a goat in the fastest possible time. Rodeo competitors were protected from getting hurt by rodeo clowns, some of whom were dressed up as flamboyant drag queens, including one particularly charismatic drag queen from Texas whom I adored named Chili Pepper. At night, the gay rodeos hosted parties and dances where the country western music playlist of my life blared away: "Chattahoochie," "Every Little Thing," "What Part of No," "Ain't Goin' Down ('Til the Sun Comes Up)," "One More Last Chance," Boot Scootin' Boogie," "Life's a Dance," and others. This eye-opening detour for me into gay rodeo helped rejuvenate my life. Over time, I made gay cowboy friends all over the country, including three handsome real-life cowboys whom I once met at the Oklahoma City gay rodeo as we sheltered in a hotel while an actual tornado passed through the city. All three wanted to date me, the city slicker finance guy, and one of them told me that he would sell his farm in Missouri and move to Los Angeles to be with me. The experience of being fawned over by three handsome authentic cowboys fed my thirty-one-year-old ego.

Then there was "The Dance." At the beginning of every gay rodeo, right after playing the national anthem, a rider-less horse would enter the arena to the tune of Garth Brooks's emotional hit "The Dance" while everyone remained standing to honor people who had died from AIDS. This gay rodeo ritual turned me into a bawling, blubbering, emotional mess. Every single time. Just gut-wrenching. The loss of Stephen, Joan, and so many others over the past nearly ten years was still so raw for me. I was hardly alone. Brooks's poignant song left everyone in the rodeo arena with tears streaming down their faces.

Gay rodeo saved me. It made me realize that one day life would be all right again. I was on my way.

In early 1993, I received a large bonus and a promotion at work, and I moved into a larger office in the Team Disney building, underneath the giant statue of Doc, one of the seven dwarfs from *Snow White*. After paying down a decent chunk of the debt I had accumulated caring for Stephen, I used part of my bonus to buy a brand new blue Chevrolet Silverado 1500 extended cab pickup truck for cash, and I said goodbye to my old dented black Mercury Lynx. My 1992 life-changing slap from Jessie, my trip to Australia, and my new hobby of competing in rodeos had accelerated my turning flywheel and my love of life again.

But I completely bombed at dating. I kept telling myself, "Who wants to date a thirty-one-year-old widower? What man will really ever understand everything that I lived through in my twenties? I am damaged emotional goods in so many ways." I also compared every man to Stephen, for whom I still grieved. I felt no man could really compete with him, the first love of my life. I forced myself to go through a bit of the dating ritual because I didn't want to be alone forever. But some weekend nights, I stayed home and cried to Natalie Cole's "Miss You Like Crazy" and Whitney Houston's "Didn't We Almost Have it All." I could hardly get past the first or second date with anyone. I wasn't good at dating in 1983 before I met Stephen, and I wasn't good at it in 1993 either. I still wasn't ready.

In February 1993, I received a letter from my father. In the months since Joan's death, while handling her estate, I had many uneasy conversations with my parents because I was still quite hurt and angry about their abandonment of Stephen and me as he died. I kept my telephone conversations with them brief and only about Joan's estate matters. But here was a letter to me, addressed to me in my father's handwriting. My father never wrote letters to anyone.

I opened it, and inside was a hand-written apology to me, from my father but written on behalf of both of my parents. I sat down to read it in my sister's living room and I couldn't believe its contents. He apologized for them abandoning me in my time of need. He apologized for them judging me for being gay. He apologized for the terrible things that my mother had said to me in anger on the telephone before Stephen died. He wrote that they had never seriously considered getting an abortion when my mother was pregnant with me, but that I was an unexpected child, and they had always considered me a wonderful addition to our family and were thankful that they had me. He explained that in the months since Joan's death, and because of her death, they had done a lot of research about homosexuality. They spoke to several priests, and these priests said that they should accept me for who I am and love me unconditionally. They spoke to several doctors, including a geneticist, and learned that homosexuality occurs everywhere in nature, in every species, and is not a choice. They spoke to several of their friends and learned that nearly every one of these friends had a gay or lesbian member in their family tree somewhere. In the process, my mother also learned that one of her favorite longtime work colleagues was gay. My father concluded his letter by saying that they both loved me very much and missed me, and they wanted me to be in their lives again if I would allow it, but that they would understand if I never wanted to be in contact with them again. My father ended the letter by inviting me to visit them at their home in Las Vegas. My mother signed her name at the bottom of the letter, too.

This letter blew my mind and brought tears to my eyes. First and foremost, there was the sheer fact that he wrote the letter, rather than my mother, who usually handled all matters of the heart. My father, the engineer, rarely expressed his emotions, but here he was pouring himself out in his letter.

And my parents' months of research about homosexuality? Just amazing. But thoroughly researching a subject was absolutely something that my disciplined valedictorian parents would do. They had completed a journey of discovery far beyond their humble, rigid, Vauxhall, New Jersey, roots. I cried my eyes out. I was so proud of them. They had embraced unconditional love. I knew that I needed to see them as soon as possible. I instantly forgave them for everything.

In that moment, I was no longer an orphan. My mother and father became my mom and dad again.

I flew to Las Vegas the next weekend and reconciled with my mom and dad. We hugged each other and we all cried. I had never seen my dad cry before. We had long talks about everything—our family, Stephen and his death, my lawsuit with his parents, what it was like for me to be gay, my finance career and Disney, and my new interest in rodeo. My parents finally had learned to see the shades of color in the world, instead of only black and white. They told me that they were unhappy living in Las Vegas and wanted to move back to California, to Carpinteria Beach near Santa Barbara where we had often vacationed as a family during my childhood. I encouraged them to do this. These were the first real, adult, mature conversations that my mom, dad, and I ever had together in our lives.

At one point during that weekend, they took me to see a show at the three-year-old Mirage Hotel, built by the Mirage Resorts cofounders and casino moguls Elaine and Steve Wynn. The Siegfried and Roy show, with their famous white tigers. As we drove to the hotel, my mom gleefully boasted to me from the front seat of the car:

"You know, Chris, Siegfried and Roy are partners. They are gay. They have been a couple for a very long time. And they're performing at the Mirage making millions of dollars. Isn't that fantastic?"

Then she winked at me. I tried to absorb her new worldly outlook. It sure was a whole new world in the Zyda family.

I completely forgave my parents, but to make sure we were on the same page, I asked them to sign an agreement of rules we would all follow in our relationship going forward. A settlement agreement of sorts. They willingly and instantly agreed. Rule number one was "unconditional love only." From that weekend on, we enjoyed a real, adult, mature relationship of equals. Unfortunately, no one can take back hurtful words said in anger. In the wake of such missteps, all people can do is choose to apologize, forgive, heal, and move forward. Too often, this proves impossible, as people rarely have the courage my dad displayed in writing that letter. But as George Eliot wrote, "It's never too late to be what you might have been." My mom and dad moved back to California and bought a house in Carpinteria. I had nearly five more years with my dad, and eleven more years with my mom, and I cherished every minute.

◆◆◆

THROUGHOUT 1993, MY FINANCE career continued to accelerate. The early 1990s were the dawn of alternative investments in the institutional investment world. Hedge funds, portable alpha, distressed and credit, private equity, venture capital, and real estate. All of it incredibly fascinating to me. I studied hard so that I could stay on top of these emerging investment trends. I was especially drawn to distressed and credit investing, venture capital, and the emerging internet industry. Through all of these new investments, I made several good friends including the distressed credit genius John Angelo, who cofounded the successful Angelo Gordon & Co., and Meryl Witmer, a brilliant woman whose small-cap equity hedge fund made Disney a fortune, and who now sits on the board of directors of Warren Buffett's Berkshire Hathaway and is also a longtime member of *Barron's* Roundtable.

At the age of thirty-one, now responsible for managing almost $2 billion of investments, I had entered the big leagues in the institutional investment world, and headhunters asked me regularly to interview for jobs at high profile endowments and foundations, all of which I turned down because I was so happy at Disney.

Instead, I dreamed of a promotion into an operating finance role at Walt Disney World and moving to Orlando. In Orlando in 1993, a great house cost around $100,000, a lot less than one in Los Angeles, plus there was no state income tax in Florida. Judson Green, Disney's former CFO, was now the president of Theme Parks and Resorts and he wanted me to join his finance team in Orlando. But Richard Nanula, Judson's successor and the current CFO, wanted me to stay in my role in Burbank. Richard treated me so well in my position that I stayed put.

Five years into my career at Disney, I was far down the road of a successful corporate finance executive and far afield from the writing career I had abandoned in 1986. But my investor relations responsibilities sometimes allowed me a creative writing outlet. My colleague Kelley and I ghostwrote humorous fictitious shareholder letters for Richard to read at the company's annual stockholders' meetings to illustrate how well Disney stock had performed for investors over long time periods. In one shareholder meeting, our fictitious shareholder letter, playing on the recent fall of Soviet Communism, came from a Bulgarian man whose father had purchased some Disney stock and hid the stock certificate in a vault in his Bulgarian village during the Cold War, where the certificate sat untouched for decades. When Communism fell, the Bulgarian man discovered his father's long-lost stock certificate, realized that he was a multimillionaire, and then promptly went out and bought Levi's jeans for his entire village. Clearly fake.

Except CNN didn't think that it was fake. The CNN reporter covering the shareholder meeting thought the Bulgarian villager story was real, and that night, Lou Dobbs reported the story on *Moneyline*, CNN's financial television show, as an uplifting story about the fall of communism. The next day, CNN called Disney to find out the name of the Bulgarian villager so that they could interview him for a follow-up story. Of course, the man didn't exist. That night, Lou Dobbs, with egg on his face, issued a retraction of the Bulgarian villager story on his show. Long before the term "fake news" was even invented, I accidentally fooled CNN.

In June 1993, at my weekly psychotherapy appointment with Guy, our usual back-and-forth conversation came to an unexpected pause. After some silence, Guy said, "I think that there's one more topic that you and I haven't discussed."

I was stumped; I couldn't think of anything. Guy and I had discussed everything under the sun about my life since early 1991.

I replied, "I can't think of anything. What is it?"

Guy responded, "You're done with therapy. You don't need to see me anymore. Get out of here."

Then Guy threw me out of his office in the middle of my hour, but he still made me pay him for a full session. That's the thing that I love about Guy. He never minces words. In that moment, Guy transformed from my psychotherapist into my lifelong friend.

With my therapy finished, I conducted a personal "damage assessment" of how the past ten years of the storm had permanently affected me in addition to changing the road that I took in my life.

First and foremost, I had developed a fear of sex. AIDS had fused sex to death in my mind. This deadly virus was now everywhere in the world around me, and I had to learn how to navigate having sex and enjoying it even though it felt like playing Russian roulette with bullets in four chambers of the gun. It was easy to completely protect yourself from AIDS; all you had to do was not have sex with anyone or kiss anyone. But could you do that and still live a human life? I couldn't. Practicing safe sex, the best advice from the medical community, didn't guarantee protection from AIDS. People had to draw their own line in the sand of the risks they were willing to take in order to live a full life and engage in sex with this lethal virus still in the world. I needed to do a lot of work for many more years to overcome these fears.

Next, bullies. I had no patience for bullies. Unfortunately, the world is full of them. Doctors who stole their patient's medicine. Thieves who lied in court. A health insurance company that denied medical claims in the hope that their policyholder would die and not fight back. There will always be people in the world who choose to do the wrong thing and seek to steal from the people around them. In my future life, I would encounter more bullies, but I was more than ready to fight them, and I did.

Next, homophobia. This became a lightning rod for me. Today, much less homophobia exists in the worlds in which I live, but it's still out there and something deep inside me is triggered whenever I encounter it. Yes, I have encountered it again, and in the most unlikely place, too: Hawai'i.

Finally, I suffer from survivor's guilt. Part of me still feels guilty that I remained healthy while Stephen, and so many others, died. I do not understand why I never tested HIV positive, the great unanswered question of my life. The hypochondriac in me still believes that someday I will seroconvert. All I can conclude is that the universe has other plans for me. But when I think about Stephen and all the people that I knew who were lost to AIDS, the guilt of surviving really hits me. It stops me in my tracks. I miss them all, mowed down so long before their primes. I am, in fact, AIDS affected. But I do know that life is for the living and, guilty though I may feel, I appreciate being alive. That gets me moving again.

The winds really started to change for gays and lesbians in the early 1990s. The Third National March on Washington for Lesbian and Gay Rights occurred on April 25, 1993. Over one million people attended this time, thirteen times the number who participated in the first march in 1979, and more than three times the number who participated in the second march in 1987. Jackie Goldberg became the first openly lesbian woman elected to the Los Angeles City Council on April 20, 1993.

Then, on October 1, 1993, President Bill Clinton instituted the "Don't Ask Don't Tell" policy for the US military, which allowed gays and lesbians to serve in the military as long as they didn't disclose their sexual orientation. Four months earlier, the Israeli military had allowed gays and lesbians to serve openly. Throughout the early 1990s, several countries in Europe also allowed gays and lesbians to serve openly in their militaries. The US military was playing catch-up, but it was progress. The world was really starting to change its attitudes.

After 1993's Old Topanga wildfire burned 16,800 acres in the Santa Monica Mountains and canyons all the way down to the Pacific Ocean at Malibu Beach, destroying 369 homes along the way, I spent Thanksgiving with my brother and his family in Carmel. I got to know Michael's college friends Bud and Susan, who both had been early employees at Apple and who lived a few blocks away. Susan was a well-connected chief financial officer in Silicon Valley, and seemingly knew everyone in the tech industry. She and I bonded over corporate finance, and we bored everyone else at the dinner table with our conversation.

Shortly after Tonya Harding's boyfriend famously clubbed the knees of Nancy Kerrigan, the Olympic ice skater, Los Angeles experienced its own clubbing. At 4:31 a.m. on January 17, 1994, all of Los Angeles was jolted awake with a strong magnitude 6.7 earthquake, which killed sixty people and caused widespread damage. The earthquake shook me from my bed and caused significant damage to my sister's house. A sculpture of three distressed ancient Corinthian Greek columns that I had recently purchased at the Pacific Design Center to remind me of my Greece vacation with Stephen fell off a desk and became really distressed—breaking into pieces on the floor. The new chips and cracks on the columns only added more patina to the sculpture after I glued it back together.

Los Angeles is a city of periodic earthquakes, but this one, named the Northridge Quake, was by far the largest since the February 9, 1971, magnitude 6.6 Sylmar Quake, which occurred when I was nine years old. Whenever Los Angeles has one of its large earthquakes, three things happen. First, people who have moved to Los Angeles from elsewhere, and particularly from the East Coast, freak out, their fears made even more terrifying by Lucy Jones, the earthquake queen and longtime California Institute of Technology seismologist, who then warns on television news programs about dozens or perhaps hundreds of upcoming aftershocks, and also fields questions on whether the earthquake might merely be just a small foreshock to the inevitable "big one" that someday will split the State of California in two along the San Andreas Fault line and plunge its entire coast into the frigid depths of the Pacific Ocean. Second, just as Lucy the earthquake queen predicts, the main earthquake indeed is followed by dozens, if not hundreds, of aftershocks over the next several weeks, sometimes even while Lucy speaks on live television, while the earth's tectonic plates settle into their new positions. These aftershocks cause all Angelenos to live in suspense waiting for the next earth tremor, which can occur at any moment. Third, after a large quake, Los Angeles home prices plummet, particularly in the city's hillside neighborhoods. Between 1991 and 1994, Los Angeles home prices already had declined precipitously because of the Savings and Loan Crisis, the US economic recession, and layoffs in the defense industry, and the Northridge Quake finished the job, bringing prices to levels not seen since the early 1980s.

A bit after Randy Shilts, the author of *And the Band Played On*, the bestselling book about the early years of the AIDS crisis, died from AIDS on February 17, 1994, my friend Kevin from college contacted me—the man who had coaxed me out of the closet in the spring of 1983 after we saw *Sophie's Choice*, my coming-out film. Kevin now lived in San Francisco, and he was visiting LA for a few days with his partner, Brian, a San Francisco emergency room doctor. The three of us had a lovely dinner together. I was so happy that Kevin had found a wonderful partner. But mostly, I was simply relieved that Kevin was still alive.

By early 1994, Euro Disneyland in Paris, which had opened two years earlier, was in deep financial trouble and its financial restructuring became a huge company project. As we neared its completion, I came up with a morale-boosting idea that also served as a creative writing outlet for me: writing and producing a short company video called "Financial Fairy-Tale Theater" that told the financial story of Euro Disneyland with some twisted inside Disney humor. Richard, the CFO, approved the project. We planned for him to unveil it at the closing dinner.

I wrote a script with the help of my colleague Kelley. Our fairy-tale story would use clips from Disney's animated films with a voiceover by a narrator. For the narrator, I reached for the stars, literally, to get the great Betty White. She had just completed her run on Disney's television show *The Golden Girls*, so I called our Television group and found out the name of her talent agent: Tony. I phoned him out of the blue and, incredibly, he took my call. I told Tony about the project and sent him the script.

The next morning, my office telephone rang, and when I answered, the instantly recognizable voice on the line said, "Hi, Chris, this is Betty."

It was *the* Betty White, calling me. She said she loved the script, and agreed to do the project.

A few days later, Betty White, a team of people from Studio Operations, my colleague Kelley, and I met in one of the Disney soundstages at 2:00 a.m., the only time that we could get, and we shot the video. Betty was incredible. So gracious, and kind, and such a trooper to work from 2:00 a.m.– 4:00 a.m. on a silly corporate video project. As expected, her comedic delivery was spot-on and she improvised her own extra humor to the story masterfully.

Everyone at the Euro Disneyland closing dinner loved Richard's surprise video, and it boosted the team's morale after working for months on such a difficult financing restructuring. I sent a copy of it to Betty White. Tony, Betty's agent, telephoned me and told me that she said that my video was one of the funniest things that she had ever done. Then he added, "You're in the wrong profession, Chris. If you ever write anything, I hope that you'll let me know because I'll get you signed here at the William Morris Agency."

Whoa. Hearing these words from a top agent at one of Hollywood's top talent agencies now eight years after I shelved my dream of a writing career blew me away.

I wondered if Tony's comment was a sign from the universe that I should ditch my finance career and pursue writing again. I had gone so far down the corporate finance road that I was on, and it had turned out to be a fantastic road, and now my writing road was far off in the distance. But by 1994, I was no longer skeptical about signs in my life, since I kept noticing them. There had been many signs, or odd coincidences, since Stephen's death. I came to believe that this was his way of letting me know that he was watching over me. To this day, rabbits have a strange way of appearing in my life when times get difficult, or when something great in my life is about to happen. There is another sign that Stephen sends me quite frequently—it's a three-digit number that appears to me in all sorts of unexpected ways. It's been hard for me to ignore these frequent strange coincidences, and so I've become a believer in signs.

After the Northridge Quake, I had many repairs to do at my sister's house, including rebuilding brick walls, fixing the broken chimney, repairing broken pipes, replacing broken dishes, patching cracked drywall, and repainting. Early one morning in February 1994, as I waited there for a contractor to arrive, the telephone rang. It was my long-lost friend Bryn! Finally! He was still alive! Six years after he moved out of my house to live with his sister in Minnesota, he finally called me. Thank God I kept my name listed in the phone book.

I could tell immediately from his voice that he was in very bad shape. It was weak and hoarse. He said, "Chris, I'm not doing well here in Minneapolis and I don't have anyone to turn to. My sister is tired of taking care of me and she is evicting me from her house at the end of this week. I don't have any money for an apartment, and there's no other place for me to live here, and I'm going to end up dying on the streets of Minneapolis. I want to get to my mom's house in Tucson, Arizona, so that I can die there. Can you help me get there?"

My heart instantly broke, all over again.

"Of course I will help you, Bryn," I replied. "Does your mom really want you to come? Will she take good care of you when you get to Tucson?"

If Bryn had answered no, I would have flown him to Los Angeles to live the rest of his life with me.

"Yes, she wants me to come," Bryn answered. "She just doesn't have any money to pay for an airline ticket. All I need is an airline ticket, Chris."

I was so angry at Bryn's sister, whom I didn't even know, evicting Bryn into the snow in the middle of the Minnesota winter. What fucking horrible concept of family was that? God damn it, the AIDS virus sure made people treat other people terribly. But now was not the time to debate any of this with my dying friend, Bryn.

"Of course I will buy you an airline ticket, Bryn," I responded. "How soon do you want to go?"

"As early as tomorrow, Chris," he said.

After we hung up, I called the Disney travel department and bought Bryn a one-way ticket from Minneapolis to Tucson for two days later. I Federal

Expressed him the ticket in those days before electronic ticket delivery, along with cash for food and taxis. I spoke to Bryn the next day to confirm that the package had arrived. He flew to Tucson the following day.

Bryn spent the short remainder of his life living with his mom. He died two months later on April 15, 1994, at the age of thirty-two, one of the 270,870 deaths out of 441,528 cases of AIDS reported in the US by the end of 1994 since the inception of the AIDS pandemic, according to amfAR.[11] His mom called to deliver the news to me, his one remaining friend, and she thanked me for being there for him in his time of need. When she called, I was home sick with pneumonia from overwork and not taking care of myself. This was an especially tough time, since Frank Wells, Disney's brilliant and charismatic president and chief operating officer, had died in a helicopter crash while skiing almost two weeks earlier on Easter Sunday. I was in my office working that day when Richard, our CFO, called me with the devastating news. Everyone at Disney took Frank's tragic death hard. I never had pneumonia before, or since. After I hung up from Bryn's mom, I cried for my friend Bryn, and hoped that, just maybe, this could be the final death.

Then, miraculously, it was. Bryn was the last of my gay friends from my twenties to die from AIDS. Within about a year, newly discovered HIV anti-retroviral therapies dramatically lowered the AIDS mortality rate, turned HIV into the manageable disease that it is to this day, and patients on their deathbeds miraculously sprang back to life like someone had hit the rewind button on their illness. AIDS was no longer a certain death sentence.

I may have been sick with pneumonia, but this moment marked a rebirth for me. The storm was finally clearing for good for me. That summer of 1994, I traveled to New York City to celebrate the twenty-fifth anniversary of the 1969 Stonewall Riots and all the progress gay and lesbian rights had made since that important uprising. I partied there like Prince, just like it was "1999."

◆◆◆

ALTHOUGH THE STORM HAD damaged me in several key aspects, it also forged me into a man. I learned how to take care of myself, and to be afraid of no one. I learned to not give up when life got tough. I learned that I was a much stronger person than I ever imagined. Most importantly, I learned to be my own hero, like in Mariah Carey's 1993 megahit song "Hero," the lyrics of which serve as an anthem to my life. Like the lyrics of her song, I saw the truth that the hero lies in me. A hero, in fact, lies in each one of us—if we accept the responsibility to save ourselves.

As the end of 1994 approached, my second mom Margaret and I celebrated her sixty-fourth birthday on Christmas Eve with a prix fixe dinner and Dom Perignon champagne at L'Orangerie Restaurant, the ultra-expensive West Hollywood restaurant behind my old dumpy studio apartment on West Knoll Drive, where ten years earlier I could not even afford an appetizer. I still have the dinner menu in my scrapbook. I had certainly traveled a heart-wrenchingly long path over those ten years.

But I could see the sun on the horizon.

CHAPTER 12
SUN AGAIN

After Bryn died, I received a large raise and bonus from Disney that enabled me to pay off all my remaining debts from Stephen's medical care as well as all my remaining business school loans, with money still left over for a down payment on a house. It was time for me to move on from my sister's house now that I had completed the administration of her estate.

I wanted to take advantage of the drop in LA housing prices in the wake of the Northridge Quake, particularly in the Hollywood Hills. So in January 1995, as O. J. Simpson's televised murder trial began in downtown Los Angeles, I looked for homes in the Hills, and specifically in Beachwood Canyon, because it was close to my work in Burbank.

I came across a bank-owned foreclosed three-bedroom house on Hollyridge Drive at the top of Beachwood. It had a full-on view of the Hollywood sign and the canyon. Because of the Northridge Quake, prospective buyers were staying far away from any house that looked like it could fall down a hillside. I hired a structural engineer who confirmed the house was built on concrete pilings sunk thirty feet down into the bedrock below, and that it was completely secure. The house was listed at less than 50 percent of what it sold for in 1987. I offered even less than that, plus I asked for a 5-percent down payment and advantageous mortgage financing from the bank. Glendale Federal Savings, still struggling from the Savings and Loan Crisis, was desperate to sell and agreed to all of my terms, including helping me purge my credit history of my prior defaulted mortgage with Home Savings. So, at the age of thirty-two, I moved into the Hollywood Hills home I had dreamed of owning ever since the summer of 1983. I played

Sheryl Crow's Grammy Award winning hit "All I Wanna Do" over and over as I moved in and unpacked. Anthony Kiedis, the lead singer of the Red Hot Chili Peppers, lived across the street from me, and young women tried to climb over his security gate at all hours of the day and night so that they could try to meet him. Hollywood Hills entertainment at its best.

The icing on the cake: during escrow, I received a copy of my credit report that showed that my student loans were "paid as agreed" and "never late." Somehow, all of my late payments and non-payments while Stephen was dying got purged from my record. My FICO credit score leapt back to a pristine level.

After I moved in, I threw a housewarming party and invited everyone from my life: my mom and dad; my second mom Margaret; my UCLA mentor, Liz, who still paid my bills and did my income taxes; my other UCLA mentor, Cid, who encouraged me to go to business school; my friend Erika and her husband, Rick; my friend Robert; Robert's mom and dad; my mom and dad's best friends Annette and Leila and Gigi; my sister's ex-partner, Jane; my attorney, Lloyd, and his wife; my friend from college and former roommate, Sandy; my friends from Saint Andrew Church, Noel, Chris, and Jenise; my gay rodeo posse; and my colleagues from Disney. Nearly everyone from every part of my life, all together, mingling effortlessly.

At one point, I heard my mom's voice coming from the den as she held court with her best friends Annette, Leila, and Gigi. She bragged, "I always knew that Chris would be successful."

Given everything that had happened between my mom and me, I peered around the corner and jokingly said, "Really? Hmmm, you always knew that I would be successful. Really, mom?"

She did not miss a beat with her response. "That's how I remember it, Chris. Now let me talk to my friends. Shoo."

Then my mom smiled at me and waved me away, and I laughed. Amazing how life can be resilient if we let it.

There was one more important guest at my housewarming party: Paul, my new boyfriend. Yes, I fell in love again in March 1995, nearly four years after Stephen's death. Paul was a widower just like me. He and I had what is known as a "growing relationship" for several years. We helped each other complete our grieving processes. Ultimately, we realized that we were wrong for each other and split up, amicably, and remain friends.

As for Stephen's parents, his mother developed pancreatic cancer in early 1995, and she quickly died at her Yorktown, Virginia, home on May 11, 1995, at the age of sixty-seven. Six months later, his father, on November 24, 1995, the day after Thanksgiving, killed himself with a gun in the town of Richmondville, New York, at the age of seventy-five.

I found this all out from Marc, the only friend of Stephen's from Washington, DC, who did not abandon him, and my only remaining link to news regarding Stephen's parents. He telephoned to tell me the shocking and sad news.

I can only imagine the pain of life and sense of aloneness that Stephen's father must have felt as he struggled to pull the trigger. His father had no Jessie, as I did, to shake him and lead him out of his grief.

The obituary for Stephen's mother highlighted her extensive work in local Episcopal churches and with several AIDS support groups. It also mentioned that she was survived by her husband, her mother, and her brother. But no mention at all of Stephen, her son and only child. No mention about him predeceasing her. The omission of him from his mother's obituary seemed odd to me given how she professed that she would never be separated from her son again. Perhaps this omission was intentional if his father wrote the obituary and didn't want to acknowledge his son.

His father's obituary, after highlighting that he had served in the Army in the Southwest Pacific and received five battle stars, stated that he was survived by his brother, and that he was predeceased by his wife and his son "Steve." This was odd because Stephen always insisted that his name be written as "Stephen" and not "Steve," even though he allowed people to call him "Steve" in conversation.

Until I wrote this memoir, I didn't know where Stephen's ashes ended up. However, through Google searching, I found an entry for his mother on the Find-a-Grave website, which listed St. Martin's Episcopal Church in Williamsburg, Virginia, as her final resting place. I telephoned the church, and the staff confirmed for me that his mother's ashes were scattered there, as were the ashes for his father, and Stephen's ashes, too.

In February 2018, I visited the memorial garden at St. Martin's. It's a beautiful, peaceful spot where their ashes are scattered underneath large pine trees. I found a plaque on the bell tower that listed all three of their names. But strangely, Stephen's name was misspelled as "Steven," suggesting that whoever ordered the plaque didn't know Stephen at all, or at least didn't know how to correctly spell his name.

Nothing annoys an English literature major quite like a typo. I pointed out the spelling error to the church, and they replaced it with a new plaque, and I mailed them a check to pay for it. The right thing to do—one final act of taking care of Stephen, my first love, nearly twenty-seven years later. I placed a dozen red roses beneath their plaque, and I said a prayer for all three of them.

When Stephen was alive, we had our "song," "There's Me," from the Broadway musical *Starlight Express*. A song about being there for someone when the chips are down, a time capsule of my relationship with Stephen from 1986 onward. But two years after he died, I discovered another song to capture my relationship with him and my life during my twenties: "I Remember L.A.," by Celine Dion. This song laments a lost love, a lost time, and Lost Angeles. The music from both songs streamed through me in that memorial garden while my heart replayed memories of Stephen. I did not cry. Instead, I felt peace.

By the mid-1990s, societal attitudes toward homosexuality started evolving at a rapid pace. Acceptance seemed to be happening everywhere. Now, being gay was "cool." Gay and lesbian celebrities—k.d. lang, Melissa Etheridge, Greg Louganis, Ellen DeGeneres, George Michael, Nathan Lane—came out of the closet in the nineties and their careers didn't end. Some of them actually got more work. RuPaul, the drag queen, released his hit song "Supermodel" and achieved international fame. These brave celebrities joined the even braver ones who came out during the 1980s or even earlier—Billie Jean King, Martina Navratilova, Elton John, Ian McKellen, Boy George, Rupert Everett, and Harvey Fierstein.

Disney instituted same-sex partner health benefits for its cast members in January 1996. On January 18, 1996, the hugely popular *Friends* television show aired the episode titled "The One with the Lesbian Wedding" on NBC. The iconic gay-themed television series *Will and Grace* premiered on September 21, 1998. On May 20, 1996, the US Supreme Court, in its *Romer vs. Evans* decision, struck down Colorado's Amendment 2 as unconstitutional, ruling that states could not pass laws to prevent their cities from protecting the rights of gays and lesbians. The back-and-forth culture wars were in full swing, but the pendulum over time was swinging toward more acceptance of gays and lesbians, even if it backtracked a bit every once in a while, as it did on September 21, 1996, when President Bill Clinton signed the Defense of Marriage Act into law to "protect" states from having to recognize other states' same-sex marriages in the event that Hawai'i's State Circuit Court soon ruled that same-sex marriages were legal (on December 3, 1996, the Hawaii Circuit Court ruled in favor of same-sex marriage). Or later in the 1990s when fundamentalist Reverend Jerry Falwell claimed a scandal over Tinky Winky, the cute purple character on the *Teletubbies* children's show that Mr. Falwell was certain was gay and corrupting young children through their television sets.

I call this period "The Wonderful Thing that Happened During the 1990s." The world changed very quickly in a very short period of time, but this change was only possible because of a foundation painfully built by many gays and lesbians over several decades, including the Mattachine Society and the Daughters of Bilitis of the 1950s, the transgender women and men at the Cooper's Donuts uprising in 1959, the nearly 600 activists who protested at the Black Cat in 1967, the brave drag queens at the 1969 Stonewall Riots, the gay activist who pushed a banana cream pie into Anita Bryant's face on October 14, 1977, and the fearless work of the members of ACT UP in the 1980s who helped battle the AIDS crisis even as they fought AIDS themselves. Every one of these gay and lesbian trailblazers upon whose shoulders I stand today was infinitely much braver than I could ever be. These groundbreaking Americans made the world in which I live today possible. I also believe that a contributor to these changes was the AIDS crisis itself because, as people fell ill, many people discovered they had gay family members, gay friends, and gay work colleagues. Once homosexuality had a personalized face, it became much harder to hate, and many people chose unconditional love—the right choice—rather than the judgment espoused by fundamentalist religious conservatives. And the world changed for the better.

In mid-1995, I had dinner with an old friend from UCLA student government whom I hadn't seen since graduation since he lived overseas. He was the same age as me and married with three children. At the end of our dinner, he told me that he was gay. This was surprising, but then again, I do have the world's worst gaydar. He went on to tell me that he had been in love with me since we met in college. Even more surprising. And so sad. At the center of my friend's life was a big lie that prevented his true happiness.

As he spoke, I realized that I was looking into a mirror of who I could have become if I had chosen to stay in the closet in 1983. After all, that was a completely valid choice in that era: a choice to live a lie out of self-protection. My friend and I had chosen completely different roads at a critical and defining time of our lives.

He told me that he had no plans to leave his wife, that he loved her and had never strayed, and that he loved his three children very much. He lamented that the world had changed so much since we were in college, and now that gays and lesbians were more accepted by society he realized he had made the wrong choice so long ago. He was determined to stay with his wife and family. He tried to be an honorable man, even to his own detriment to his own truth and happiness.

I left this dinner with a heavy heart. I realized that my friend's confession to me that he was gay and felt such affection for me was likely the closest he would ever come to having a gay experience in his life. It was hard to look into this mirror. Sadly, a few years later he committed suicide.

Also in 1995, I was asked to make a presentation to Disney's Board of Directors about the performance of the company's various investment portfolios. Normally, Richard Nanula, the CFO, would do this, but he was out of town so I got the assignment. I covered our portfolios' performance, investment theory, a history of alternative investments, how my investment approach emulated David Swensen's Yale Endowment investment model, and how our investment returns even sometimes beat Yale's. When I finished, the directors spontaneously applauded. Then one of the directors stood up and told the group that I had given the clearest financial presentation that anyone had ever made to the Board. His name was Irwin Russell, one of the top entertainment attorneys in the country. He went on to become my close friend and mentor for the next eighteen years. A wonderful, brilliant man. I also met Sidney Poitier that day, another Disney Board member. First Betty White and now Sidney Poitier.

I left that board meeting so happy, so confident, so grounded. At the age of thirty-three, life had become so fulfilling for me, and all because of that fateful decision I made at the fork in my road in 1986 in the dark shadow of AIDS.

Robert Frost's famous poem, "The Road Not Taken," is such a relevant metaphor for my life. That inspiring poem concludes with:

"I shall be telling this with a sigh
Somewhere ages and ages hence:
Two roads diverged in a wood, and I—
I took the one less traveled by,
And that has made all the difference."

Frost's poem can be interpreted many ways. It's clear that when we are young and choosing our roads that we can't later on teleport backward in time and live our lives again through our roads not taken—we only get one life to live. But Frost's poem doesn't say the road that we take can't loop back to our road not taken at some future point in life. Maybe the road we choose to take can turn out to be a convoluted detour, a decades-long roundabout bypass, that eventually connects us back into our road not taken. There are many roads to many destinations in life. As Frost understood, the important thing is to keep walking and, as I would come to discover, it may even someday lead you to your original destination.

In July 1995, Disney announced the acquisition of Capital Cities/ABC, at that time the largest corporate acquisition in history. The stockholders' meeting to approve the acquisition was scheduled for January 1996 at the Waldorf Astoria Hotel in New York City, and I had a significant planning role in it. For the meeting, I produced a video to highlight the expected synergies from the purchase. In the process of creating this video, I got to know several senior executives who worked at the ABC network.

A huge snowstorm hit New York City right before the meeting, the third-worst snowstorm on record and the worst in forty-nine years at the time, with 20.2 inches of snow falling in Central Park. Luckily, I was already at the Waldorf. The entire city shut down. I remember seeing almost two feet of snow outside the hotel. There was no traffic. At one point, my colleagues and I threw snowballs and built snowmen in the middle of Park Avenue as the snow fell around us. Magical.

But I still had plenty of work to get ready for the meeting. I needed to make edits to the corporate video. The company hired an off-road vehicle to shuttle me back and forth in the snowstorm between the Waldorf and the ABC Network's main offices near Lincoln Center. Two feet of snow was no obstacle for this vehicle.

ABC assigned me a group of production people and an editing bay where the company produced its newsmagazine show, *20/20*. By now, I knew my way around an editing bay fairly well, and I directed the efforts of the talented production team. They were surprised when I told them that I worked in corporate finance, and specifically in investments. One of them was quite senior, and privately pulled me aside and said, "You're in the wrong profession. Why don't you come work at ABC at *20/20* and move to New York? I would hire you tomorrow to be a producer here."

Whoa! Was this another sign that I should ditch my finance career and try writing again? By this time, I had made peace that if I ever pursued any writing at all, it would be many years into my future, when life finally slowed down for me, and when—or if—I ever figured out how to bridge the chasm between the incredible corporate finance road that I was on back into my road not taken.

In October 1996, I visited Washington, DC, to witness the final display of the entire AIDS Memorial Quilt, now 38,000 panels large, which covered the entire National Mall from the Washington Monument to the foot of Capitol Hill. My first ever visit to see the AIDS Quilt was an incredibly moving experience. For Thanksgiving that year, I hosted my mom and dad and some friends, and I served pumpkin soup in small bowls that I painstakingly carved out of real pumpkins at Martha Stewart's suggestion. Her hit television show made it look so simple. At dinner, however, I noticed that something was a bit off with my dad. He didn't eat his usual large portions, and he was quieter. Shortly afterward, he was diagnosed with colon cancer.

He died in Santa Barbara on January 28, 1998, right after California banned smoking in all bars and restaurants, and President Clinton's Monica Lewinsky scandal broke, causing the Republican Party to once again lose its mind about Clinton and demand his impeachment over the indiscretion. The Republican Party had long hated President Clinton, almost instantly after his 1993 inauguration after he asked his wife, Hillary, to spearhead healthcare reform legislation efforts. Republicans indignantly cried, "How dare a President appoint one of his own family members to work on projects for the American people?" I handled all of my dad's funeral arrangements. My brother Michael and his family attended the funeral service and internment at Carpinteria Cemetery. My mom finally got to spend some time with her grandchildren, whom she hadn't seen for most of their lives, and my dad's funeral represented the first step in the healing of her long-strained relationship with my brother. My family finally had come to understand the importance of unconditional love, and decades-old judgment and fighting just wasn't worth anyone's energy anymore. The church overflowed with flowers from my friends, my Disney colleagues, and Wall Street firms. The outpouring of love blew me away. Disney's Chairman and Chief Executive Officer Michael Eisner sent to my home a handwritten note of condolence from himself and his wife Jane. So classy, and so unexpected.

In the spring of 1998, I approached my ten-year anniversary working at Disney and now invested more than $4 billion for the company, and I also provided investment advice to the Amateur Athletic Foundation (today called the LA84 Foundation), the endowment created with the profits from the 1984 Los Angeles Olympics, where I once worked at age twenty-two. I also had moved into the best office in the front of the Team Disney building, underneath and between the dwarf statues of Doc and Sneezy from *Snow White*, with large windows that had a fantastic view of the reflecting pool below. I still occasionally thought about an operating finance role in Theme Parks and Resorts so that I could move to Orlando, but I knew that a company transfer was unlikely. One day, Richard, the CFO, announced that he was leaving Disney to join Starwood Hotels and Resorts. This was the latest in a string of finance departures from the company, several of them for jobs in Silicon Valley and the internet 1.0 gold rush.

With Richard's impending departure, I wondered whether it was time for me to consider an opportunity outside the company, too. By 1998, all of the Silicon Valley venture capital funds in my investment portfolios were making huge financial bets on the internet. These firms were managed by smart people, and I followed their portfolio companies and investment decisions closely. The emerging internet industry called to me.

I turned to my brother's knowledgeable and well-connected friend Susan for some finance career advice. She emphatically told me, "Silicon Valley and technology is where you need to be, Chris."

One week later, Susan's favorite headhunter grilled me in his San Mateo office during a stress interview. His interview reminded me of my time in business school when recruiters berated me for majoring in English literature. He picked my résumé apart. Thinking that I would never see this headhunter again, I argued back forcefully. Point by point, and without giving him any opportunity to interrupt me, I refuted every negative point he had made. I argued that the entire point of every finance job on the planet is to make sure that a company delivers a good return on investment, and that no one knew investments better than I did. As I finished my impassioned rebuttal and prepared to politely leave his office, his demeanor completely changed. He smiled and he said, "Well done. I think that you would be a perfect fit for Amazon.com. Have you heard of it? Amazon sells books on the internet. Would you be willing to fly to Seattle for an interview there?"

I had definitely heard about Amazon.com. It was a company in one of the venture capital funds in my investment portfolios, and was founded only three years earlier. In fact, I had purchased a book from Amazon.com to test if the website actually worked: *Europe* by Norman Davies (an incredible book about European history, one of the clearest and best written, really). It arrived at my office, like magic. I knew that Amazon had recently gone public, but it was still a small company and not very well-known.

I flew to Seattle the next Friday morning. A rare sunny day in that city, but I didn't appreciate this at the time. It looked beautiful to me in the sun. I interviewed all day long at Amazon's four-story headquarters building at 1516 Second Avenue, between Pike Street and Pine Street, two blocks from Seattle's popular Pike Place Fish Market. Each Amazon executive on my interview loop took me for a walk outside the building to get coffee because it was a sunny day, which amused me. I especially connected with Joy Covey, Amazon's brilliant and charismatic chief financial officer. She was an amazing force of nature. As you may remember, I have a special weakness for brilliance. I spent the weekend in Seattle and toured neighborhoods a bit.

When I returned to Los Angeles on Sunday afternoon, the Mickey Mouse luggage tag that had been on my suitcase for nearly ten years snapped off as my bag tumbled down the ramp of the baggage carousel at Burbank Airport. I wondered to myself, "Is this a sign?"

On Monday afternoon, Randy, Amazon's treasurer, offered me a job to become Amazon's first assistant treasurer. The cash compensation was a 70-percent pay cut from what I made at Disney, but it included a lot of Amazon stock options and a large one-time cash signing bonus. I ran all the numbers and slept on it overnight.

The next morning, I called Randy and accepted his offer. Then I resigned from Disney. All hell broke loose. Paul, Disney's recently hired treasurer, panicked and told me that he was promoting me effective immediately with a huge compensation increase and a brand new company car. Richard, the CFO who had already resigned himself, tried to convince me to stay. The corporate treasury department buzzed with news of my resignation—apparently, I was the guy who everyone expected to be a Disney lifer. My telephone rang off the hook as the Disney grapevine spread my news and colleagues called to congratulate me. Then, Disney's CEO Michael Eisner telephoned me. The grapevine had reached all the way up to him. He told me that later that same day he would name one of my colleagues, Tom, as the company's new chief financial officer to succeed Richard, and if I stayed I could have my pick of senior finance jobs in the company.

Well, in 1998, Michael Eisner was the most powerful man in Hollywood, and he was calling me personally to say that I could have my pick of senior finance jobs. At the age of thirty-five, I was on the receiving end of the phone call that everyone in Hollywood dreamed of. I couldn't believe it. All I did was go on one job interview and get an offer. Now, if I stayed, I would finally have a shot at my dream finance job in Theme Parks and Resorts and be able to move to Orlando.

Since I was stunned by this sudden turn of events, and since Michael Eisner is not a person to whom you can easily say "no," I replied, "Okay, Michael, I will stay at Disney. Thank you so much for calling me."

I hung up the phone and leaped out of my chair. I bolted to my office window and looked down at the peaceful reflecting pool below me in front of the Team Disney Building and tried to calm myself down. I was at a huge crossroads in my life, at this incredible company that had been a rock for me for the past ten years, and its CEO had just asked me to stay. I had just quit and then unquit my Disney job within the span of about two hours. My head spun with confusion and emotions. Am I taking the right road?

Then I telephoned Randy, Amazon's treasurer, told him what had happened, unaccepted my Amazon job offer, and thanked him for the opportunity to interview there.

Well, it turned out that Randy did not take no for answer, either. He said: "Well, we're not going to take this lying down, Chris. I'll be right back to you."

About fifteen minutes later, my office phone rang and it was Jeff Bezos, the Chairman and Chief Executive Officer of Amazon.com. I hadn't interviewed with him when I was in Seattle, but I already knew his name from studying the company's financials. He said, "Chris, Joy and Randy really want you on our team, so we are going to sweeten the deal. If you accept our job offer within the next twenty-four hours, we will double the amount of your stock options."

This blew me away. Double the amount of stock options for me? If this little internet company ended up being successful, these stock options would translate into a huge amount of money. Dumbfounded, I didn't know what to say, but it popped into my head that I probably could negotiate for more. So I asked him, "Can I also trade my cash signing bonus for more stock?"

"Yes, of course you can," replied Jeff Bezos. "I like how you're thinking, Chris. Randy and Joy will work it all out with you."

I hung up. Two CEOs, one road to choose! And I only had twenty-four hours to make up my mind. Talk about stress!

That evening as I drove home over Burbank's Barham Pass, I spoke with Joy, Amazon's CFO, as she tried to seal the deal with me. She had earned a joint JD–MBA degree at Harvard, and also was a certified public accountant, and in the short time I had known her it was clear she was one of the smartest people I had ever met.

"You strike me as a builder, Chris," Joy said. "There are probably still great things for you to do at Disney, but at Amazon you can help us build everything from scratch. This is a once-in-a-lifetime opportunity. Come build with us."

Joy's passionate argument resonated with me. I knew that joining Amazon, this little start-up company that only sold books over the internet and operated at gigantic net losses, was a huge career gamble for me. But I also knew that the internet sector was destined to be big, and that Amazon had a chance to be successful. I was fully back in life. I felt safe in life again, safe enough to take this risk. I didn't need to stay at Disney for its great health insurance plan any longer because I wasn't going to die from AIDS. I was thirty-five years old, still young enough to recover if Amazon went bankrupt or otherwise didn't work out. I had lived my entire life in Los Angeles, too, and thought that it might be interesting to live in Seattle for a few years, even if I would rarely see the sun. I remembered my Mickey Mouse luggage tag falling off my suitcase at the baggage carousel. It seemed to be another sign, and by now I had learned to pay attention to the signs in my life. I thought to myself, "Chris, it's time to leave Disney and take a career risk. That luggage tag fell off your suitcase for a reason. Follow the sign, and go work with Joy."

As you can imagine, I didn't sleep very much that night. But this time I stuck to my decision and the next morning, I resigned from Disney one last time. Everyone understood that my decision was final and no one argued with me about it. Sandy Litvack, Disney's General Counsel, called me up to his office to thank me for my work and wish me luck. Michael Eisner called me at home later that night, and he congratulated me, and wished me well. Once again, a very classy thing to do. I said to him, "Thank you, Michael. Who knows, maybe we will work together again in the future."

He replied, "Yes, maybe we will."

On my last day of work on Monday, June 29, 1998, Disney threw a goodbye party for me in the studio commissary, and the theme was—get this—Christopher Zyda's Funeral Service! My colleagues decorated the commissary to look like a mortuary, including an actual open casket with a dummy's dead body inside of it, all provided by the studio props department. Posted around the room were photos of me in various poses at prior work events, a blown-up cranky complaint letter that I had written to United Airlines about some travel screwup, and other funny work memories. My colleagues one by one stood at the lectern next to the dummy in the open casket and told humorous stories about working with me, and how they would miss me, and they gave me a framed animated cel of Mickey Mouse and Pluto that everyone in my department had signed as my going away gift. At last, a funeral I enjoyed attending!

The most wonderful goodbye party imaginable, for me, the English literature major who literally begged Human Resources for a job at Disney ten years earlier. Me, a living, breathing example of the American Dream, only two generations away from my four very poor grandparents—two of them immigrants—who worked as laborers, truck drivers, painters, and maids.

Then, after the party was over, I finished my last bit of work, completed my exit interview with Human Resources, and, as required, I turned in my cast member badge (but between you and me, Cindy from Human Resources let me keep it). I left my office underneath and between Doc and Sneezy on the third floor of the front of the Team Disney building, and I drove my blue Chevy Silverado pickup truck off the studio lot one final time. As I stopped my truck at the security booth to say goodbye to the guards, I looked back at the iconic building that had been my work home, my rock, for so many years. I felt incredibly thankful for my time at Disney, the place that sheltered me during the storm. And I felt hopeful for my future at this little internet company in Seattle that sold books. I felt grateful for everything in my entire life, and for the sun that shined upon me again. My fifteen-year journey into the storm, and through it, and out of it, and now beyond it.

The next morning, Tuesday, I left Los Angeles and drove to Seattle in my pickup truck. I started my new job as Amazon's first assistant treasurer three days later on Friday, at the age of thirty-six. And to my delight, my new office desk at Amazon was made from a solid door and four 4"x4" posts for legs, nearly identical to the desk that I had built in 1985 when I moved in with Stephen. Every Amazonian had one. The company called them "door desks." A wonderful welcome mat, and a sign from Stephen. I was sure of it.

Sunny days again, indeed.

CHAPTER 13
AFTER

The NEXT TWENTY-TWO YEARS of my life seem to have passed in an instant. And it has been mostly sunny on this road I have traveled. After leaving Disney, my life continued getting better as fate stepped in to see me through. I am grateful that I persevered in the face of my life's adversity, and that, thanks to my friend Jessie, I chose happiness. I came of age in the early era of AIDS, and the AIDS virus derailed my life plan, but I have lived my life like I promised Stephen I would when he was on his deathbed. I have lived a very lucky and wonderful life, on many levels, with multiple lightning bolts of good health[31] and fortune. When I was a young boy, my Czech grandmother told me that our ancestors came from the Arabian Peninsula. In Arabic, my last name Zyda ("Zayda" in Arabic) means "lucky" or "good fortune." On balance, I would say this has proved to be an appropriate namesake.

My finance career led me to dreams that I didn't even know I had. Assistant Treasurer, then to Treasurer, then to Vice President and International Chief

---

31   Despite my hypochondria, my health is strong (knock on wood) and my lifelong medical history can be summarized in a few sentences. Tonsils and adenoids removed at age five. Wart on my right pinky finger burned off at age eight by a sadistic doctor who did not believe in anesthesia. Childhood mumps, but no measles. Periodic head and chest colds, but hardly ever the flu. Lifelong allergies and asthma, relieved only by Zyrtec. Chicken pox, as you know, at age twenty-three. Occasional bronchitis. Pneumonia, as you also know, at age thirty-one. Concussion and sprained wrist from a rodeo accident at age thirty-two. Four wisdom teeth removed at age thirty-four. Sinus surgery also at age thirty-four to improve my breathing, which didn't work. Five colonoscopies since age forty, with nothing of note found. Prescription for fifteen Ambien pills at age fifty-three to help me sleep when I travel, and because I sleep mostly like a baby I still have nine pills left (they are expired now). I take a group of vitamins twice a day: B complex with C, glucosamine, ginger, turmeric, krill oil, and tart cherry. My blood pressure is 120/74 and my cholesterol is normal. All my bloodwork is normal and "boring" according to my doctor. There, now you know my entire medical history as of this writing.

Financial Officer, then to Vice President of Financial Planning and Analysis, and then to Chief Financial Officer where I led a company's initial public offering (IPO) and rang the bell on the New York Stock Exchange trading floor that I first visited with my Disney boss, Marcia. After retiring from Corporate America, I then founded an investment advisory firm and became a Chief Executive Officer. And remember that conversation I had with Disney CEO Michael Eisner about possibly working with him again? Well, we did.

I have maintained my lifetime commitment to carpe diem, one of the most important lessons that I learned with Stephen from the storm. In that spirit, I have traveled all over the world, and have enjoyed river rafting, scuba diving, surfing, swimming with dolphins in the open ocean, and boating in my yacht. I also competed in the 2013 CrossFit Open and placed twenty-first in the Southern California region and 212th in the world for men aged 50–54. Carpe diem can be such a wonderful, life-affirming, rejuvenating force for us all.

In 2012, I threw a fiftieth birthday party for myself at the Los Angeles Natural History Museum in the middle of its dinosaur gallery. The theme was the "Zydasaurus" dinosaur birthday celebration, in honor of the fact I wasn't extinct. The universe even sent me an unexpected beautiful supermoon on the evening of the party.

In 2013, the UCLA English department invited me to be its commencement speaker. A wonderful experience. My speech is on YouTube. If you watch it, you will hear references to the storm, Stephen, Joan, my friend Bryn, my mom and dad, carpe diem, Robert Frost's "The Road Not Taken," and even Stephen's mother, to whom I referred as "Grendel, the Monster's Mother from *Beowulf*." Now you know why.

Also in 2013, I returned to my UCLA fraternity and served as its chapter advisor for several years. Life came full circle for me as I returned to my fraternity where this story began, where I came out of the closet to my fraternity brothers decades ago—a moment of my history that they still fondly talk about at alumni events.

I lived full-time in San Francisco from 2003 to 2008. I still own a beautiful home there on Seward Street in the hills over the Castro District with a breathtaking view of the city and the Bay Bridge below. While I lived there, I also fell in love for a third time, with Michael, the best man in the entire city. Another brilliant attorney! And also a talented real estate developer, architect, interior designer, and chef.

I marvel at the increased acceptance of gays and lesbians over the past twenty-two years. Today, we have been assimilated in many places throughout the world and it's wonderful. Michael and I attended World Pride in New York City in 2019 to celebrate the fiftieth anniversary of the Stonewall Riots, which was a huge city party for everyone: straight, gay, and in between. Even the police force and fire department joined in the fun. Every business flew rainbow flags that weekend, including Wall Street firms. In honor of the Stonewall anniversary, the Russell Reynolds executive search firm published an article about LGBTQ+ executive recruiting and talent strategy. Such love, acceptance, and progress.

I lived in San Francisco during that daring time in 2004 when Mayor Gavin Newsom started issuing gay marriage certificates, lighting the fuse for the final pitched battles in the fight for gay marriage. These battles played out like a masterful chess game simultaneously in courtrooms and in legislatures across the country. The inspirational lyrics of "You Can't Stop the Beat" from the musical *Hairspray* underscored this march from 2000 onward: "You can't stop today as it comes speeding down the track."

And today certainly sped down the track. Although President Bill Clinton's Defense of Marriage Act had existed since September 1996, fundamentalist religious conservatives worried that California would overturn it. So in March 2000, they placed Proposition 22 on the California ballot, which stated that only a marriage between a man and a woman was valid. Proposition 22 passed, becoming another roadblock for gay marriage. Four years later, San Francisco Mayor Newsom simply ignored the law and started marrying gay couples in City Hall. Religious conservatives had a meltdown. For days, the Mayor couldn't even be served with an order to stop issuing marriage licenses because San Francisco's elected officials hid him from process servers through an elaborate game of hide-a-mayor. One month later, the California Supreme Court ordered San Francisco to stop marrying gay couples. One month after that ruling, the Commonwealth of Massachusetts legalized gay marriage, becoming the first state to do so (Vermont, in 2000, through a civil union bill, was the first state to give full marriage rights to same-sex couples, but stopped short of calling it gay marriage).

After these initial clashes over gay marriage, in an episode of mind-blowing hypocrisy, on June 11, 2007, Larry Craig, a conservative Republican US Senator from the State of Idaho who had ardently opposed rights for gays and lesbians throughout his eighteen-year senate career and who criticized President Clinton as a "nasty, bad, naughty boy" during the Monica Lewinsky scandal, was arrested in the Minneapolis–St. Paul International Airport for soliciting sex from an undercover police officer in an adjoining stall in a men's restroom. Even while proclaiming, "I am not gay, I have never been gay," Senator Craig—who rushed to propose to and marry his wife Suzanne shortly after he publicly denied being one of the members of Congress involved in the 1982 congressional teenage male page sex scandal—pled guilty to disorderly conduct and it ended his senate career.[32] After his guilty plea, several gay men stepped forward to say they had engaged in sex with Senator Craig or that he made a sexual advance toward them.[33] This man has lived much of his life in a self-loathing prison constructed of deeply buried negative tapes.

By 2007, all eyes had turned toward California's Proposition 22—overturning it, and defending it. Fundamentalist religious conservatives worried that the law would be overturned, so they crafted a new one, called Proposition 8, and placed it on the November 2008 ballot. A fierce campaign battle ensued. The proponents were largely bankrolled by the Roman Catholic Church and the Church of Jesus Christ of Latter-Day Saints. I looked inside a Catholic church near San Francisco's financial district and saw a banner imploring the congregation to vote yes on Proposition 8 to "protect marriage." I shook my head when I witnessed, once again, how far the corrupt Church had fallen away from what should be its true mission, now misusing its tax-exempt status to politically lobby for legislation to hurt me.

Six months before the November 2008 election, the California Supreme Court struck down Proposition 22 as unconstitutional and in its *In Re: Marriage 2008* ruling allowed gay marriages to resume. Eighteen thousand more gay marriages took place before the election. Proposition 8 passed in November, erecting a new roadblock to gay marriage in California. But the winds of the nation continued to shift, and quickly. Despite Proposition 8's passage, by November 2008, two states—Massachusetts and Connecticut—had legalized gay marriage. Over the next year, Iowa, Vermont, New Hampshire, and Washington, DC, all legalized it, too.

---

32   August 28, 2007, "Senator, Arrested at Airport, Pleads Guilty," *The New York Times.*

33   December 2, 2007, "More Gay Men Describe Sexual Encounters with US Senator Craig," *The Idaho Statesman.*

In May 2009, California's Supreme Court upheld Proposition 8 under the state's constitution, but it didn't invalidate the gay marriages that occurred before the proposition passed. So, for several years there was a special group of grandfathered married gay couples in California. California's elected officials had refused to defend Proposition 8 in court challenges. This left only fundamentalist religious conservatives to defend it, unmasking them and making it crystal clear that this was about forcing their strict religious beliefs on the citizens around them.

At one point, Dolly Parton, a very wise woman from America's heartland, weighed in on gay marriage, saying, "I think that they should be able to suffer just like us heterosexuals." Dolly Parton's statement was the best, funniest, and most honest argument uttered by anyone during the gay marriage war.

A separate fight over Proposition 8 brewed in Federal Court, and in 2010 US District Judge Vaughn Walker struck down the proposition as unconstitutional. Furious fundamentalist religious conservatives instantly appealed the decision to the US Supreme Court. Judge Walker issued a stay on more gay marriages in California pending the US Supreme Court's final decision on the matter.

But as Proposition 8's appeal wound its way up to the US Supreme Court, the country's political winds shifted even more. In December 2010, the US Senate voted to allow gays and lesbians to serve openly in the military, allowing the United States to catch up to the rest of the free world's militaries. The states of New York, Maryland, Washington, and Maine all legalized gay marriage during 2011 and 2012. The US Supreme Court already had ruled, in its 2003 *Lawrence vs. Texas* decision, that laws against gay and lesbian sex were unconstitutional. Homophobia seemed in retreat everywhere. Legal protections for gays and lesbians throughout the country changed quickly, and the courts involved in the gay marriage war scrambled to catch up with the rest of the country in their legal rulings.

The case for and against gay marriage was argued in the US Supreme Court on March 26, 2013, which would have been Stephen's sixty-third birthday. On June 26, the Court issued two landmark rulings: *United States vs. Windsor*, and *Hollingsworth vs. Perry*. The first ruling allowed married gay and lesbian couples to receive the same federal benefits as heterosexual married couples if their states allowed gay marriage. The second ruling affirmed that California's Proposition 8 was unconstitutional and cleared the way for gay marriages to begin again in California.

When the US Supreme Court announced its historic decisions, I was in the middle of one of my early morning CrossFit workouts. The entire gym cheered the news of the rulings. I took a break from my workout and called Michael and proposed to him on my iPhone:

"The Supreme Court ruled that we can get married now. Will you marry me?"

Michael said yes, and then we hung up and I finished my CrossFit workout. Such a romantic engagement story, right? But so fitting if you know me, which by now I hope you do. We tied the knot in December that year in our living room with an officiant I found on Yelp who married us for $150. Michael is my husband now, something that I never dreamed would be possible when I made my first terrified steps out of the closet in 1983. His name is Michael Joseph. My brother is named Michael Joseph, too. My dad was named Joseph Michael. My Roman Catholic confirmation name is Michael, too. Nice coincidences, right? My husband Michael was my biggest cheerleader as I wrote this memoir, even when I woke him up typing notes on my iPhone memo app at 2:32 a.m. so that I wouldn't forget to include an important detail. I am so lucky to have him in my life.

Finally, on June 26, 2015, the US Supreme Court ruled, in *Obergefell vs. Hodges,* that gay marriage was legal in all fifty states, and the nationwide battle for gay marriage in the culture wars was over.

It's stunning, and depressing, how much fundamentalist religious conservatives have fought to force their religious beliefs upon the rest of America. All rooted in their homophobia, their peculiar reading of the Bible, and because of the Missing Commandment. These people, and their churches, spent millions upon millions of dollars—not to help the poor, not to help people overcome their addictions, not to help young single mothers raise and educate their unplanned children, not to help the struggling unemployed, but instead to deprive people who love each other the opportunity to get married and have their rights respected and protected. In the end, love won, as it should. Meanwhile, the poor, the addicted, the young single mothers, and the struggling unemployed still suffer. Misguided organized religions and fundamentalist religious conservatives continue to miss the point. Now, we have gay marriage but argue about who will bake and decorate the wedding cake.

I'm better at hugging today, and I'll hug you if you don't have a cold. I'm still a hypochondriac and germophobe and I still frequently run to Michael Marsh, my doctor in Burbank across the street from the Disney Studios lot, even though today it takes me over an hour to drive the nearly ten miles to his office from mine because the Waze app has ruined all of my shortcuts.[34] My doctor of more than thirty years is on to me, though. When I ask him my perennial question, he says, "Yes, Chris, you are going to die. But not from this." Then, he pivots into asking me questions about his investment portfolio.

I ran into one of Stephen's parents' attorneys at Spago Restaurant in Beverly Hills one afternoon around 2010. The woman whose picture I took at my deposition. She remembered me and we shook hands. We noted how we were both doing well enough to afford lunch at pricey Spago. I told her that Stephen's parents had both died. She said to me, "I hope that you realized that I was just doing my job, Chris. I had no ill will toward you." I already knew that, but it was nice to hear it from her directly.

A moment of corporate America karmic justice happened on December 8, 2008, when the Tribune Company, owner of the *Chicago Tribune* that fired my sister for being a lesbian, filed Chapter 11 bankruptcy. Long delayed karma, but karma nonetheless. I made money trading in *Tribune*'s bank debt, which sold for pennies on the dollar while the *Tribune*'s management team was fired, and later my friend John Angelo took over the bankrupt company. The despicable homophobic *Tribune* editor who judged and fired Joan and destroyed her journalism career was inducted into the Chicago Journalism Hall of Fame, received a lifetime achievement award from the Chicago Headline Club, won the Excellence in Journalism award from the City Club of Chicago, and earned the James C. Craven Freedom of the Press Award from the Illinois Press Association—in 2019 he died from pancreatic cancer, the same disease that killed Stephen's mother.

I finally left the Roman Catholic Church in 2002 after a priest propositioned me during my behind-the-screen confession in Menlo Park, California. My confession was hijacked, and suddenly I was consoling this poor man over his lonely life and also chastising him for using insider information to hit on gay men in the confessional booth. That was my final straw.

---

34   In my opinion, Los Angeles shortcuts should be earned by learning how to drive the city's streets, and not be given away for free by an app.

I am still a registered Democrat, but I vote as an Independent. The last remaining tatters of the Republican Party from my youth finally died in 2016 when the party leapt off the cliff and abandoned all morality. There is no American political party for a fiscally conservative and socially liberal, hardworking, taxpaying, and intensely patriotic citizen like me, but at least I appear to be in the majority.[35] Someone, please start a political party for us. Even the Supreme Court today has been sullied by a seemingly unhinged man who screamed during a tantrum in the US Senate on national television, proving to me that he likely will never render impartial justice for Americans. Only time will tell if this man will ever rule with the prudence of Hugo Black.[36] Ah, the Age of Truthlessness.

One thing is for sure, and that's the fact that I know a lot of dead people. Almost every person in this memoir is gone. David, Stephen's Yale University roommate, in 1990, at the age of forty. Stephen in 1991, at the age of forty-one. My sister in 1992, at the age of forty. My friend Frank, who watched *Beauty and the Beast* on his deathbed, in 1992, at the age of thirty-seven. Michael, Stephen's psychotherapist, in 1992, at the age of forty-eight. Erwin Okun, Disney's senior vice president of corporate communications, in 1992, at the age of fifty-eight. My friend Bryn in 1994, at the age of thirty-two. Frank Wells, Disney's charismatic president and chief operating officer, in 1994, at the age of sixty-two. Stephen's mother in 1995, at the age of sixty-seven. Stephen's father also in 1995, at the age of seventy-five. My dad in 1998, at the age of seventy-two. My friend Jessie in 2002, at the ripe old and wise age of ninety-six. My mom in 2004, at the age of seventy-eight. My friend Basil the monk in 2005, at the age of seventy-three. Joy Covey, my friend and

---

35 According to a Gallup poll taken from March 1–8, 2018, regarding political party affiliations, forty-five percent of Americans classified themselves as Independents like me, twenty-nine percent classified themselves as Democrats, and twenty-three percent classified themselves as Republican Party members.

36 Hugo Black was appointed to the US Supreme Court by President Franklin D. Roosevelt, and served from 1937 to 1971. He was a member of the Democratic Party in an era when America's racists and misogynists largely were Democrats (it was not until the 1960s, when the Democratic Party and Republican Party swapped much of their respective political platforms, that America's racists and misogynists became members of the Republican Party). After Justice Black was appointed to the Supreme Court, it was discovered that he had been a member of a racist American terrorist group called the Ku Klux Klan and the country demanded his resignation, but President Roosevelt continued to support him. Justice Black remained on the court, and then surprised everyone by not making racist rulings, but instead becoming one of the great civil libertarians in Supreme Court history and a champion of the First Amendment.

Amazon's rock star chief financial officer, in 2013, at the age of fifty. Irwin Russell, my friend and mentor, also in 2013, at the age of eighty-seven. John Angelo, my friend and mentor and distressed credit genius, in 2016, at the age of seventy-four. Lloyd, my friend and attorney, in 2018, at the age of fifty-seven. Jeff, David's boyfriend, in 2020, at the age of sixty-eight. Judson Green, Disney's president of theme parks and resorts, in 2020, at the age of sixty-eight. May their memories be eternal.

So many other people from my twenties completely scattered from my life because of the storm. But I haven't forgotten them. The lyrics of "Disappear" from *Dear Evan Hansen* underscore how I feel:

> *No one deserves to be forgotten.*
> *No one deserves to fade away.*
> *No one should come and go,*
> *and have no one know*
> *he was never even here.*
> *No one deserves to disappear.*
> *To disappear.*
> *Disappear.*

Thinking about all the people that I knew in my early twenties, and leafing through my old green address book of friends I knew in that carefree summer of 1983, I can recall several names of men who simply disappeared from my life because of the AIDS virus. So many young men. Now, decades later I can't recognize all of their names or picture all of their faces. I don't know if all of the men listed below actually died or not, and I'll never know. Dozens of handsome, vibrant young men frozen in the time capsule of my memory.

Tony, who worked as a personal assistant to a major pop star.

David, from USC who wanted to become a pharmacist.

John, from USC and my former roommate.

Nils, my workout partner at The Athletic Club.

Peter, the son of old Hollywood royalty, too sweet beyond words.

Devon, the brave blond president of the UCLA gay student union.

Rocky, the handsome Latino who always flashed the sexiest smile at me at the Revolver video bar on *Dynasty* nights.

George and Dan, the handsome couple from UCLA.

Bob, the attorney whom I met at The Athletic Club who helped Stephen find a job after he was laid off by California Federal Savings and Loan.

Bob's partner, Peter.

Jim, the very tall blond man who lived on Charleville Boulevard in Beverly Hills.

Salvador, who cut my hair back when I still had it.

David, the friendly and very tall blue-eyed bodybuilder whom everyone admired.

David the bodybuilder's friend, another David, a UCLA theater major who produced the student film that I wrote that won first place.

The interesting and mysterious handsome brown-haired high-fashion model who spent an afternoon in the summer of 1983 touring Los Angeles with me and who crazily traded his clothes for mine in a West Hollywood alley before he left town. That sure was fun!

Chris, my former roommate who introduced me to my friend Bryn.

Alex and Danny, the couple who worked out at the Holiday Spa Health Club in Hollywood.

Phil, the African American personal trainer at The Athletic Club.

Chet, the Navy dentist who lived in San Diego.

Chet's other Navy dentist friend from San Diego, whose name I can't remember.

Mike, the friendly bartender at the Rose Tattoo Restaurant.

Matt, who knew Gloria Swanson and who worked on the film *Sunset Boulevard* with her.

Worrell, the gregarious bartender at the Mother Lode bar.

JV, who worked with me at *The Los Angeles Herald-Examiner*.

Bill, the blond man who was married to a woman but still hung out in West Hollywood all the time.

Don, who owned a restaurant.

Dick, and Dennis, and another Bill, and Grant, and Hughes, and Owen, and another Bill, and Leonard, and another Mike, and another Tony.

And Wayne Burgos, whom I dated a bit in the summer of 1983, who has a plaque on the AIDS Memorial Walk just east of the corner of Santa Monica Boulevard and Westmount Drive on the sidewalk in front of the Body Energy Club, almost right across the street from the apartment building where he once lived. Wayne died on July 16, 1994, at the age of thirty-four. He worked as a talent agent. I see Wayne's plaque every time I visit the Body Energy Club, and I clean it when it's dirty.

That's all from just one address book that I used for one summer of my life. May their memories be eternal, too.

Everyone has their own list.

Some of my gay friends made it through the storm and did not disappear. My friend Robert survived, became an exceptional interior designer, and today runs a successful home design business in Red Bank, New Jersey, called Red Ginger Home. Kevin, my college friend who coaxed me out of the closet in 1983—he survived, too, and became a psychotherapist in San Francisco. His house is only fourteen houses away from our San Francisco house, but sadly I have lost touch with him and never see him anymore. Thanks to Google, I know that Marty, my first boyfriend during the summer of 1983 who thankfully introduced me to the Bodhi Tree Bookstore, also survived and now lives in Houston and works as a lighting designer. He still looks great.

My wonderful lifelong friend, first boss, and second mom, Margaret, is still in my life at the age of nearly ninety!

I'm still in touch, as friends, with the people who helped me save myself: Guy, my psychotherapist; Christine, my shiatsu practitioner; and Dr. Jackie, my grief hypnotherapist.

On August 13, 1998, an amazing thing happened: San Francisco's *Bay Area Reporter*, for the first time in more than seventeen years since the AIDS pandemic began, reported zero AIDS obituaries.[37] Wow! What a nice milestone.

In 2014, researchers published in *Science* about the early spread of HIV-1 in human populations, and they traced AIDS all the way back to chimpanzee hunters in Cameroon and in Kinshasa in the Republic of the Congo before 1920.[38] They proved that AIDS was never a "gay disease" at all as those fundamentalist religious conservatives railed about for years in their efforts to discriminate against gay men. Instead, the researchers confirmed that AIDS was just a serious disease that can infect anyone regardless of their sexual orientation. A serious *human* disease. I sometimes wonder how people would behave if another deadly virus ever appeared in the world, but one that

---

37 Timothy Rodrigues, August 13, 1998, "Death Takes a Holiday," *Bay Area Reporter*.

38 Nuno R. Faria, et al., October 3, 2014, "The early spread and epidemic ignition of HIV-1 in human populations," *Science*, Volume 346, Number 6205, 56–61.

affected everyone and quickly transmitted through casual contact. Would people lose their minds like they did with AIDS? Would leaders politicize the virus? Would people come together and support one another? Or would such a virus cause division between people?

Today, people with HIV can now take medicines that render their HIV undetectable and not infectious to others with one pill per day. If they can afford it. The retail price of one pill is over sixty dollars. According to the World Health Organization, more than forty million people worldwide are living with HIV. Yes, people can, and do, still die from AIDS.

It does not surprise me that nearly forty years after the first cases of AIDS, still no AIDS vaccine or cure has been announced.

What a test of humanity the world received from the universe with the AIDS pandemic. Ask yourself: which side of history were you on? Did you do the right thing? Are you proud of how you acted? Two data points from my life experience stand out clearly. (1) The entertainment industry, perpetually vilified by fundamentalist religious conservatives as godless and having no morality, jumped headfirst into compassionately fighting the AIDS pandemic and supporting those affected by it. (2) Fundamentalist religious conservatives, hiding behind the "cloak of God," stood by and laughed at the plight of people dying from AIDS and actively sought to make their suffering worse: the polar opposite of God's teachings. Fundamentalist religious conservatives and their judgmental organized religions have always thrived on corrupt moral hypocrisy. If you're not sure about this, just ask Jerry Falwell, Jr. about his alleged hunky Miami pool boy throuple boyfriend, Giancarlo Granda.

In writing about the storm, I have unlocked, explored, swept, and vacuumed nearly every cobwebbed corner of my memory. But what incredible, cathartic therapy for me. To some extent, I fooled myself into thinking the storm was over, but it still churned within me until I purged it through writing this book and directly confronting my long-buried AIDS pandemic post-traumatic stress disorder.

Along the way, many signs encouraged me to keep writing. The most important sign, however, occurred for me at Winterskol in Aspen, Colorado. As I stood in the nighttime sky at the base of Aspen Mountain's gondola, a mountain that I have skied dozens of times, while skiers traversed down the slopes carrying lighted candles and fireworks burst in the sky above them, I experienced a powerful realization. All of the memories from the storm that I had stuffed deep inside me for decades, and that I had been painfully and emotionally digging out, suddenly integrated into me and locked into place. I realized that all of the memories of my life, even the painful ones, were a part of me forever, and that I didn't need to hide from them anymore. They couldn't hurt me anymore. As I stood at the bottom of that Aspen gondola, I allowed every emotion from my life to flow through me all at once—everything, whether good or heartbreaking—and I felt an emotion even better than happiness. I felt joy, gratitude, peace, knowing, acceptance, and love all rolled into one. It felt utterly exhilarating. Suddenly my entire life made sense. I felt lighter. I realized that I didn't need to lock the memories up or even release them. I could allow them to be a part of me, and to feel them, forever. My spiritual epiphany. I had reclaimed my lost decade of my own history.

This, I believe, is the most important message in this memoir: if you can allow yourself to remember and feel all of the emotions from all of your life experiences, from the best to the worst, all at the same time, and accept them as a part of your personal history in this world, I promise you that you will experience an emotion beyond any other. You will know your own truth. I also promise you that this is as California woo-woo as I'm going to get in this memoir. I won't digress into my meditation, acupuncture, yoga, or periodic veganism.

I now understand that I was supposed to exist after all. My own George Bailey *It's a Wonderful Life* realization. I was meant to be in this world for Stephen, Joan, Bryn, my mom and dad, and countless other people whom I have tried to help along their way. My Roman Catholic namesake, Saint Christopher, whom the Pope demoted to folk hero status in 1969, turned out to be the perfect saint name for me, too. You see, Saint Christopher was known for helping people cross a dangerous river where many people had died. His large size and strength allowed him to safely escort travelers through the treacherous currents. As the legend goes, one day a small child asked Saint Christopher to help him cross the river. As he crossed the river with the child on his shoulders, the child became heavier, as if made of stone. Upon reaching the other side of the river, Saint Christopher asked the child why he became so heavy. The child told him that he was the Christ Child, and that he carried the weight of the entire world with him. Christopher actually means "Christ bearer" in Greek. Because of this legend, Saint Christopher became the patron saint of travelers. Interestingly, he's also the patron saint of storms, too, specifically lightning and floods. I felt the weight of the world on my shoulders at times, too, as I lived through the storm, and I am proud to have helped a few people during their time in this world. So, my Roman Catholic saint namesake is perfect for me. Who cares that the Pope demoted him? My birth was not a mistake. I was supposed to be here for everything that happened in the storm, and beyond it.

Even for screwing up my mom's funeral. Oh, yes, when I was forty-two years old I royally messed up my mom's funeral after she died in Santa Barbara on August 5, 2004. One mistake by Chris to last for all eternity.

At the time she died, I was working in San Francisco, and I couldn't immediately travel to Santa Barbara. So I asked Jean, my mom's longtime nurse, to pick out one of Mom's favorite outfits so that she could be dressed in it for the rosary service. Jean had taken great care of my mother for years, and I considered her as part of our family. I trusted her implicitly.

On the night of my mom's rosary, I got to Welch-Ryce-Haider Mortuary in Santa Barbara forty-five minutes early, before any of the guests arrived. The funeral director ushered me into the room with my mom's casket, closed. The room was beautifully decorated and full of flowers. For the service, I even brought my own rosary beads, from my confirmation at Our Lady of Lourdes Catholic Church in 1974, even though I was no longer a Roman Catholic.

The funeral director asked, "Are you ready to see the body?" In Roman Catholic funerals, the rosary service is almost always done with an open casket so that mourners can view the earthly remains. It's a Roman Catholic tradition. I answered, "Yes," and then he opened the casket.

My mom looked so beautiful and peaceful, and just like I remembered her from the week before she died when I had visited her. Her makeup and hairdo were perfect. She would be so happy with how good she looked. There was just one thing out of place:

She was dressed in a purple velour track suit.

I stared with my mouth agape. The funeral director stood next to me, expecting compliments for his great work. But all I could focus on was the purple velour track suit.

My mom was about to spend eternity in Carpinteria Cemetery buried next to my dad wearing a purple velour track suit! Oh, no, I had asked Jean to dress my mom in one of her favorite outfits, but I didn't specify "a nice beautiful dress for all of eternity." Why did I delegate this? How would I ever explain this to our guests arriving any minute? Especially to Annette, my mom's best friend in the whole world, and really an aunt to me, who surely would never forgive me for dressing her in this highly inelegant couture.

I suddenly heard Annette's distinctive voice off in the distance, so she had arrived, early as usual. I turned to the funeral director and said, "My mom looks beautiful. You did a fantastic job. Close the casket. We are going to do the rosary with the casket closed. If anyone asks to see inside, tell them that my mom didn't look very good at the end of her life, and our family has requested that the casket remain closed. Don't open it for anyone. Not even my brother. Even if they beg you. Understand?"

The puzzled funeral director nodded and shut the casket. I walked out to the lobby and intercepted Annette, and told her that the casket would be closed for the rosary service because they just couldn't make my mom look as she deserved to be seen. I asked her to spread the word to the other guests as they arrived. Annette responded, "I just visited your mother a couple weeks ago and she looked fine," but she nodded and followed my request. Phew!

Then, I ran into the men's bathroom. There wasn't even time for me to change my mom's clothes before her funeral service and internment the next morning. There really was no way for me to fix this mess. My mom was destined to spend eternity in Carpinteria Cemetery wearing a purple velour track suit, dressed ready to go for a run on Carpinteria Beach, lying next to my dad, who was wearing his business suit and tie.

Then I lost it, and I started to simultaneously cry and laugh in the mortuary's men's bathroom. "Laughter through tears is my favorite emotion," said Truvy, the character played by Dolly Parton in *Steel Magnolias*, and Truvy was right. I imagined my mom and dad standing there laughing at me, and laughing with me, too: my mom modeling and showing off her purple velour track suit, my dad complimenting her on how good she looked, and the two of them singing "purple rain, purple rain," the chorus from Prince's 1984 hit song. At that point, I made peace with my unfortunate, royal mistake, because in the big scheme of life, it didn't matter. And because I had to, since my mom's rosary service was starting any minute. I bargained with myself: "Well, as track suits go, it is a really nice one," and, "Velour will be fashionable again someday, I'm sure of it." Eventually, I composed myself.

Lessons learned: (1) I'm far from a perfect human being, and (2) be careful what you delegate to others!

After that screwup, I didn't feel guilty one bit bribing the church's piano player with a $300 bonus to play my mom's favorite song, "When Irish Eyes Are Smiling," at the end of her funeral service the next morning even after the parish priest warned me that the song could not be played inside the church because it wasn't an official Catholic song. The pianist played the song as requested, everyone sang the lyrics, the priest glared at me, and I shrugged and smiled back from my pew.

In another full-circle moment, my mom and my brother Michael fortunately healed their relationship at the end of her life. About one year before she died, she suffered a mini-stroke and it only affected the portion of her brain that housed memories of her decades-long strained relationship with my brother. Suddenly, my mom was unconditionally happy to see my brother, and they could be together and have normal conversations with no stress whatsoever. There wasn't even a need for either of them to apologize to each other for the past—the mini-stroke deleted all of it from her mind as if nothing bad had ever happened between them. Michael was wonderful about it, and the two of them got to share some quality time together during her last year of life. He was able to share with my mom his phenomenal success as the head of the video game degree program in the University of Southern California's Computer Science department, and my mom was so genuinely happy for him, and proud of him. Such a gift.

I am now more than twice as old as I was when Stephen died. I have lived a great portion of a life that I once thought I would never have. The small potted Ficus plant that one of my Wall Street friends sent me when my dad died in 1998 now lives in a giant pot and has grown into a tree nearly fifteen feet tall. This Ficus has followed me through many of my twenty-two lifetime moves up and down the West Coast, finally to my Outpost Canyon home on Senalda Road in the Hollywood Hills again, in a celebrity-packed enclave just below the famed Mulholland Drive where my high school friends and I used to cruise in our parents' cars, and where tour buses drive down my street all day long hoping for a celebrity sighting.

Per Stephen's request, I never made an AIDS quilt panel to honor him. But Stephen never asked me to not write a book about him. And on his deathbed, he did ask me to write something someday. So, this memoir shall serve as my own version of an AIDS quilt panel to honor him and tell his story. Our story. One story from the AIDS generation. After all, that's what Horatio did for Hamlet—he lived to tell Hamlet's story. Besides, you can fit a lot more story into a book than on an AIDS quilt panel. I am truly grateful that Stephen fell in love with me, and that we had our life together even when the whole world was against us. Stephen, the first love of my life, wherever you are hanging out in the universe today, I hope that you know that I will always love you.

Everyone's first love in life is special. It doesn't make the loves that follow afterward any less important, or real, or rich. I am incredibly lucky to have found love three times in my life, and the third time with my husband Michael has been the best of all.

I have achieved so many dreams in my unexpected and wonderful life, and I am grateful for everything. The only major dream that I haven't achieved, until now, was to write something. Writing is my biggest unfulfilled carpe diem. But that is now about to change. You see, I never completely buried the writing dream of my youth, and it's never too late to resurrect and realize your life dreams if you continue to believe in yourself. After decades of detours on the unexpected but fantastic road in life that I took because of AIDS, I am finally veering that road back toward my road not taken. Through my tears of joy, I can see my road not taken appearing on the horizon as I write the last sentences of this memoir, the only thing I am likely to write in my life. The uplifting songs from the playlist of my life are cheering me on to finish. I hear Barbra Streisand belting out "Don't Rain on My Parade." I hear Cyndi Grecco singing "Making Our Dreams Come True," the inspiring theme song from the iconic television series of my youth, *Laverne and Shirley*. I hear Hoku's "Perfect Day" inspiring me to cross the finish line. I hear Mariah Carey's beautiful voice singing "Hero."

So, on a perfect warm sunny spring Sunday morning with no storm in sight, on the couch in my living room, after 177 days of writing at night and on weekends, and with my husband Michael sitting next to me, at long last I have connected the road that I took in life because of the AIDS virus into my road not taken. I did it. I have finally written a book.

THE END